AUTOMATED WEB SITE EVA~

HUMAN-COMPUTER INTERACTION SERIES

VOLUME 4

The titles published in this series are listed at the end of this volume.

Automated Web Site Evaluation

Researchers' and Practioners' Perspectives

by

Melody Y. Ivory
University of Washington,
Seattle, U.S.A.

KLUWER ACADEMIC PUBLISHERS
DORDRECHT / BOSTON / LONDON

A C.I.P. Catalogue record for this book is available from the Library of Congress

ISBN   978-90-481-6446-2

Published by Kluwer Academic Publishers,
P.O. Box 17, 3300 AA Dordrecht, The Netherlands.

Sold and distributed in North, Central and South America
by Kluwer Academic Publishers,
101 Philip Drive, Norwell, MA 02061, U.S.A.

In all other countries, sold and distributed
by Kluwer Academic Publishers,
P.O. Box 322, 3300 AH Dordrecht, The Netherlands.

Printed on acid-free paper

Contents

List of Figures

List of Tables

For Allum and Angelo

Acknowledgments

Thanks to the most high for the strength and determination to conduct the research presented in this book.

We thank our family and friends for their support: Allum Ross Ndiaye, Angelo Ivory-Ndiaye, LaVance Ivory, Ronald Ringo and family, Damesha Ringo, Betrand Gaskin, Teddy and Teresa Gaskin, Lin Covington, Janice Sherman, Carmen Anthony, Richard Freeman, Dr. Carla Trujillo, Dr. Johnathan Reason, Dr. Adrian Isles, Dr. John Davis, Roy Sutton, Dr. Sheila Humphreys, Reggie Walker, and other members of BGESS. We also thank all our supporters within the University of Washington community and our Information School colleagues.

We thank members of the Web Portal Services Group at Kaiser Permanente and others who facilitated our research: Mary-Anna Rae, Dani Tobler, Mark Randall, Arturo Delgadillo, Kayvan Sootodeh, Royce Everone, Gaston Cangiano, Bryan Merrill, Lisa Washington, Katrina Rosario, Anthony Harris, Santhosh Pillai, Cheryl Rucks, Kelly Albin, Ron Dolin, Bob Dolin, Doug Shelton, Ric Leopold, Kayvan Sotoodeh, Ben Say, Dr. Henry Neidermeier, and Barbara Andrews.

We thank researchers within the HCI community who have provided support and guidance throughout our research endeavors: Marti Hearst, Jim Demmel, James Landay, Ray Larson, William Kahan, Rashmi Sinha, Ben Shneiderman, Jean Scholtz, Sharon Laskowski, B.J. Fogg, and Jean Vanderdonckt. Thanks to all the Berkeley GUIR people for your invaluable input over the years.

We thank everyone who has contributed to the WebTango Project, including: Marti Hearst, Rashmi Sinha, Roderick Megraw, Alissa Harrison, Young-Mi Shin, Shiquing Yu, Mary Deaton, Nicole Elger, Tina Marie, Wenchun Wang, Deep Debroy, Toni Wadjiji, Chantrelle Nielsen, Wai-ling Ho-Ching, Stephen Demby, David Lai, Judy Ramey, Jennifer Turns, Beth Kolko, David Farkas, and Aline Chevalier. We thank Maya Draisin and Tiffany Shlain at the International Academy of Digital Arts and Sciences for making the Webby Awards data available. We thank Lincoln Stein for his assistance with an early version of the Metrics Computation Tool and Tom Phelps for his assistance with the extended Metrics Computation Tool. WebTango research was supported by a Hellman Faculty Fund Award, a Microsoft Research Grant, a Gates Millennium Fellowship, a GAANN fellowship, and a Lucent Cooperative Research Fellowship Program grant.

We thank Chantrelle Nielsen for her editing and indexing assistance. Last, but not least, we thank Jean Vanderdonckt for the invitation to write this monograph and for writing the Foreword. We thank Robbert van Berckelaer at Kluwer for publishing this work.

Foreword

Among all information systems that are nowadays available, web sites are definitely the ones having the widest potential audience and the most significant impact on the everyday life of people. Web sites contribute largely to the information society: they provide visitors with a large array of services and information and allow them to perform various tasks without prior assumptions about their computer literacy.

Web sites are assumed to be accessible and usable to the widest possible audience. Consequently, usability has been recognized as a critical success factor for web sites of every kind. Beyond this universal recognition, usability still remains a notion that is hard to grasp. Summative evaluation methods have been introduced to identify potential usability problems to assess the quality of web sites. However, summative evaluation remains limited in impact as it does not necessarily deliver constructive comments to web site designers and developers on how to solve the usability problems. Formative evaluation methods have been introduced to address this issue.

Evaluation remains a process that is hard to drive and perform, while its potential impact is probably maximal for the benefit of the final user. This complexity is exacerbated when web sites are very large, potentially up to several hundreds of thousands of pages, thus leading to a situation where evaluating the web site is almost impossible to conduct manually. Therefore, many attempts have been made to support evaluation with:

- *Models* that capture some characteristics of the web site of interest.

- *Methods* that guide the evaluator to assess the usability of the web site based on the previously established model.

- *Tools* that provide evaluators with assistance in conducting the evaluation process.

Due to the above characteristics, web sites have drawn considerable attraction from both the research domain and the practitioners' community, thus providing different viewpoints on how to assess usability. This book is dedicated to those models, methods, and tools that support usability engineering of web sites: for the first time in the history of Human-Computer Interaction in general and in Usability Engineering in particular, there is a fundamental work trying to improve the validity and the applicability of these models, methods, and tools.

Melody Ivory's book is pioneering the field of automated web site evaluation. Not only has she contributed largely to this field by developing WebTango, a tool that automatically captures values of some metrics. But also, she has conducted experimental studies to show how these metrics are correlated with the usability of web sites, depending on their site type and on the context of use.

The big hope behind automated web site evaluation is that the models, the methods, and especially the tools will be able to perform the tedious part of the work of gathering information about the web site, trying to condense it, and bring it into light for the eyes of the evaluator. Farenc *et al.* [1999] showed that automatic evaluation of graphical user interfaces against guidelines would reach a plateau effect around 44%, thus meaning that only one part of guidelines can be checked automatically. In Cooper *et al.* [1999], it was shown that more than half of usability guidelines for web sites could be addressed, automatically, semi-automatically, or in a mixed-initiative fashion. The portion was more important due to the fact that web sites are more accessible and analyzable in principle than compiled applications running on top of a window manager. This sustains a strong desire that web sites can be assessed more thoroughly. It is expected that other evaluation methods will be able to expand their evaluation capability and scope to evaluate more and more aspects relevant to usability. This is especially interesting since many disciplines, so diverse as cognitive psychology, ethnography, and graph theory, can contribute towards the ultimate goal of assessing the true essence of web site usability.

The goal of such tools is *not* to replace the human intervention, but to complement it, if not to augment it. If an evaluator is responsible for a very-large web site, she would appreciate being able to locate the portions of the web site to look at, rather than being forced to examine systematically all parts of the web site. Similarly, if a tool can identify potential areas of usability flaws, the evaluator can have the attention attracted and verify its plausibility.

Having tool support is certainly desirable and helpful, but there is a big risk that some designers or developers will completely rely on the results provided by such tools. Transferring the responsibility for evaluating and ensuring the usability from the designers to the tool is not acceptable, even when the tool provides us with validated results on how to improve the usability of the web site. For this to happen, quality models should be introduced and validated. Anyway, existing tools suffer from shortcomings as highlighted and discussed in this book: tools produce usability reports that may appear inconsistent with each other, their effectiveness remains to be documented and empirically validated not only in the research domain, but also in the real world, it is unclear yet to what extent tools largely or slightly contribute to improving usability. Briefly said, this field is very promising in practices and contents, leaving ample room for further work.

With this book, Melody Ivory introduced this new discipline of automated web site evaluation, one that is of a crucial importance to both researchers and practitioners as reflected into the two main parts dedicated to these two audiences. To me, this book is today the most extensive, comprehensive, and up-to-date source of information to get when someone is seriously interested in evaluating a web site. Having monitored Melody Ivory's work for more than three years now, I have witnessed some significant advances in this field, shedding light on obscure parts. Therefore, I warmly recommend this invaluable volume to everyone who wants to research, conduct, or understand web site usability evaluation, especially with some degree of automation.

Professor Jean Vanderdonckt
Louvain-la-Neuve
June 10, 2003

Introduction

Melody Y. Ivory

We can define universal usability as more than 90 percent of all households being successful users of information and communication technologies at least once a week.
—Shneiderman, pg. 36 [2002]

Why are there so many web sites that are difficult to use, especially considering that we "know" how to design sites that are easy to use? Just today (December 16, 2002), I attempted to find guidance on constructing an effective index for this book. Although Google[TM] returned many links for this search, none of the top sites, including the ones geared toward book writers, had readily usable information. For example, one site had a section with a long list of links to articles, thus requiring extensive scrolling. To make matters worse, the page designer used a small font size and crammed the links close together, which made them even more difficult to read. On another site, the color combinations made it impossible to read the text or navigate through the site.

Given that these site designers did not address the needs of the "typical" web user, one can only imagine how poor the experience might be for a user with visual, learning, or other impairments. We clearly have a long way to go toward creating a universally beneficial[1] Web, wherein all users (regardless of backgrounds, education, and abilities) can benefit from the vast amount of information and services that are available on-line. What will it take for all users to be able to find the information that they need and to accomplish the tasks that they need to complete with minimal effort?

Several approaches have been explored in an attempt to improve the current state of the Web, most of which provide extra support (e.g., guidelines, templates, authoring tools, training, and site generators) to practitioners. Automated web site evaluation has also emerged as a way to better support practitioners in creating usable and accessible sites. Although early evaluation methodologies focused on ensuring that the HTML code conformed to valid coding practices, more recent tools examine usability, accessibility, and other design issues. Research and development in this area has proceeded rapidly; at publication time, there were over 70 automated web site evaluation methodologies and tools. Now is the time for researchers, tool developers, and practitioners to assess where we are in this area.

This book is a culmination of over five years of research and practical experience in the Web domain. As researchers, we have conducted surveys and analyses of automated web site evaluation methodologies and tools, developed an automated evaluation approach (the WebTango approach), conducted empirical studies of automated evaluation tools, and conducted empirical studies on the web site design process. As web site design and usability engineering practitioners, we have experienced and observed the difficulties that practitioners face when they strive to produce usable and accessible web sites. From these two perspectives, we document the current state of automated web site evaluation.

Audience for this Book

We designed this book primarily to support researchers and practitioners in the Web domain. For researchers, we provide an overview of the approaches that have been explored for automated web site evaluation and their effectiveness; we also highlight open research problems. For practitioners, we provide an overview of the tools that have been developed for automated web site evaluation and their effectiveness. We compare and contrast tools in several ways, which can help practitioners to choose the tools that are most appropriate for their web site design context.

This book contains information that is also relevant to developers of automated web site evaluation tools. For instance, we discuss limitations of existing tools and several ways in which they can be improved. Tool developers can use study results and comparative tool assessments to inform future development efforts.

Organization of this Book

Figure I.1 depicts the organization of the book and shows several paths through it. We suggest that researchers and practitioners begin by reading the chapter in Part I, as it describes the work practices of practitioners, including their reported used of automated web site evaluation tools. We suggest that researchers read both Parts II and III to gain a thorough understanding of the methodologies that have been developed, their instantiation as tools, and the effectiveness of the resulting tools. Part III contains information that we think is of benefit to practitioners. However, we suggest that practitioners review the

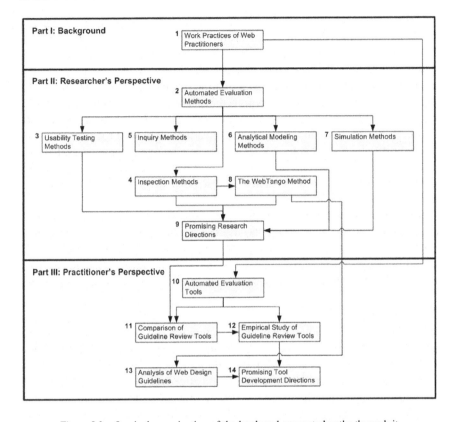

Figure I.1.   Logical organization of the book and suggested paths through it.

chapter on the WebTango method (Chapter 8) prior to reading the chapter on web design guidelines (Chapter 13).

Part I provides background information on the work practices of web practitioners. We summarize surveys and studies that provide insight on: the use of automated evaluation methods, relative to non-automated approaches; work practices that need to be supported; and the challenges that practitioners face, in particular with applying design guidelines.

Part II discusses the automated evaluation methodologies. Chapter 2 presents a taxonomy for describing automated and non-automated evaluation methods and summarizes the classification of 84 methods. Chapters 3–7 provide methodology details and summative assessments for the five major classes of techniques: usability testing, inspection, inquiry, analytical modeling, and simulation. We elaborate on one approach—the WebTango method for deriving design guidance from empirical data—in Chapter 8. We discuss other promising approaches in Chapter 9.

Part III discusses the automated evaluation tools that have been developed. Chapter 10 describes the structure of an automated evaluation tool and discusses the five types of evaluation tools. It also presents survey results on the use of these tools and discusses their current role in the work practices of web practitioners. Chapter 11 compares evaluation results reported across ten tools for a single web page. Chapter 12 reports the results of a study wherein designers used several tools to modify sites and diverse users tested the original and modified sites to determine whether modifications improved the usability and accessibility of sites. Chapter 13 demonstrates how one automated evaluation tool—the WebTango prototype—can be used to provide concrete thresholds for web design guidelines. Chapter 14 discusses ways in which to improve automated evaluation tools.

Appendix A provides an exhaustive list of the methodologies and tools that are discussed in this book; it can be used as a quick reference to learn about specific methods or tools. For each approach, we the provide name, reference, and a brief description of the approach's automation support. The reader can use the index or bibliography to find out more information about each approach.

In Summary

It is our belief that automated web site evaluation has merit as one way to address the usability and accessibility lag on the Web. However, we think that the methodologies and tools are still in their infancy. More research and development is needed to expand their usefulness and effectiveness so that practitioners can integrate them into their web site design processes. It is our hope that the information that we present in this book will facilitate major advances in the state-of-the-art of automated web site evaluation and, consequently, move us closer toward a universally beneficial Web.

Notes

1 Many terms are used to describe the performance objective of web sites, including usability, accessibility, universal usability, universal accessibility, and others. We introduce the term *universal benefit* to encompass these related objectives.

I

BACKGROUND

Chapter 1

WORK PRACTICES OF WEB PRACTITIONERS

Creating a site that is of universal benefit to its users is a far more complex task than most new (and some experienced) web practitioners[1] realize. Although it may be straightforward to code HTML pages, creating an effective site requires practitioners to follow practices, such as user-centered design or guideline application. In this chapter, we discuss the web site design and development process and the incorporation of usability engineering into it. We describe several studies of web practitioners that were aimed at understanding the steps that they take to ensure that their sites are universally beneficial, including following a user-centered design process, using design guidelines,[2] and using automated evaluation tools. We also surmise the effect of these work practices on the current state of the Web.

Both researchers and developers of automated web site evaluation methodologies and tools need to be cognizant of the surveys and studies that we summarize in this chapter. They provide insight on: (1) the current adoption of these approaches, relative to the use of non-automated approaches; (2) the work practices that need to be supported; and (3) some difficulties that practitioners face, in particular with applying design guidelines. The quality of the Web should improve with the deployment of methodologies and tools that better support these work practices and help practitioners to overcome challenges that arise during the web site design and development process.

1. Web Site Design Process

To gain insight about the process of creating sites, Newman and Landay [2000] conducted an ethnographic study of professional web site designers. They discovered that designers go through several design iterations with paper sketches and create different representations of a site—site maps depicting the site organization, storyboards depicting task completion steps, and schemat-

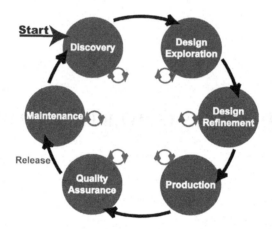

Figure 1.1.   Web site design and development process.

ics illustrating page layouts. Other literature sources (e.g., [De Troyer and Leune, 1998; Ford and Boyarski, 1997; Fuccella, 1997; Heller and Rivers, 1996b; Nielsen, 2000; Sano, 1996; Shneiderman, 1997; van Duyne *et al.*, 2002]) describe similar web site design and development processes. Figure 1.1 summarizes the phases that are often mentioned.

Site requirements are identified during the discovery phase; requirements need to address many issues, such as who the intended users are, what tasks they need to accomplish, what constraints need to be met, and so on. Several design alternatives may be explored during the design exploration phase. However, one design idea is chosen and improved upon during the design refinement phase. Site implementation typically occurs during the production phase; design templates or style guides may be developed initially to guide the implementation effort. The implemented site is tested and repaired, if necessary, during the quality assurance phase; afterwards, it is released for broad use. Once the site is released, it undergoes continuous maintenance (e.g., updating content). Iteration may occur during each of these phases, as depicted in Figure 1.1.

To ensure that sites will be of universal benefit to their users, web practitioners may employ a number of practices during this design and development process. For instance, they may follow a usability engineering process (Figure 1.2). (Ivory [2003d] provides an expanded discussion of the process depicted in Figure 1.2.) To characterize the use of practices like usability engineering, we summarize an early survey that Vora [1998] conducted, as well as a more recent survey that we conducted [Ivory and Chevalier, 2002; Ivory *et al.*, 2003].

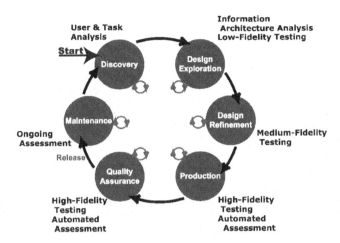

Figure 1.2. Usability engineering incorporated into the web site design and development process.

2. Early Survey of Work Practices

From December 17, 1997 until January 15, 1998, Vora [1998] surveyed 138 web designers to understand how the web authors (or designers) design web pages and to provide guidance to developers so that they could design usable web page development tools. The survey included questions about the designers' professional background, motivation for designing web pages, and design experience. The designers came from a variety of professional backgrounds, with 42 and 32 percent coming from user interface design and human factors, respectively. At least half of them designed web pages as their primary job responsibility and 70 percent had more than two years of design experience.

Although the survey delved into the details of the designers' design activities and their use and assessments of authoring and other other tools, we do not focus on these aspects here. Instead, we focus on survey questions that examined designers' work practices with respect to the design and evaluation of web sites. The survey inquired about how often designers used design guidelines, optimized pages for fast download, designed pages for accessibility, and conducted usability evaluations. Table 1.1 shows that over half of the designers always optimized pages for fast download and at least 30 percent used guidelines or conducted usability evaluations. Less than twenty percent of designers always considered accessibility issues when designing web pages. These results suggest that designers were not consistently or adequately applying work practices that could produce sites that are of universal benefit.

Table 1.1.   Work practices used in the design and evaluation of web sites.[a]

Work Practice	Frequency of Use		Total
	Always	Sometimes	
Design Guideline Use[b]	30%	59%	89%
Download Speed Optimization	57%	42%	99%
Accessibility Optimization	17%	50%	67%
Usability Evaluation[c]	30%	69%	99%

[a] Results are from a survey of 138 web designers [Vora, 1998].
[b] Design guideline use includes the use of both guidelines and style guides.
[c] We aggregrated responses to the survey's question about usability evaluation. The Always column reflects the percentage of designers who stated that they employed usability evaluation all the time (29.7 percent). The Sometimes column reflects the percentage of designers who stated that they employed usability evaluation almost all the time (39.9 percent), often (14.5 percent), and sometimes (15.2 percent).

2.1   Influences of Work Practices

A survey of web users, the Graphics, Visualization, and Usability Center's (GVU) 8th WWW User Survey [GVU Center, 1997] conducted from April 10, 1997 through May, 1997, provides some insight on the influences of the work practices employed during the time frame of Vora's survey. In addition to inquiring about the demographics and interests of 7220 web users, the GVU survey inquired about problems encountered in using the Web (e.g., not being able to find information or return to a page previously visited, waiting too long for pages to download, or visiting broken links). In comparison to the preceding semi-annual surveys, the eighth survey suggested several trends, including the three trends discussed below.

- Download speed was still a problem for 63 percent of users, but the percentage was declining annually. As shown in Table 1.1, designers consistently worked to reduce page download speed, which made some contribution to the decline. The decline could also be attributed to the simultaneous increase in modem connection speed.

- At least 50 percent of users had problems with broken links; there was a 10 percent decrease from the preceding survey.

- Finding known and new information afflicted 32 and 50 percent of users, respectively. Only 30 percent of respondents reported finding known information as problematic in the preceding survey.

Although the survey did not inquire directly about web site usability or accessibility, the first two trends suggest a positive effect attributable, at least in part, to the reported work practices. However, a subsequent web user survey (conducted a year later from October 10, 1998 through December 15, 1998 [GVU Center, 1998]), included questions pertaining to usability and accessibility (e.g., visiting pages that use bad HTML, are not compatible with all browsers, or have too many or useless graphics) and suggested that the work practices were inadequate. Of the 3291 users who responded to the questions, 30 percent reported problems with bad HTML, 43 percent had problems due to scripts, 26 percent had problems due to incompatibility issues, and 49 percent due to graphics. There has not been a subsequent study; thus, it is not possible to determine whether the trends improved or not.

3. More Recent Survey of Work Practices

Similarly to Vora's survey, we conducted a survey of web practitioners in August of 2002 [Ivory and Chevalier, 2002; Ivory *et al.*, 2003]. We recruited participants by sending email announcements to mailing lists (e.g., CHI-Web, ASIS IA, ASIS HCI, and many others) and by posting announcements on web sites, such as SpiderMetrix.com. Respondents included 169 practitioners who had a role in developing sites for use by broad user communities. Almost an equal number of males and females responded. They represented a broad range of practitioners (web designers, information architects/designers, usability analysts/human factors, and other roles). They had varying design expertise (beginner: 31 percent, intermediate: 51 percent, and expert: 18 percent) with 57 percent of them having worked in the field for more than three years and 46 percent of them having designed more than ten sites. Participants worked in many environments, including corporations, academic institutions, and independently; they worked on education, e-commerce, intranet, health, and other types of sites.

We asked the practitioners about their work practices related to creating usable and accessible sites. We used several questions from Vora's survey for comparison purposes (e.g., the use of guidelines, usability evaluation, download speed optimization, and accessibility optimization). We also asked survey respondents about their usage and assessment of twenty-five automated evaluation tools; we discuss the latter results in detail in Chapter 10.

Table 1.2 compares 1997 and 2002 responses to these questions and shows that work practices have not changed dramatically. About the same percentage of practitioners reported optimizing pages for fast download and accessibility, and conducting usability evaluations, but there was a four and six percent increase in the number of respondents who stated that they always optimize for accessibility or used design guidelines, respectively. These increases are related and attributable most likely to the Section 508 standards that required Federal agencies to make their electronic and information technology, including web

Table 1.2. Work practices used in the design and evaluation of web sites (1997 and 2002).[a]

Work Practice	1997 Frequency of Use[b]			2002 Frequency of Use[c]		
	Always	Sometimes	Total	Always	Sometimes	Total
Design Guideline Use[d]	30%	59%	89%	36%	60%	96%
Download Speed Opt.	57%	42%	99%	52%	46%	98%
Accessibility Opt.	17%	50%	67%	21%	72%	93%
Usability Evaluation	30%	69%	99%	28%	68%	96%
Automated Evaluation	–	–	–	15%	67%	82%

[a] The 1997 results are from a survey of 138 web designers [Vora, 1998]. The 2002 results are from a survey of 169 web practitioners [Ivory and Chevalier, 2002; Ivory et al., 2003].
[b] We aggregated responses to the 1997 survey's question about usability evaluation. The Always column reflects the percentage of designers who stated that they employed usability evaluation all the time. The Sometimes column reflects the percentage of designers who stated that they employed usability evaluation almost all the time, often, and sometimes. The 1997 survey did not inquire about the use of automated evaluation tools.
[c] We aggregated responses to the 2002 survey's questions. The Always column reflects the percentage of practitioners who stated that they employed the practice all the time. The Sometimes column reflects the percentage of practitioners who stated that they employed the practice often, occasionally, and rarely.
[d] Design guideline use includes the use of both guidelines and style guides.

sites, accessible to people with disabilities [Center for Information Technology Accommodation, 2002] and provided guidelines for doing so.

Unlike the other practices, only fifteen percent of respondents reported that they always used automated evaluation tools. Furthermore, respondents had mixed opinions about the automated evaluation tools that they had used. At least half of them thought that the tools were helpful in creating usable and accessible sites and in learning about effective design practices. However, the majority of them did not think that using the tools produced better sites than those produced without using tools. They did not think that the tools had adequate functionality or support or that they were easy to use. Practitioners' responses suggest that it is helpful for them to have another way to check their designs, after making changes in particular, but the tools are currently too difficult and too limited to use.

It is difficult to assess directly the effect of the work practices on the usability and accessibility of web sites; however, we are launching a study to do so. Several recent studies (see [Shneiderman et al., 2003] for examples) suggest that usability and accessibility problems still persist, despite the work practices. In the remainder of this chapter, we discuss several studies that we have conducted to examine the effect of one of the most prevalent work practices—design guideline use—on produced designs. We examine the effect of automated evaluation tools in Chapter 12.

4. Studies of Design Guideline Use

Both surveys showed design guideline use to be one of the most prevalent practices that practitioners use to ensure that their sites are of universal benefit to users. Interface designers have historically experienced difficulties using guidelines [Borges *et al.*, 1996; de Souza and Bevan, 1990; Lowgren and Nordqvist, 1992; Smith, 1986], and our recent studies of novice and professional web designers demonstrate that they experience cognitive difficulties when using them as well [Chevalier and Ivory, 2003a]. We have conducted four experimental studies to gain insight on the use of guidelines during the design and evaluation processes of novice[3] and professional web site designers. Our studies examine guideline use when designers have and have not undergone training in how to apply them.

4.1 Use of Guidelines Without Training

In our first study [Chevalier and Ivory, 2003b], fourteen web designers (eight novices and six professionals) designed a car dealer's web site in conditions with or without eleven client-prescribed constraints (e.g., the web site must be short: 10-15 pages maximum; and the on-line services must be presented: to arrange an appointment, to ask questions, etc.). Designers articulated (i.e., used a think aloud protocol [Ericsson and Simon, 1993]) the constraints that they were applying as they developed the site. Two experts analyzed the designers' verbal protocols and classified them as being relevant to the client-prescribed constraints or to user constraints (i.e., ergonomic aspects like web site navigation).

We found that professional designers articulated nearly twice as many client constraints as novices in both study conditions, and they articulated more user constraints than novices. We found that when novice designers had to consider client-prescribed constraints, they experienced difficulties in considering user constraints or anticipating users' activities. Analysis of designers' web sites showed that all designers experienced difficulties in implementing articulated constraints in their designs, especially ergonomic constraints (i.e., guidelines typically enumerated in the web site design literature); novice designers respected significantly fewer articulated constraints in their designs than professionals. Expert analyses of all web sites revealed that there was an average of fifteen ergonomic violations on each.

We formulated several hypotheses to explain these results, including a hypothesis that both the novice and professional designers had become super web users via practice, and as such, ergonomic aspects that would be problematic for novice web users are not problematic for them and are consequently overlooked. To test our hypotheses, we conducted a second study wherein we asked twenty-eight designers (half novices and half professionals) to evaluate a web site in conditions with or without the same eleven client-prescribed constraints [Chevalier and Ivory, 2003b]. The web site was for a music store, which exhibited the ergonomic problems identified in the sites produced during the first study. Designers articulated the constraints (client-prescribed and ergonomic) that they thought the site violated. We found that novices and professionals articulated a significantly larger number of constraints linked to ergonomic aspects than to the client-prescribed constraints. However, they only identified 5–7 percent of the ergonomic problems that the site exhibited.

In our third study [Chevalier, 2002], we asked sixteen designers (half novices and half professionals) to develop a car dealer's web site in conditions with eleven ergonomic constraints or with half ergonomic and half client-prescribed constraints. Ergonomic constraints represented the most common problems that designers identified in the second study. Designers articulated the constraints that they were applying as they developed the site. All designers in the condition with only ergonomic constraints managed to respect them in their sites, and they inferred a large number of client constraints. Designers in the other condition experienced difficulties considering both the users' and the client's needs. Sites in both conditions had a large number of ergonomic problems.

4.2   Use of Guidelines With Training

Results of the three studies led us to conclude that guidelines are difficult to apply in the Web domain and that training is required to make them accessible to novice designers. Hence, our fourth study examined the effect of a short training program in applying usability criteria and recommendations on the evaluation and improvement of a web site that contained usability problems [Chevalier and Ivory, 2003a]. The training program presented web site usability criteria along with recommendations and examples. Seven untrained and six trained novice designers participated in the study. Study results showed that the trained novices identified 31 percent more usability problems than the untrained novices. Moreover, the trained novices managed to make several modifications to the site's home page to improve its usability. Sites in both conditions still exhibited usability problems.

Although guideline use is a prevalent work practice, the four studies show that even though designers attempt to apply guidelines and to consider users' needs, they have difficulty addressing them. Training novice designers to apply guidelines improves their ability to do so, but it is still not enough to help them to produce sites without usability problems.

5.   Discussion

We summarized the results of two surveys that show that web practitioners take various steps to ensure that sites are of universal benefit: (1) at least half of them always optimize pages for fast download, and (2) at least 30 percent of them always use design guidelines. How frequently practitioners employ these approaches has not changed much from 1997 to 2002; however, there is slightly more effort to make sites accessible, seemingly by using design guidelines. Only fifteen percent of practitioners reported using automated evaluation tools all the time. In Chapters 9 and 14, we discuss ways in which to improve automated evaluation methods and tools and to consequently expand their adoption and use.

We also summarized four studies on the use of design guidelines, which show that although guideline use is a prevalent practice, practitioners, novices in particular, experience difficulty in adhering to guidelines. Novices, and perhaps professionals, need more support in designing universally beneficial sites. We think that design and evaluation tools that are more effective than the existing ones can provide this much needed support.

Notes

1 We use the term practitioner to refer to designers, usability engineers, information architects, webmasters, and other professionals who participate in the design and development of web sites
2 Web design guidelines are recommendations, heuristics, or criteria that prescribe design choices at many levels from the overall design approach to specific interface details (e.g., font sizes or color combinations to use). They can be determined from empirical studies (e.g., [Bernard *et al.*, 2001; Bernard and Mills, 2000; Boyarski *et al.*, 1998; Larson and Czerwinski, 1998]) or from the experiences of experts in practice (e.g., [Nielsen, 2000; Spool *et al.*, 1999]). They can also arise from broader efforts lead by standardization committees or organizations like the World Wide Web Consortium (e.g., [World Wide Web Consortium, 2001c]) or the International Organisation for Standardisation (e.g., [International Organisation for Standardisation, 2002]).
3 Novice designers in all our studies had recently completed an HTML authoring class, but they had not built a professional site or worked with a client.

II

RESEARCHER'S PERSPECTIVE

Chapter 2

AUTOMATED EVALUATION METHODS

This chapter provides the foundation for our discussion in Part II of automated web site evaluation methods. We discuss frameworks for describing evaluation methods in general, and automated evaluation methods in particular. We point out the limitations of existing frameworks and describe an expanded taxonomy for classifying evaluation automation. We summarize the application of this taxonomy to 84 methods, and in the process, we characterize the state-of-the-art in automated web site evaluation. We include approaches that were developed after our original survey of 58 methods [Ivory and Hearst, 2001; Ivory, 2001], but suggest that the reader refer to these prior surveys for a more comprehensive discussion of automated and non-automated methods for evaluating both graphical and web interfaces. Chapters 3–7 provide methodology details, including summative assessments of the techniques.

Survey results suggest promising ways to expand existing approaches to better support automated web site evaluation. We elaborate on one such approach— the WebTango method for deriving design guidance from empirical data [Ivory and Hearst, 2002a]—in Chapter 8. We discuss other promising approaches in Chapter 9. We refer the reader to Appendix A for an exhaustive list of methodologies and tools that are discussed in this book.

1.   Early Surveys of Automated Evaluation Methods

Several surveys of evaluation methods for graphical interfaces exist; Hom [1998] and Zhang [1999] provide a detailed discussion of inspection, inquiry, and testing methods (these terms are defined in Section 2). Several taxonomies of evaluation methods have also been proposed. The most commonly used taxonomy is one that distinguishes between predictive (e.g., GOMS analysis and cognitive walkthrough, also defined in Section 2) and experimental (e.g., usability testing) techniques [Coutaz, 1995]. Whitefield *et al.* [1991] present another classification scheme that is based on the presence or absence of a user and a computer. Neither of these taxonomies reflect the automated aspects of evaluation methods.

The first survey of evaluation automation, by Balbo [1995], uses a taxonomy which distinguishes among four approaches to automation:

- **Non Automatic**: methods "performed by human factors specialists."

- **Automatic Capture**: methods that "rely on software facilities to record relevant information about the user and the system, such as visual data, speech acts, and keyboard and mouse actions."

- **Automatic Analysis**: methods that are "able to identify usability problems automatically."

- **Automatic Critic**: methods which "not only point out difficulties but propose improvements."

Balbo uses these categories to classify thirteen common and uncommon evaluation methods. However, most of the methods surveyed require extensive human effort, because they rely on formal usability testing or require considerable evaluator interaction. For example, Balbo classifies several techniques for processing log files as automatic analysis methods despite the fact that these approaches require formal testing or informal use to generate those log files. What Balbo calls an automatic critic method may require the evaluator to create a complex interface model as input. Thus, this classification scheme is somewhat misleading, because it ignores the non-automated requirements of the evaluation methods.

2.   Taxonomy of Automated Evaluation Methods

We group methods along the following four dimensions:

- **Method Class:** describes the type of evaluation conducted at a high level (e.g., usability testing or simulation);

- **Method Type:** describes *how* the evaluation is conducted within a method class, such as thinking-aloud protocol (usability testing class) or information processor modeling (simulation class);

- **Automation Type:** describes the evaluation aspect that is automated (e.g., capture, analysis, or critique); and

- **Effort Level:** describes the type of effort required to execute the method (e.g., model development or interface usage).

Figure 2.1 demonstrates this classification scheme. We describe each taxonomy dimension in the remainder of this section.

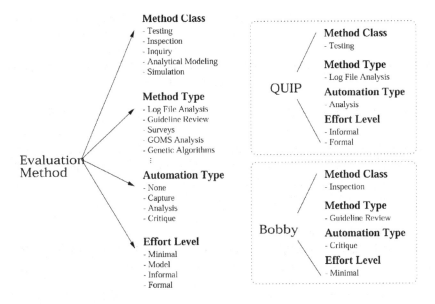

Figure 2.1. Taxonomy for classifying evaluation methods. The right side of the figure demonstrates the taxonomy with two approaches that are discussed in later chapters.

2.1   Method Class

We classify evaluation approaches into five method classes: testing, inspection, inquiry, analytical modeling, and simulation.

- **Testing:** an evaluator observes participants interacting with an interface (i.e., completing tasks) to determine usability problems.

- **Inspection:** an evaluator uses a set of criteria or heuristics to identify potential usability problems in an interface.

- **Inquiry:** participants provide feedback on an interface via interviews, surveys, etc.

- **Analytical Modeling:** an evaluator employs user and interface models to generate usability predictions.

- **Simulation:** an evaluator employs user and interface models to mimic a user interacting with an interface and report the results of this interaction (e.g., simulated activities, errors, and other quantitative measures).

Evaluation methods in the testing, inspection, and inquiry classes are appropriate for formative (i.e., identifying specific usability problems) and summative (i.e., obtaining general assessments of usability) purposes. Analytical modeling and simulation are engineering approaches to evaluation that enable evaluators to predict usability with user and interface models. Software engineering practices have had a major influence on the first three classes, while the latter two, analytical modeling and simulation, are quite similar to techniques used to analyze the performance of computer systems [Jain, 1991].

2.2   Method Type

There is a wide range of evaluation methods within the testing, inspection, inquiry, analytical modeling, and simulation classes. Rather than discuss each method individually, one or more related methods are grouped into method types, which typically describe *how* an evaluation is performed. Chapters 3–7 present these method types.

2.3   Automation Type

We adapt Balbo's automation taxonomy (described in Section 1) to specify the aspect of an evaluation method that is automated: none, capture, analysis or critique.

- **None:** no level of automation supported (i.e., evaluator performs all aspects of the evaluation method).

- **Capture:** software automatically records usability data (e.g., logging interface usage).

- **Analysis:** software automatically identifies potential usability problems.

- **Critique:** software automates analysis and suggests improvements.

2.4   Effort Level

Balbo's automation taxonomy is also expanded to include consideration of a method's non-automated requirements. Each evaluation method is augmented with an attribute called **effort level**, which indicates the human effort required for method execution:

- **Minimal Effort:** does not require interface usage or modeling.

- **Model Development:** requires the evaluator to develop an interface model or a user model to employ the method.

- **Informal Use:** requires completion of freely chosen tasks (i.e., unconstrained use by a user or evaluator).

- **Formal Use:** requires completion of specially selected tasks (i.e., constrained use by a user or evaluator).

These levels are not necessarily ordered by the amount of effort required, because it depends on the method used.

2.5   Summary

The taxonomy consists of: a method class (testing, inspection, inquiry, analytical modeling, and simulation); a method type (e.g., log file analysis, guideline review, surveys, etc.); an automation type (none, capture, analysis, and critique); and an effort level (minimal, model, informal, and formal).

3.   Overview of the Surveyed Methods

We surveyed 84 methods applied to web sites and analyzed them using our taxonomy. Table 2.1 shows surveyed approaches for each method class (bold entries in the first column) and the method types within each class (entries that are not bold in the first column). Each entry in columns two through five depicts specific evaluation methods along with the automation support available and the human effort required to employ automation. For some evaluation methods, we discuss more than one approach; hence, we show the number of methods surveyed in parentheses beside the effort level. Some approaches provide automation support for multiple method types (see Appendix A). Table 2.1 also summarizes the number of non-automated and automated capture, analysis, and critique method types surveyed. Table 2.2 provides descriptions of all method types.

There are major differences in automation support among the five method classes. For instance, analytical modeling and simulation classes are far less explored. Table 2.1 shows that automation in general is greatly underexplored. Methods without automation support represent 67 percent of the approaches surveyed, while methods with automation support collectively represent only 33 percent. Of this 33 percent, capture methods represent 15 percent, analysis methods represent 13 percent, and critique methods represent 3 percent. All but one of the capture methods require some level of interface usage; information scent modeling uses simulation to generate usage data for subsequent analysis. Of all the surveyed methods, only 18 percent are free from requirements of formal or informal interface use.

To provide the fullest automation support, software would have to critique interfaces without requiring formal or informal use. The survey revealed that this level of automation has been developed for only two method types: guideline review (e.g., [RetroAccess, 2002; Scholtz and Laskowski, 1998; WatchFire, 2002]) and cognitive walkthrough (e.g., [Blackmon *et al.*, 2003]). Guideline review methods automatically detect and report usability violations and then make suggestions for fixing them (discussed further in Chapter 4). The automated cognitive walkthrough approach can identify potential navigation problems and

Table 2.1. Automation support for 84 web evaluation methods.[a,b]

| Method Class | Automation Type | | | |
Method Type	None	Capture	Analysis	Critique
Testing				
Thinking-aloud Protocol	F (1)			
Question-asking Protocol	F (1)			
Shadowing Method	F (1)			
Coaching Method	F (1)			
Teaching Method	F (1)			
Co-discovery Learning	F (1)			
Performance Measurement	F (1)	F (4)	(2)	
Log File Analysis			IFM (18)[c]	
Retrospective Testing	F (1)			
Remote Testing		IF (3)		
Inspection				
Guideline Review	IF (4)		(10)	(15)
Cognitive Walkthrough	IF (2)			(1)
Pluralistic Walkthrough	IF (1)			
Heuristic Evaluation	IF (1)			
Perspective-based Inspection	IF (1)			
Feature Inspection	IF (1)			
Formal Usability Inspection	F (1)			
Consistency Inspection	IF (1)			
Standards Inspection	IF (1)			
Inquiry				
Contextual Inquiry	IF (1)			
Field Observation	IF (1)			
Focus Groups	IF (1)			
Interviews	IF (1)			
Surveys	IF (1)	IF (2)		
Questionnaires	IF (1)	IF (2)		
Self-reporting Logs	IF (1)			
Screen Snapshots	IF (1)	IF (1)		
User Feedback	IF (1)			
Analytical Modeling				
No Methods Surveyed				
Simulation				
Information Proc. Modeling			M (1)	
Information Scent Modeling		M (1)	M (3)	
Method Types Surveyed				
Total	26	6	5	2
Percent	67%	15%	13%	5%

[a] A number in parentheses indicates the number of evaluation methods surveyed for a particular method type and automation type. The effort level for each method is represented as: minimal (blank), formal (F), informal (I), and model (M).

[b] Seven software tools provide automation support for multiple method types.

[c] Methods may or may not require a model.

Table 2.2.   Descriptions of the web evaluation method types depicted in Table 2.1.

Method Class Method Type	Description
Testing	
Thinking-aloud Protocol	user talks during test
Question-asking Protocol	tester asks user questions
Shadowing Method	expert explains user actions to tester
Coaching Method	user can ask an expert questions
Teaching Method	expert user teaches novice user
Co-discovery Learning	two users collaborate
Performance Measurement	tester records and analyzes performance data
Log File Analysis	tester analyzes usage data
Retrospective Testing	tester reviews videotape with user
Remote Testing	tester and user are not co-located during test
Inspection	
Guideline Review	expert checks guideline conformance
Cognitive Walkthrough	expert simulates user's problem solving
Pluralistic Walkthrough	multiple people conduct cognitive walkthrough
Heuristic Evaluation	expert identifies heuristic violations
Perspective-based Inspection	expert conducts narrowly focused heuristic evaluation
Feature Inspection	expert evaluates product features
Formal Usability Inspection	experts conduct formal heuristic evaluation
Consistency Inspection	expert checks consistency across products
Standards Inspection	expert checks for standards compliance
Inquiry	
Contextual Inquiry	interviewer questions users in their environment
Field Observation	interviewer observes system use in user's environment
Focus Groups	multiple users participate in a discussion session
Interviews	one user participates in a discussion session
Surveys	interviewer asks user specific questions
Questionnaires	user provides answers to specific questions
Self-reporting Logs	user records interface operations
Screen Snapshots	user captures interface screens
User Feedback	user submits comments
Analytical Modeling	
No Methods Surveyed	
Simulation	
Information Proc. Modeling	mimic user interaction
Information Scent Modeling	mimic web site navigation

provide guidance for correcting them [Blackmon *et al.*, 2002; Blackmon *et al.*, 2003].

Of those methods that support the next level of automation—analysis—Table 2.1 shows that log file analysis, guideline review, and simulation methods represent the majority. Most of these methods do not require formal or informal interface use. However, they do require the site to be implemented.

Subsequent chapters describe evaluation methodologies surveyed, and the emphasis is on methods that support automated analysis and critique of web sites. (There are no automated analysis or critique methods for the analytical modeling and inquiry classes, so we describe briefly these approaches.) The discussion also presents assessments of these automated evaluation techniques using the following criteria:

- **Effectiveness:** how well a method discovers usability problems,

- **Ease of use:** how easy a method is to employ,

- **Ease of learning:** how easy a method is to learn, and

- **Applicability:** how widely applicable a method is to web sites other than those originally applied to.

We highlight the effectiveness, ease of use, ease of learning, and applicability of automated assessment methods in our discussions of each method class.

Chapter 3

USABILITY TESTING METHODS

Usability testing with human participants is a fundamental evaluation method [Nielsen, 1993; Shneiderman, 1998]. It provides an evaluator with direct information about how people use web sites and the problems that they encounter with the sites being tested. During usability testing, participants use the site or a prototype to complete a predetermined set of tasks, while the tester or software records the results of the participants' work. The evaluator then uses these results to determine how well the site supports users' task completion and to derive other measures, such as the number of errors encountered and task completion time.

Our survey revealed methods to support automated analysis of web sites, but we are not aware of methods to support automated critique. We summarize the automated analysis methods and conclude with an assessment of the surveyed approaches.

1. Synopsis of Automated Analysis Methods

Automation is used in three ways within usability testing: automated monitoring or measurement of web server performance, automated capture of usage data, and automated analysis of this data according to some metrics or a model (referred to as log file analysis in Table 2.1). In rare cases, methods support both automated capture and analysis of usage data (e.g., [Al-Qaimari and McRostie, 1999; Hong *et al.*, 2001]).

Table 3.1 provides a synopsis of the automated analysis method types that we discuss in this chapter—performance measurement and log file analysis. Log file analysis is the predominate approach, mainly because web servers automatically log client requests [Drott, 1998; Fuller and de Graaff, 1996; Hochheiser and Shneiderman, 2001; Sullivan, 1997]. However, server log files are not very accurate. They do not capture user interactions that occur only on

Table 3.1.   Synopsis of automated analysis support for usability testing methods.[a]

Method Class:	Testing
Automation Type:	Analysis
Method Type:	Performance Measurement—analyze performance data (2 methods)

Evaluation Method	Effort
Monitor web server availability	
Measure web server performance	

Method Class:	Testing
Automation Type:	Analysis
Method Type:	Log File Analysis—analyze usage data (18 methods)

Evaluation Method	Effort
Use of task models (AWUSA, QUIP, WebQuilt, KALDI, WebRemUSINE)	IFM[b]
Statistical analysis (traffic- and time-based)	IF
On-line analytical processing ([Büchner and Mulvenna, 1998], WebLogMiner)	IF
Usage mining (AWUSA, LumberJack, MiDAS, SpeedTracer, WUM, WEBMINER, WebLogMiner)	IFM[b]
Visualization (pattern-, behavior-, usage-, and evolution-based)	IF

[a] The effort level for some methods is minimal, which is denoted by the missing entries in the Effort column.
[b] Methods may or may not require a model.

the client side (e.g., use of within-page anchor links or the back button) and their validity is questionable due to caching by proxy servers and browsers [Etgen and Cantor, 1999; Scholtz and Laskowski, 1998]. Server logs may not reflect usability, especially because these logs are often difficult to interpret [Schwartz, 2000] and users' tasks may not be discernible [Byrne *et al.*, 1999; Schwartz, 2000]. Client-side logs capture more accurate, comprehensive usage data than server-side logs, because they allow all browser events to be recorded. Such logging may provide more insight about usability. On the downside, it requires every web page to be modified to log usage data, or the use of an instrumented browser or special proxy server.

The survey revealed four general approaches for analyzing log files: metric-based, pattern-matching, task-based, and inferential [Ivory, 2001; Ivory and Hearst, 2001]. Only task-based and inferential approaches have been applied to web log files; thus, we discuss them in this chapter.

2.   Performance Measurement of Web Servers

Web server unavailability or inadequate performance negatively affects web site usability [Wilson, 1999; Zona Research, Inc., 1999; Zurier, 1999]. Hence, numerous tools and services are available to monitor web server availability (e.g., [AlertSite, 2002; Bacheldor, 1999; BMC Software, 2002; Exodus, 2002; Freshwater Software, 2002; Keynote Systems, Inc., 2002]) and to measure web server performance (e.g., [Keynote Systems, Inc., 2003; Paessler GmbH, 2003; WebPartner, 2002]). For instance, Keynote's Red Alert [Keynote Systems, Inc., 2002] can send a request to a web server every 5 or 15 minutes to determine if the server is responsive. If the server is non-responsive, then it will attempt to diagnose the source of the failure (e.g., network or server problems) and send an email or phone message about the problem to the webmaster. It is also possible to monitor individual pages in the site like purchase pages or scripts to ensure that they are functioning properly. Tools like BMC Software's SiteAngel [BMC Software, 2002] and Freshwater Software's SiteSeer [Freshwater Software, 2002] can collect performance measures from multiple geographical locations under various access conditions. Most commercial web servers include tools to assess server availability and performance. One example is the Resource Analyzer [IBM, Inc., 2002] that accompanies IBM WebSphere.

Performance measurement approaches stress the web server to determine how much traffic it can handle and its response time under heavy loads. Both performance monitoring and measurement approaches allow evaluators to pinpoint performance bottlenecks, such as slow server response time, that may negatively affect the usability of a web site. They do not require any additional effort to use, once the site has been implemented. However, they focus on server and network performance and provide little insight on the usability of the site itself.

3. Task-Based Analysis of Log Files

Task-based approaches analyze discrepancies between the designer's anticipation of the user's task completion steps (represented as a task model) and what a user actually does while using the site. The QUIP (Quantitative User Interface Profiling) tool [Helfrich and Landay, 1999] and KALDI (Keyboard/mouse Action Logger and Display Instrument) [Al-Qaimari and McRostie, 1999] support task-based, log file analysis for Java interfaces. Java interfaces, such as applets and Java server pages, are often used in the web domain. The remaining task-based approaches in Table 3.1 are applicable broadly to sites that are implemented in HTML.

QUIP aggregates traces of multiple user interactions and compares the task flows of these users to the designer's task flow. QUIP encodes quantitative time-based and trace-based information into directed graphs (see Figure 3.1). For example, the average time between actions is indicated by the color of each arrow, and the proportion of users who performed a particular sequence of actions is indicated by the width of each arrow. The designer's task flow is

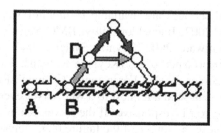

Figure 3.1. QUIP usage profile contrasting task flows for two users to the designer's task flow (diagonal shading) [Helfrich and Landay, 1999]. Each node represents a user action, and arrows indicate actions taken by users. The width of arrows denotes the fraction of users completing actions, while the color of arrows reflects the average time between actions (darker colors correspond to longer time). Reprinted with permission of the authors.

indicated by the diagonal shading in Figure 3.1. Currently, the evaluator must instrument the interface to collect the necessary usage data, and must manually analyze the graphs to identify usability problems.

WebQuilt [Hong *et al.*, 2001] provides a graphical depiction of usage data captured via a special proxy server. The visualization is very similar to QUIP, in that it aggregates usage data and summarizes task completion with arrows showing actions taken by users, the percentages of users taking the actions (width), and the average times users spent on pages before selecting links (color). Web-Quilt also enables the evaluator to view the usage data at multiple levels of detail using a zooming interface. For example, if users spent a considerable amount of time on a web page, the evaluator could view the actual page within the interface.

KALDI [Al-Qaimari and McRostie, 1999] captures usage data and screen snapshots for Java applications. It also enables the evaluator to classify tasks (both manually and automatically via filters), compare user performance on tasks, and playback synchronized screen shots. It depicts logs graphically to facilitate analysis.

WebRemUSINE (Web Remote USer Interface Evaluator) [Paganelli and Paternò, 2002] is an approach for capturing client-side log files and comparing usage patterns to specified task sequences. Evaluators use the ConcurTaskTrees [Paternò *et al.*, 1997] editor to express web site tasks as a series of temporal relationships among a collection of pages. Using this information, WebRemU-SINE looks for precondition errors (i.e., task sequences that violate temporal relationships) and also reports quantitative metrics (e.g., task completion time) and information about task patterns, missing tasks, and user preferences reflected in the usage data. Studies with a system for graphical interfaces (USINE) [Lecerof and Paternò, 1998]) showed that USINE's results correspond with empirical observations and highlight the source of some usability problems. To

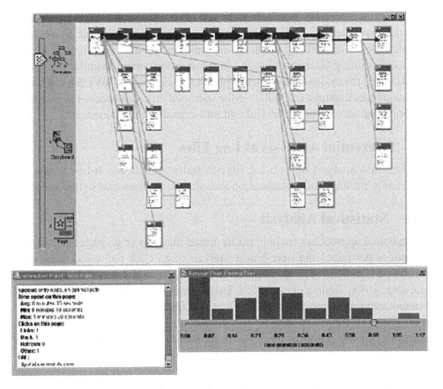

Figure 3.2. WebQuilt visualization contrasting task flows for twelve users to the designer's task flow (path across the top). Each node of the graph in the top window is a thumbnail image corresponding to a web page and the arrows are actions taken by users to transition between pages. Nodes are outlined with a color based upon the aggregate time spent on the page (e.g., green indicates a relatively fast speed and red a relatively slow speed); colors are controlled by the window on the lower right (the slider filter panel). Special entry and exit nodes are highlighted with shaded and colored outlines. The width of arrows corresponds to the relative number of users traversing the path; the color blue is used to distinguish the designer's designated path (path across the top). When a node is selected, specific information regarding that web page (e.g., the minimum, maximum, and average time that users spent on the page) is displayed in the information panel in the lower left window. The interface enables evaluators to zoom in and out of the graph so that they can view usage data at different levels of detail (e.g., page- and site-levels). This figure is a more recent and unpublished version of the figure presented in [Hong *et al.*, 2001]. Reprinted with permission of the authors.

use the system, evaluators must create task models using the ConcurTaskTrees editor and specify mappings between log file entries and the task model. We-bRemUSINE can analyze multiple log files (typically captured remotely) to enable comparisons across users [Paternò and Ballardin, 1999].

Unlike the preceding approaches, the AWUSA (Automated Website USability Analysis) [Tiedtke *et al.*, 2002] framework integrates multiple assessment techniques—task-based log file analysis, guideline review (see Chapter 4), and web usage mining (discussed later)—into one environment. Similarly to Web-RemUSINE, the evaluator specifies explicit task sequences. AWUSA compares task sequences captured in log files to the specified task sequences. For instance, it reports the number of successful and unsuccessful task sequences.

4.   Inferential Analysis of Log Files

Inferential analysis of web log files includes statistical, on-line analytical processing, mining, and visualization techniques, as discussed in this section.

4.1   Statistical Analysis

Statistical approaches include traffic-based analysis (e.g., pages-per-visitor or visitors-per-page) and time-based analysis (e.g., click paths and page-view durations) [Drott, 1998; Fuller and de Graaff, 1996; Sullivan, 1997; Theng and Marsden, 1998; Tiedtke *et al.*, 2002]. In the recent past, most methods required manual preprocessing or filtering of the log files before analysis [Cooley *et al.*, 1999]. However, current tools automate most preprocessing. Statistical analysis typically produces quantitative measures that an evaluator must interpret to identify usability problems. Software tools, such as WebTrends [NetIQ, 2002], NetGenesis [CustomerCentric Solutions, 2002], and NetTracker [Sane Solutions, LLC, 2002], facilitate analysis by presenting results in graphical and report formats (i.e., static tables and charts).

Statistical analysis is largely inconclusive for web server logs, given that they provide only a partial trace of user behavior and timing estimates may be skewed by network latencies. Server log files are also missing valuable information about what tasks users want to accomplish [Byrne *et al.*, 1999; Schwartz, 2000]. Nonetheless, statistical analysis techniques have been useful for improving usability and enable ongoing, cost-effective evaluation throughout the life of a site [Fuller and de Graaff, 1996; Sullivan, 1997].

4.2   On-Line Analytical Processing

On-Line Analytical Processing (OLAP) is an approach for interactively exploring multidimensional data [Chaudhuri and Dayal, 1997]. It enables the analyst to construct custom views of the data (referred to as data cubes; Figure 3.3) so that she can explore relationships among various dimensions to make inferences about the data. There are four basic OLAP operations that analysts can use to explore a data cube: drill-down (explore along one dimension), roll-up (reverse of drill-down), slice (define a sub-cube along one dimension), and dice (define a sub-cube along multiple dimensions). The analyst can make

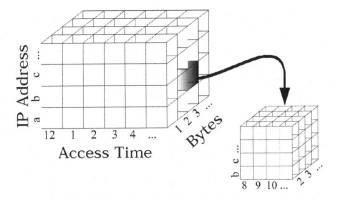

Figure 3.3. Three-dimensional data cube for a web log file. The sub-cube on the right depicts the results of a dice operation.

hypotheses about the data (e.g., correlations between two dimensions) and use these operations to test these hypotheses.

Zaïane *et al.* [1998] and Büchner and Mulvenna [1998] proposed the use of OLAP in the analysis of web log files; Dyreson [1997] proposed an approach for constructing data cubes specifically for this task. WebLogMiner [Zaïane *et al.*, 1998] enables evaluators to explore relationships among various dimensions (e.g., the time of web site use, the amount of bytes transferred, and the user's IP address) to make inferences about how users access a site. For example, the evaluator can explore access patterns or user behaviors over time (Figure 3.3). Büchner and Mulvenna [1998] propose an OLAP tool that integrates data from web server logs, web metadata (i.e., information about the topology of the site, labels for content areas, and characteristics of pages), and marketing data to discover marketing trends, such as how customers are attracted to the site, how they are retained, and which cross-sales are successful.

OLAP may enable the evaluator to identify areas of the site that need to be improved. The interactive exploration and summarization of web log data that is possible with OLAP is in stark contrast to statistical analysis approaches; the latter simply generate static tables or graphs of access trends. OLAP approaches are still affected by the limitations of server log files.

4.3 Web Usage Mining

Web usage mining entails the application of data mining techniques, such as deriving association rules or decision trees, to the analysis of user behavior captured in log files [Cooley *et al.*, 1997; Etzioni, 1996; Kosala and Blockeel, 2000; Spiliopoulou *et al.*, 1999; Spiliopoulou, 2000; Zaïane *et al.*, 1998]. After processing a log file to reconstruct usage sessions [Cooley *et al.*, 1999; Srivastava *et al.*, 2000], the evaluator can use machine learning techniques to develop predictive models of user behavior. For example, the evaluator may derive association rules to show that large percentages of users access the same sequence of three pages; in this case, server pre-fetching may be used to preload pages or the site may be adapted dynamically or redesigned based on such use profiles [Masseglia *et al.*, 1999; Spiliopoulou, 2000]. Although researchers have applied traditional data mining techniques to web log files, new techniques have been developed (e.g., [Borges and Levene, 1999; Gaul and Schmidt-Thieme, 2000; Heer and Chi, 2002a]). In addition, researchers have developed both automated (unsupervised) and supervised mining tools for web log file analysis.

There are numerous web usage mining tools available, and we survey a few of them in this section. All tools are concerned with identifying navigation paths and then discovering navigation patterns across users. SpeedTracer [Wu *et al.*, 1997] derives association rules and generates statistical reports to summarize characteristics of frequently traversed paths. WebLogMiner [Zaïane *et al.*, 1998] provides both OLAP (see preceding section) and data mining support; the data mining techniques include the derivation of association rules, decision trees, and transition matrices to reflect correlations between accessed pages. WEBMINER [Cooley *et al.*, 1997; Cooley *et al.*, 1999] provides similar functionality, as well as a way for the evaluator to query and analyze the discovered patterns to better inform site changes.

LumberJack [Chi *et al.*, 2002; Heer and Chi, 2002b] applies clustering analysis to derive major groupings of user traffic and then computes statistical measures for each group (e.g., number of sessions, percentage of site visitors, and keywords that characterize the group). Unlike other data mining approaches, LumberJack considers the content on web pages, the structure of the site, and the log file data in its clustering algorithms [Heer and Chi, 2002a]. The authors have shown through several empirical studies that the clustering approach yields good results (99 percent accuracy in some cases) and that LumberJack can help to inform site improvements. AWUSA (discussed in Section 3) takes a related approach to web usage mining, in that it considers the web site's structure and the evaluator-specified tasks in its analysis of usage patterns.

The preceding mining approaches are all unsupervised, which means that they do not enable the evaluator to influence how predictive models are derived. M*i*DAS [Büchner *et al.*, 1999; Spiliopoulou, 2000] and the Web Utilization Miner (WUM) [Spiliopoulou and Faulstich, 1998; Spiliopoulou, 2000] enable evaluators to supervise the mining process. M*i*DAS enables the evaluator to specify patterns that are potentially interesting using a mining language. In addition, it enables the evaluator to specify what constitutes a navigation pattern as opposed to using default pattern extraction rules. An empirical study showed that the developers could use the tool to gain insight for improving the design of an educational web site [Berendt and Spiliopolou, 2000; Spiliopolou and

Pohle, 2001]. WUM does not support the specification of navigation pattern constraints, but it does enable evaluators to specify criteria to guide the discovery process.

Although web usage mining may provide more insight than the other inferential analysis approaches provide, it requires considerable data mining expertise to use. Furthermore, it may be difficult to interpret the discovered knowledge to make corrective changes to the web site. Most mining tools provide some way to visualize the discovered patterns and related statistical measures, which may help to facilitate the analysis process.

4.4 Visualization

Visualization is also used for inferential analysis of web log files [Chi *et al.*, 2000; Cugini and Scholtz, 1999; Guzdial *et al.*, 1994; Hochheiser and Shneiderman, 2001]. It enables evaluators to filter, manipulate, and render log file data in a way that ideally facilitates analysis. Our survey revealed four major visualization approaches—pattern-, behavior-, usage-, and evolution-based. We describe these approaches in this section. In general, it would be beneficial to employ a statistical analysis or mining approach to study traffic, clickstreams, and page views prior to exploring visualizations.

4.4.1 Pattern-Based

Pattern-based visualizations attempt to provide an overview of usage patterns reflected in log files. They fall in the continuum between statistical analysis (i.e., static charts and graphs) and OLAP approaches (i.e., interactive exploration of multiple dimensions). Starfield visualization [Hochheiser and Shneiderman, 2001] is one example that enables evaluators to interactively explore web server log data to gain an understanding of the human factors issues related to visitation patterns. This approach combines the simultaneous display of a large number of individual data points (e.g., URLs requested versus time of requests) in an interface that supports zooming, filtering, and dynamic querying [Ahlberg and Shneiderman, 1994]. Visualizations provide a high-level view of usage patterns (e.g., usage frequency, correlated references, bandwidth usage, HTTP errors, and patterns of repeated visits over time) that the evaluator must explore to identify usability problems.

4.4.2 Behavior-Based

Behavior-based visualizations characterize user behavior during a usage session, but the emphasis is not on how users' task completion steps correspond with the designer's task completion (i.e., task-based analysis; see Section 3). For example, Card *et al.* [2001] developed a protocol analysis approach for aggregating client-side log file data, verbal protocols, and eye-tracker data such

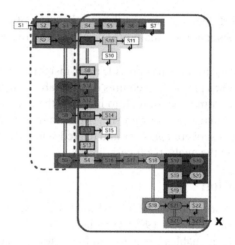

Figure 3.4. Web behavior graph for a usage session. Each rectangle corresponds to a state in the task completion process, and ovals indicate a list of keywords specified during a search operation. Arrows depict the user's movements to new states; double vertical lines indicate the return to previous states. Each state is shaded to indicate the strength of the information scent between pages; darker colors indicate higher information scent. Each group of states that are shaded similarly corresponds to a different web site. The dotted lines on the left indicate searching behavior, and the solid lines on the right indicate browsing behavior. The X indicates that the user did not complete the task. Adapted from [Card *et al.*, 2001] with the authors permission.

that users' information-seeking behavior could be analyzed. More specifically, the authors attempt to infer the information "scent" [Chi *et al.*, 2000; Furnas, 1997; Pirolli and Card, 1995] or cues that users follow during task completion. The authors developed web behavior graphs (WBG) to depict information-seeking behavior (Figure 3.4). WBGs summarize user movements (searching and browsing) and the strength of information scent at each step. Figure 3.4 shows, for example, that when the information scent gets lower on a site (indicated by states with lighter colors), users switch to a different site. The evaluator can use these graphs to determine areas that need improvement on the site.

4.4.3   Usage-Based

Similarly to behavior-based visualizations, usage-based visualizations summarize web site navigation. However, they depict this information in the context of the site's structure. For example, WebViz [Pitkow and Bharat, 1994] provides a graphical view of the site and allows the evaluator to map attributes to visual aspects of the graph. The evaluator can use colors to reflect the frequency or recency of access to pages and links. WebViz also enables the evaluator to animate the graph to show patterns of site use for a specified time interval.

MIR (Metaphorical Information Representation) [Kizhakke, 2000] examines the use of spatial metaphors to represent information. It provides a three-dimensional virtual world that the evaluator can use for exploring log file data, although it is not clear whether the approach is usable in practice. Each web page is represented as a building in a spatial layout, and there are links between buildings. As the user moves through the virtual world, the view reflects the current viewpoint along with links that the user can traverse from each building. The author claims that the virtual web site walkthrough should help designers to determine whether the site's structure is effective.

The dome tree visualization [Chi *et al.*, 2000; Chi, 2002] provides an insightful representation of simulated (see Chapter 7) and actual web site usage captured in server log files. This approach maps a web site into a three-dimensional surface representing the hyperlinks (Figure 3.5). The location of links on the surface is determined by a combination of content similarity, link usage, and link structure of web pages. The visualization highlights the most commonly traversed subpaths. An evaluator can explore these usage paths to possibly gain insight about the information "scent" (i.e., common topics among web pages on the path) as depicted in Figure 3.6. This additional information may help the evaluator to infer what the information needs of site users are, and more importantly, may help them to infer whether the site satisfies those needs. The dome tree visualization also reports a crude path traversal time based on the sizes of pages (i.e., number of bytes in HTML and image files) along the path. Server log accuracy limits the extent to which this approach can successfully indicate usability problems.

ScentViz [Chi, 2002] incorporates the dome tree visualization as well as others into an environment for supporting interactive log file analysis. For instance, the disk tree visualization shows the home page in the center of a disk with links emanating from this center, based on usage patterns. This visualization provides the evaluator with information about how traffic flows from the home page, but it does not provide usage paths. It uses colored links to indicate web site changes like the addition or deletion of content. Similarly to OLAP, the evaluator can drill down into the log file data from the graph.

VISVIP [Cugini and Scholtz, 1999] is a three-dimensional tool for visualizing log files compiled by the WebVIP (Web Visual Instrumentor Program) [Scholtz and Laskowski, 1998] tool during usability testing. WebVIP is a visual tool that enables the evaluator to specify the types of user events to log (e.g., link selection, use of back button, or window resizing). These choices are converted to JavaScripts which are then inserted into each page of the site, after it is copied. This code automatically records the page identifier and a time stamp in an ASCII file every time a user selects a link.

Figures 3.7 and 3.8 show VISVIP's web site and usage path depictions to be similar to the dome tree visualization approach. VISVIP generates a two-

Figure 3.5.   Dome tree visualization [Chi *et al.*, 2000] of a web site with a usage path displayed as a series of connected lines across the left side. Reprinted with permission of the authors.

dimensional layout of the site where adjacent nodes are placed closer together than non-adjacent nodes. A third dimension reflects timing data as a dotted vertical bar at each node; the height is proportional to the amount of time that users spent on a page. Unlike the dome tree visualization, it can only depict one usage path at a time. VISVIP provides animation facilities for visualizing path traversal. Because WebVIP logs reflect actual task completion, prior statistical analysis is not necessary for VISVIP usage.

4.4.4   Evolution-Based

Given the rapid changes and growth in Internet use, evolution-based visualizations help evaluators to analyze changes in web traffic over time. As one example, ScentViz (discussed in the preceding section) [Chi, 2002] enables evaluators to compare disk tree visualizations for a specified time period. The

```
DocID   Freq   Size SA URL

33775     63    2445        docs/investor/sharinfo.htm
36369    168    3028        docs/factbook/1998/index.htm
33775     63    2445        docs/investor/sharinfo.htm
33778     58   20537        docs/investor/sitemap.htm
33780     26    2313        docs/investor/orderdoc.htm
Total Path Bytes: 30768 (17 Seconds)
Keywords for 33775 36369 33775 33778 33780:
reinvestment 7.230992
stock 6.651224
brochure 6.307321
dividend 5.522883
shareholder 5.165537
preferred 4.850075
automatic 4.215094
contacts 4.163801
```

Figure 3.6. Dome tree information about the usage path depicted in Figure 3.5, including an estimated navigation time and information scent (i.e., common keywords along the path). Reprinted with permission of the authors.

author refers to these slices of disk trees as a time tube visualization. ScentViz also contrasts usage patterns reflected in dome trees over a time period. For example, it can show both increases and decreases in usage on a weekly basis. Areas of the site with decreased activity may indicate usability problems or perhaps content that can be removed from the site.

Anemone [Dodge, 2001; Fry, 2000] generates a dynamic depiction of changes in web site usage patterns. It grows the site layout genetically as new pages are added to the site. When pages receive frequent visits, the corresponding nodes are enlarged in the visualization. Similarly, nodes shrink in size and disappear as pages receive fewer visits. The current implementation does not enable the evaluator to control the animation, and the evaluator must click on nodes in the graph to show the correspondence between each node and the page in the site.

5.   Discussion

Table 3.1 summarizes automated analysis methods discussed in this chapter. Although the techniques vary widely on the four assessment criteria (effectiveness, ease of use, ease of learning, and applicability), all approaches offer substantial benefits over the alternative—time-consuming, unaided analysis of potentially large amounts of raw data. Task-based techniques like WebQuilt and VISVIP are the most effective (i.e., provide clear insight for improving

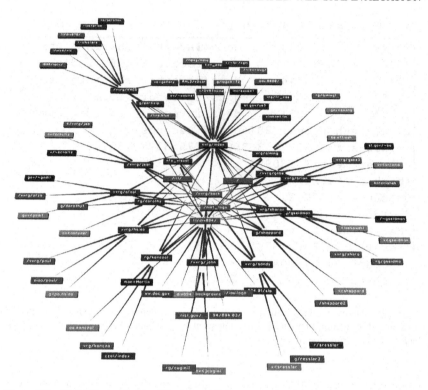

Figure 3.7. VISVIP visualization [Cugini and Scholtz, 1999] of a web site. Each node corresponds to a web page, and each arc reflects linking structure. Reprinted with permission of the authors.

usability via task analysis) and do not require additional effort to develop task models. WebRemUSINE can be highly effective, provided the evaluator accurately specifies task models and mappings between these models and log file entries. The task-based approaches do require informal or formal web site use.

Performance measurement techniques focus on server and network performance, which provides little usability insight. Similarly, inferential analysis of web server logs is limited by their accuracy and may provide inconclusive usability information. Nonetheless, web usage mining is the most effective inferential analysis approach, but it is not easy to use. Data mining is a complex process, which requires the evaluator to develop substantial expertise to build accurate models and to translate them into design changes.

The techniques surveyed in this chapter could be applied broadly to web interfaces. The current trend is to aggregate multiple approaches into one tool. For example, AWUSA incorporates both task-based and web usage mining

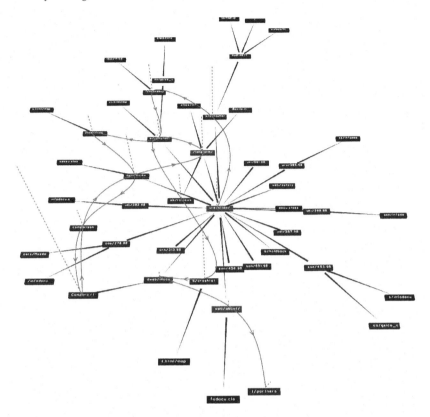

Figure 3.8. VISVIP visualization [Cugini and Scholtz, 1999] of a usage path (series of directed lines on the left site) laid over the site. Reprinted with permission of the authors.

techniques. As another example, WebLogMiner incorporates both OLAP and web usage mining approaches. Such aggregation should promote tool adoption, provided the tools are easy to use.

Chapter 4

INSPECTION METHODS

A usability inspection is an evaluation methodology whereby an evaluator examines the usability aspects of a web site with respect to its conformance to a set of guidelines. Guidelines can range from highly specific prescriptions to broad principles, and unlike other evaluation methods, inspections rely solely on the evaluator's judgment. A large number of detailed usability guidelines exist for evaluating web interfaces (e.g., [Comber, 1995; Detweiler and Omanson, 1996; Levine, 1996; Lynch and Horton, 1999; World Wide Web Consortium, 1999]). Common inspection techniques are heuristic evaluation [Nielsen, 1993] and cognitive walkthroughs [Blackmon *et al.*, 2002; Lewis *et al.*, 1990].

Our survey revealed methods to support automated analysis and critique of web sites. We summarize these methods and conclude with an assessment of them.

1.   Synopsis of Automated Analysis and Critique Methods

Designers have historically experienced difficulties following design guidelines [Borges *et al.*, 1996; de Souza and Bevan, 1990; Lowgren and Nordqvist, 1992; Smith, 1986]. One study has demonstrated that designers are biased towards aesthetically pleasing interfaces, regardless of efficiency [Sears, 1995]. Because designers have difficulty applying design guidelines, automation is used predominately within the inspection class to objectively check guideline conformance. Software tools assist evaluators with guideline review by automatically detecting and reporting usability violations and, in some cases, making suggestions for fixing them [Balbo, 1995; Farenc and Palanque, 1999]. There is also an automated cognitive walkthrough approach for web sites [Blackmon *et al.*, 2002; Blackmon *et al.*, 2003].

Tables 4.1 and 4.2 summarize 26 automated analysis and critique tools available for the guideline review and cognitive walkthrough method types. Assum-

Table 4.1. Synopsis of automated analysis support for inspection methods.[a]

Method Class:	Inspection
Automation Type:	Analysis
Method Type:	Guideline Review—expert checks guideline conformance (10 methods)

Evaluation Method	Effort
Analyze the structure of pages and site (HyperAT, Gentler, Rating Game, WebTango)	
Use guidelines for analysis (AWUSA, Dr. HTML, KWARESMI, WebSAT, WebTango)	
Analyze the scanning path of a page (Design Advisor)	
Analyze visual consistency across pages (Page Layout Change)	

[a] The effort level for all methods is minimal, which is denoted by the missing entries in the Effort column.

ing the site is implemented, all methods require minimal effort to employ, which we denote with a blank entry in the Effort column. Most approaches use a set of guidelines in the evaluation process, but these approaches cannot assess web site aspects that cannot be evaluated automatically, such as whether the text will be understood by users. For example, Farenc *et al.* [1999] showed that only 78 percent of a set of established ergonomic guidelines could be operationalized in the best case scenario and only 44 percent in the worst case.

The surveyed approaches support five general types of analyses: structural, HTML and CSS (cascading style sheet) coding, usability and accessibility, visual, and textual. We discuss these general approaches. For additional assessments of some of the guideline review tools that we discuss in this chapter, we refer the reader to Chapters 11 and 12 in Part III.

2.   Structural Analysis of Web Pages and Sites

The Rating Game [Stein, 1997] is an automated analysis tool that attempts to measure the quality of web pages using a set of easily measurable features. These aspects include: an information feature (word to link ratio), a graphics feature (number of graphics on a page), a gadgets feature (number of applets, controls, and scripts on a page), and so on. The tool reports these raw measures without providing guidance for interpreting them (with respect to a web page's quality) or for improving the web page.

Two authoring tools from Middlesex University, HyperAT [Theng and Marsden, 1998] and Gentler [Thimbleby, 1997], perform a similar structural analysis at the site level. The goal of HyperAT is to support the creation of well-structured hyper-documents. Its structural analysis entails verifying that the breadths and depths within a page and at the site level fall within thresholds

Table 4.2. Synopsis of automated critique support for inspection methods.[a]

Method Class:	Inspection
Automation Type:	Critique
Method Type:	Guideline Review—expert checks guideline conformance (15 methods)

Evaluation Method	Effort
Use coding standards for critique (Dr. Watson, HTML Validator, CSS Validator, Weblint)	
Use guidelines for critique (508 Suite, AccessEnble, AccVerify/AccRepair, ALTifier, A-Prompt, Bobby, Dr. Watson, EvalWeb, InFocus, LIFT, PageScreamer, WAVE)	

Method Class:	Inspection
Automation Type:	Critique
Method Type:	Cognitive Walkthrough—expert simulates user's problem solving (1 method)

Evaluation Method	Effort
Use text similarity measures for critique (CWW)	

[a] The effort level for all methods is minimal, which is denoted by the missing entries in the Effort column.

(e.g., depth less than three levels). (HyperAT also supports inferential analysis of server log files similarly to other log file analysis techniques; see Section 4 of Chapter 3.) Gentler [Thimbleby, 1997] provides a similar structural analysis but focuses on the maintenance of existing sites rather than the design of new ones. The effectiveness of these structural analyses is questionable, because the thresholds have not been validated empirically.

The WebTango prototype (discussed in Chapter 8) [Ivory and Hearst, 2002a] uses predictive models to analyze the structure of individual pages and the site overall. Similarly to the Rating Game, the methodology entails computing 157 quantitative page-level and site-level measures. The measures assess many aspects of web interfaces, including the amount of text on a page, color usage, and consistency. These measures along with expert ratings from Internet professionals are used to derive statistical models of highly rated web interfaces. The models are then used in the automated analysis of new sites. For instance, the prototype reports predicted ratings along with a rationale for the predictions. The evaluator has to interpret this information to determine the most appropriate design changes.

3.   Analysis of HTML and CSS Coding

Several automated critique tools use HTML and CSS coding guidelines for web page assessment. The World Wide Web Consortium's (W3C) HTML Validation Service[1] [World Wide Web Consortium, 2001c] checks that HTML code conforms to W3C coding standards. Similarly, the W3C's CSS Validation Service[2] [World Wide Web Consortium, 2002b] checks that style sheets conform to W3C standards. Weblint [Bowers, 1996] and Dr. Watson [Addy & Associates, 2000] also check HTML syntax and verify that links exists. In addition, Dr. Watson computes download speed and spell checks text.

4.   Analysis of Usability and Accessibility

Many of the automated analysis and critique tools analyze the HTML code to ensure that it conforms to accessibility or usability guidelines—the Section 508 guidelines (US Federal standard) [Center for Information Technology Accommodation, 2002], the W3C Content Accessibility Guidelines [World Wide Web Consortium, 1999], or both. There is a lot of similarity between these two sets of guidelines, because the Section 508 guidelines are based on the W3C guidelines. (See [Thatcher, 2002] for a side-by-side comparison.)

Overall, the tools address a broad range of user abilities [Ivory *et al.*, 2003], but they focus on ensuring access, rather than improving user experiences. To address the limitations of these guidelines, Coyne and Nielsen [2001] proposed an additional 75 guidelines (e.g., minimize the use of graphics or small font sizes for text, avoid pop-up windows, separate browser windows, or cascading menus, and minimize the number of links on a page) derived from studies of users with vision and mobility impairments. These guidelines are embedded in the LIFT tool - Nielsen Norman Group Edition [UsableNet, 2002a].

The tools are very similar in functionality. Essentially, the automated analysis tools—Automated Website USability Analysis (AWUSA) [Tiedtke *et al.*, 2002], Doctor HTML [Imageware, Inc., 2001], Knowledge-based Web Automatic REconfigurable evaluation with guidelineS optiMIzation (KWARESMI) [Beirekdar *et al.*, 2002a; Beirekdar *et al.*, 2002b; Beirekdar *et al.*, 2003], Web Static Analyzer Tool (WebSAT) [Scholtz and Laskowski, 1998], and Web-Tango [Ivory and Hearst, 2002a]—report guideline violations textually, graphically, numerically, or in some combination. The critique tools—508 Accessibility Suite[3] [Macromedia, 2001], AccessEnable [RetroAccess, 2002], AccVerify/AccRepair [HiSoftware, 2002a; HiSoftware, 2002b], ALTifier [Vorburger, 1999], A-Prompt [Adaptive Technology Research Center, 2002], Bobby [WatchFire, 2002], Dr. Watson [Addy & Associates, 2000], InFocus [SSB Technologies, 2002], LIFT [UsableNet, 2000; UsableNet, 2002a; UsableNet, 2002b], PageScreamer [Crunchy Technologies, 2002], WAVE [Pennsylvania's Initiative on Assistive Technology, 2001], and EvalWeb [Scapin *et al.*, 2000]—

also provide recommendations or assistance in correcting violations. Ivory *et al.* [2003] provide a detailed discussion of most of these tools.

The tools vary widely with respect to the type of assistance that they provide to evaluators when they attempt to correct violations. For example, the LIFT tools [UsableNet, 2002a; UsableNet, 2002b], 508 Accessibility Suite, AccVerify/AccRepair, and A-Prompt provide wizards to walk evaluators through code modifications. ALTifier and A-Prompt suggest alternative text based on the page context and other heuristics. AccessEnable is a web-based tool that can make some changes to pages automatically; the evaluator can then download the modified pages. PageScreamer [Crunchy Technologies, 2002] and InFocus [SSB Technologies, 2002] are desktop applications that can also make changes.

Conforming to the guidelines embedded in these tools can potentially eliminate usability problems that arise due to poor HTML syntax (e.g., missing page elements) or guideline violations. Research on web site credibility [Fogg *et al.*, 2000; Fogg *et al.*, 2001; Kim and Fogg, 1999] possibly suggests that some of the aspects assessed by these tools, such as broken links and other errors, may also affect usability due to the relationship between usability and credibility. However, Ratner *et al.* [1996] question the validity of HTML usability guidelines, because most have not been subjected to a rigorous development process as established guidelines for graphical interfaces. The authors' analysis of 21 HTML guidelines showed little consistency among them, with 75 percent of recommendations appearing in only one style guide. Furthermore, only 20 percent of HTML-relevant recommendations from established graphical interface guidelines existed in the 21 HTML guidelines.

EvalWeb is one automated critique approach proposed to address this issue. It provides a framework for applying established graphical interface guidelines (e.g., the Smith and Mosier guidelines [Smith and Mosier, 1986] and the Motif style guides [Open Software Foundation, 1991]) to relevant HTML components. Even with EvalWeb, some problems, such as whether text will be understood by users, are difficult to detect automatically.

KWARESMI is an extension of EvalWeb that provides a standard guideline definition language (GDL) and framework that evaluators can use to automate the assessment of guideline conformance. Unlike most guideline review approaches, it separates the guidelines from the evaluation engine. It enables evaluators to specify guidelines to use during the assessment (e.g., relevant to the type of site or users) and to express the order in which guidelines are checked. The evaluator needs to follow an extensive process to translate guidelines like the W3C or Smith and Mosier guidelines into GDL-compliant ones; the translated guidelines are expressed in XML. During the translation process, evaluators need to have detailed knowledge about the HTML elements and conditions that need to be evaluated for each guideline. However, provided that

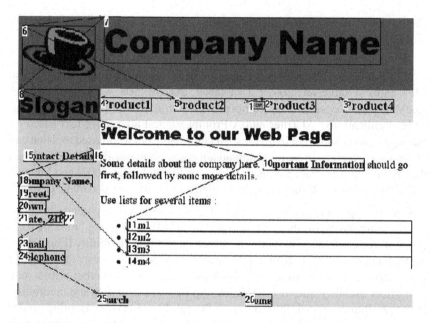

Figure 4.1. Design Advisor's scanning path for a web page [Faraday, 2000]. The numbers indicate the predicted order in which users may scan the page's elements. Reprinted with permission of the author.

an expert translates and verifies the correctness of guidelines, the translated guidelines can be used broadly by other evaluators.

5.   Visual Analysis of Web Pages

Unlike other evaluation approaches, the Design Advisor [Faraday, 2000] enables visual analysis of web pages. The tool uses empirical results from eye tracking studies designed to assess the attentional effects of various elements, such as animation, images, and highlighting, in multimedia presentations [Faraday and Sutcliffe, 1998]; these studies found motion, size, images, color, text style, and position to be scanned in this order. A preliminary eye-tracking study provides some support for the heuristics used in the web domain [Faraday, 2001]. The Design Advisor determines and superimposes a scanning path on a web page, in which page elements are numbered to indicate the order in which users are likely to scan them (Figure 5). It currently does not provide suggestions for improving scanning paths.

The Page Layout Change approach [Farkas, 2003] analyzes the consistency of layouts across pages in a site. It entails decomposing each page on a user path into a visual hierarchy [Reichenberger *et al.*, 1995], determining the type of changes (e.g., fusing of one or more regions, splitting of a region, or creation

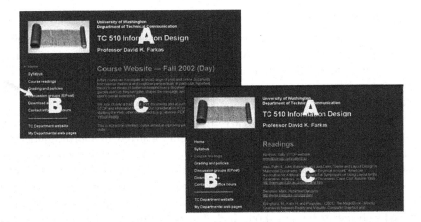

Figure 4.2. Page layout changes for a web page [Farkas, 2003]. The arrow on the left indicates the selected link. This link selection produces a change in region C of the right page. Given this minimal change, the page layout change score is 1. Reprinted with permission of the author.

of a new region) that occur within the regions that comprise the visual hierarchy, and then computing a page layout score based on the changes (Figure 4.2). The author does not provide empirically validated thresholds for the page layout scores. Currently, an evaluator has to apply the methodology manually. We included it in our discussion due to its viability as a future automated analysis approach.

6. Textual Analysis of Web Page Navigation

Cognitive Walkthrough for the Web (CWW) [Blackmon *et al.*, 2002; Blackmon *et al.*, 2003] is an automated critique approach that can identify potential navigation problems and provide guidance for correcting them. The approach entails the use of Latent Semantic Analysis [Landauer and Dumais, 1997] to contrast web page text (headings or links) to an evaluator-specified information-seeking goal (100–200 word narrative and correct link selection on the page). The LSA system computes several similarity measures for the two text inputs, based on the semantic space that the evaluator specifies (e.g., for grade nine reading ability). The authors provide LSA thresholds for three navigation problems: confusable heading or link text, unfamiliar heading or link text, and goal-specific competing heading or link text. Empirical studies have demonstrated that modifying page text to fit within these thresholds improves usability. This approach is still under development.

7.   Discussion

Tables 4.1 and 4.2 summarize the automated analysis and critique methods surveyed in this chapter. As previously discussed, the tools require minimal effort to use. In addition, they are easy to learn and apply to all basic HTML pages. They also enable ongoing assessment, which can be extremely beneficial after making design changes.

The methods appear to be highly effective at checking for guidelines (coding, usability, or accessibility) that can be operationalized, though the guidelines have not been validated empirically in most cases. For instance, it has not been established whether adhering to good coding practices will improve usability. As another example, the Rating Game, HyperAT, and Gentler use unvalidated thresholds in their structural analyses. Brajnik [2000] surveyed eleven automated web site analysis methods, including many methods that we surveyed in this chapter. The author's survey revealed that these tools address only a sparse set of usability features, such as download time, presence of alternative text for images, and validation of HTML and links. Other usability aspects, such as consistency and information organization, are addressed to a lesser degree by existing tools. We assess many of these tools in Chapters 11 and 12.

The visual analysis supported by the Design Advisor and the Page Layout Change approaches could help designers to improve web page layouts. The Design Advisor requires a special web browser for use, but it is easy to use, learn, and apply to basic web pages (i.e., pages that don't use scripts, applets, Macromedia Flash, or other non-HTML technology). The Page Layout Change approach is under development, but is very promising for assessing layout consistency across pages in a site.

Cognitive Walkthrough for the Web is the only approach that assesses the link and heading text used on web pages. Although this type of assessment is invaluable, evaluators, who are not familiar with latent semantic analysis, may find the approach to be challenging to use and learn.

We show in Chapter 11 that there is little consistency among the tools, even though the apply the same guidelines—W3C or Section 508. KWARESMI's standard guideline definition language and framework for separating guidelines from the evaluation engine could be used to unify these various evaluation engines and guidelines. This approach makes it possible to create reusable representations of the W3C and Section 508 guidelines. Furthermore, KWARESMI's evaluation engine could be used at the core of existing approaches and consequently simplify comparisons across tools.

Notes

1 We use the terms W3C HTML Validation Service, W3C HTML Validator, and W3C Validator interchangeably throughout this book.

2 We use the terms W3C CSS Validation Service and W3C CSS Validator interchangeably throughout this book.

3 We use the terms 508 Accessibility Suite and 508 Suite interchangeably throughout this book.

Chapter 5

INQUIRY METHODS

Similarly to usability testing approaches, inquiry methods require feedback from users. Evaluators use inquiry methods often during usability testing. However, the focus is not on studying specific tasks or measuring performance; the goal of these methods is to gather subjective impressions (i.e., preferences or opinions) about various aspects of a web site. Evaluators also use inquiry methods, such as surveys, questionnaires, and interviews, to gather supplementary data after a site is on-line; this feedback is useful for informing future improvements or redesigns. In addition, evaluators use inquiry methods for needs assessment early in the design process.

Inquiry methods vary based on whether the evaluator interacts with a user or a group of users or whether users report their experiences using questionnaires or usage logs, possibly in conjunction with screen snapshots. Currently, inquiry methods do not support automated analysis or critique of web sites. Automation is used to capture subjective impressions or screen snapshots during formal or informal site use. We discuss these methods in this chapter.

1.   Capture of Subjective Data

There are several web-based tools for conducting surveys and questionnaires. The two main approaches are to enable evaluators to specify instruments using an XML schema or to enable them to specify instruments using a template-based (i.e., form-fillin) interface. For example, Psychology OnLine [UWEC, 2003] is an XML-based system for specifying and conducting online surveys and questionnaires.

As another example, NetRaker's usability research tools enable practitioners to create custom HTML questionnaires and surveys via a template interface; it also provides graphical and textual summaries of results, even while studies are in progress [NetRaker, 2000]. Evaluators can interactively explore the results to segment responses by user attributes, for instance. Vividence [Vividence Corporation, 2002], Enviz Insight [Enviz, Inc., 2001], and other tools provide similar functionality. Sinha [2000] provides a comprehensive discussion and comparison of some of the available tools.

2.   Capture of Screen Snapshots

Automation has also been used to capture screen snapshots during formal or informal site use. For example, NetRaker's usability research tools include an Experience Recorder, which captures users' computer screens periodically while they participate in studies. As another example, Noldus provides an integrated hardware and software system for collecting and synchronizing behavioral data with screen snapshots [Noldus Information Technology, 2003].

3.   Discussion

Automation support for inquiry methods makes it possible to collect data quickly from a larger number of users than is typically possible without automation. However, these methods suffer from the same limitation of non-automated approaches—they may not clearly indicate usability problems due to the subjective nature of user responses. The real value of these techniques is that they are easy to use and widely applicable.

Currently, inquiry methods do not support automated analysis or critique of web sites. Similarly to task-based log file analysis approaches (see Section 3 of Chapter 3), it would be useful to compare screen snapshots generated while an expert completes a task to those generated while users complete tasks. Image processing techniques could facilitate determining automatically whether users use web pages in the same manner that they are intended to be used. Analysis of user actions within a page could complement the analysis of log files captured during the testing sessions. Automated analysis and critique approaches to support inquiry methods are open research areas.

Chapter 6

ANALYTICAL MODELING METHODS

Analytical modeling complements traditional evaluation techniques like usability testing. Given some representation or model of the interface or the user, these methods enable the evaluator to inexpensively predict usability. A wide range of modeling techniques have been developed for non-web interfaces, and they support different types of analyses as discussed in [Ivory, 2001; Ivory and Hearst, 2001]. We are not aware of analytical modeling approaches that have been developed for use in the web site evaluation domain.

Automation is used to analyze task completion (e.g., execution and learning time) within graphical interfaces. Analytical modeling inherently supports automated analysis, because the models yield quantitative performance predictions. Automated critique has not been explored for graphical interfaces.

We provide an overview of automated analysis approaches that are used in the evaluation of graphical interfaces. We then discuss the application of existing approaches and propose a new analytical modeling approach for web interface evaluation.

1. Automated Analysis of Graphical Interfaces

Most analytical modeling and simulation approaches are based on the model human processor (MHP) proposed by Card *et al.* [1983]. The MHP describes human interactions as cycles of sensing data and reacting to it (excluding any consideration of context or accumulated knowledge) and provides estimates of human performance (e.g., task completion time). GOMS analysis (Goals, Operators, Methods, and Selection rules) is one of the most widely accepted analytical modeling methods that are based on the MHP [John and Kieras, 1996]. The GOMS family of analytical modeling methods use a hierarchical task structure consisting of goals (tasks to be completed), methods (sequences of task completion steps), operators (low-level operations like moving hands or

51

typing), and selection rules (mechanisms for selecting one method to employ for task completion when there are multiple approaches). Using this task structure along with validated time parameters for each operator, the models make it possible to predict task execution and learning times, typically for error-free expert performance.

The four approaches in this family include the original GOMS method that Card *et al.* proposed (CMN-GOMS) [Card *et al.*, 1983], the simpler keystroke-level model (KLM), the natural GOMS language (NGOMSL), and the critical path method (CPM-GOMS) [John and Kieras, 1996]. These approaches differ in the task granularity modeled (e.g., keystrokes versus a high-level proce-dure), the support for alternative task completion methods, and the support for single goals versus multiple simultaneous goals. GOMS analysis has been ap-plied to all types of graphical interfaces and has been effective at predicting usability problems. However, these predictions are limited to error-free expert performance in many cases, although early accounts of GOMS considered error correction [Card *et al.*, 1983].

2.   Discussion

Approaches like GOMS analysis will not map as well to the Web domain, in particular for modeling information-seeking tasks, because it is difficult to predict how a user will accomplish the goals in a task hierarchy given that there are potentially many different ways to navigate a site. Another problem is GOMS' reliance on an expert user model (at least in the automated approaches), which does not fit the diverse user community of the Web. Hence, new analytical modeling approaches are required to evaluate the usability of web sites.

One potential solution is to use a variation of Cognitive Task Analysis (CTA) [May and Barnard, 1994], which uses a different modeling approach than GOMS analysis. CTA requires the evaluator to input an interface descrip-tion (rather than an explicit task hierarchy) to an underlying theoretical model for analysis. The theoretical model, an expert system based on Interacting Cognitive Subsystems [Barnard, 1987; Barnard and Teasdale, 1991], generates predictions about performance and usability problems similarly to a cognitive walkthrough (discussed in Chapter 4). (Interacting Cognitive Subsystems uses a computational cognitive architecture to enable evaluators to simulate inter-faces.) The system prompts the evaluator for interface details from which it generates predictions and a report detailing the theoretical basis of predictions. Such an approach could be adapted for web interfaces.

Chapter 7

SIMULATION METHODS

Simulation complements traditional assessment methods and inherently supports automated analysis. Using models of the user or the web site design, computer programs simulate the user interacting with the site and report the results of this interaction, in the form of performance measures and navigation operations, for instance. Ideally, simulators enable evaluators to input different parameters or designs so that they can study various tradeoffs and make more informed decisions about a site's implementation. However, most simulators in the Web domain require an implemented site as input. Simulation is also used to automatically generate synthetic usage data for analysis with log file analysis techniques [Chi *et al.*, 2000] or for event playback in an interface [Kasik and George, 1996]. Thus, simulation can be viewed as supporting automated capture to some degree.

Our survey revealed methods to support automated analysis of web sites. We summarize these methods and conclude with an assessment of them.

1.   Synopsis of Automated Analysis Methods

Automation is used to simulate web site navigation as depicted in Table 7.1. Although one approach is based on GOMS (discussed in Chapter 6), most approaches are based on the notion of information "scent" (i.e., common keywords between the user's goal and content on linked pages). We discuss the two approaches in the remainder of this chapter.

2.   Information Processor Modeling

WebCriteria's Site Profile [Web Criteria, 1999]   simulates web site use to estimate several metrics, such as page load and optimal navigation times. Unlike simulation approaches for graphical interfaces [Ivory, 2001; Ivory and Hearst,

Table 7.1.   Synopsis of automated analysis support for simulation methods.

Method Class:	Simulation
Automation Type:	Analysis
Method Type:	Information Processor Modeling—mimic user interaction (1 method)

Evaluation Method	*Effort*
Employ a GOMS-like model to analyze navigation (Site Profile)	M

Method Class:	Simulation
Automation Type:	Analysis
Method Type:	Information Scent Modeling—mimic web site navigation (3 methods)

Evaluation Method	*Effort*
Employ an information-scent model to analyze navigation (Bloodhound, CoLiDeS, [Miller and Remington, 2002])	M

2001], it requires an implemented site for evaluation. Site Profile performs analysis in four phases: gather, model, analyze, and report. During the gather phase, a spider traverses a site (200-600 unique pages) to collect web site data. This data is then used to construct a nodes-and-links model of the site. For the analysis phase, it uses an idealistic web user model (called Max [Lynch *et al.*, 1999]) to simulate a user's information-seeking behavior; this model is based on prior research with GOMS analysis. Given a starting point in the site, a path, and a target page, Max "follows" the path from the starting point to the target page and logs measurement data. These measurements are used to compute an accessibility metric, which is then used to generate a report. Evaluators can use this approach to compare web sites, provided that an appropriate navigation path is supplied for each.

The usefulness of this approach is questionable, because it only computes accessibility (navigation time) for the shortest path between specified start and destination pages, using a single user model [Pirolli, 2000]. Other computed measurements, such as freshness and page composition, also have questionable value in improving the web site. Brajnik [2000] showed that Site Profile supports only a small fraction of the analysis that is supported by guideline review methods, such as WebSAT and Bobby (discussed in Chapter 4). Chak [2000] also cautions that the accessibility measure should be used as an initial benchmark, not a highly-accurate approximation. Site Profile does not entail any learning time or effort on the part of the evaluator, since WebCriteria performs the analysis. Although the method is applicable to all web sites, it is no longer available for use.

3. Information Scent Modeling

Several simulators are being developed to simulate web site navigation. Unlike the information processor modeling approach, these simulators consider the common keywords (information scent) between users' information-seeking needs and content on linked pages. Bloodhound [Card *et al.*, 2001; Chi *et al.*, 2000; Chi *et al.*, 2001; Chi *et al.*, 2003] creates a model of an existing site that embeds information about the similarity of content among pages, server log data, and linking structure. The evaluator uses the simulator to either predict the likelihood that users will find information on a site or predict the information needs reflected by certain navigation patterns.

For the former case, the evaluator specifies starting points in the site and information needs (i.e., target pages) as input to the simulator. The simulator models a number of agents (i.e., hypothetical users) traversing the links and content of the site model. At each page, the model considers information scent in making navigation decisions. For instance, navigation decisions are controlled probabilistically such that most agents traverse higher-scent links (i.e., closest match to information goal) and some agents traverse lower-scent links. Simulated agents stop when they reach the target pages or after an arbitrary amount of effort (e.g., maximum number of links or browsing time). The simulator records navigation paths and reports the proportion of agents that reached target pages. Bloodhound researchers have also developed an information scent absorption rate measure to provide more accurate estimates of navigation success. Several studies of simulated and actual navigation patterns showed that the simulated patterns correspond with users' patterns in at least a third of the cases. Bloodhound does not account for the effects of various web page attributes, such as the amount of text or layout of links, on navigation behavior.

Comprehension-based Linked model of Deliberate Search (CoLiDeS) [Blackmon *et al.*, 2002; Blackmon *et al.*, 2003; Kitajima *et al.*, 2000] is a similar theoretical model of the use of information scent during the information-seeking process. Unlike Bloodhound, CoLiDeS considers web page objects (e.g., images and text areas) in its simulation. It models web page processing as a two-phase process. First, the user segments or parses the page into subregions and generates a brief description of each, based on her knowledge of page layout conventions, page titles, headings, and other cues. The user then attends to the subregion whose description is perceived as most similar to the information-seeking need. The previously discussed Cognitive Walkthrough for the Web approach (Section 6 of Chapter 4) is based on the CoLiDeS model. Blackmon *et al.* [2003] showed that their methodology could predict potential problems with confusing headings and link text.

Miller and Remington [2000; 2002] have developed an abstracted simulation model to explore the depth-breadth trade-off in information architectures

[Furnas, 1997; Larson and Czerwinski, 1998; Zaphiris and Mtei, 1997]. The researchers assign quantitative measures to each page within a site to reflect the page's relevance to an information-seeking task. The model uses the relevance measures to predict the mean search time required to navigate the site. It does not consider actual content on web sites or information-seeking goals; it only considers the hypothetical relevance estimates for pages in the site. The model makes it possible to see how search strategies and relevance distributions can inform the design of broad or deep information architectures. For instance, the evaluator could specify different relevance distributions to explore different types of information architectures.

4.   Discussion

Table 7.1 summarizes automated analysis methods discussed in this chapter. Unlike most evaluation approaches, simulators like the computational model that Miller and Remington developed can be used prior to site implementation. Hence, evaluators can explore alternative designs and optimize designs before implementation. All the simulators are still under development and have not been released for broad use; thus, it is difficult to assess how easy they are to use and learn at this time.

There is some evidence of the potential effectiveness of such simulators. For example, Bloodhound researchers showed that navigation patterns generated by their simulator are fairly consistent with actual navigation paths, at least more so when scent is "clearly visible" (i.e., links are not embedded in long text passages or obstructed by images). Similarly, CoLiDeS researchers showed that their methodology can predict potential problems with confusing headings and link text. Automated analysis and critique approaches to support simulation methods are open research areas.

Chapter 8

THE WEBTANGO METHOD

Chapter 4 described briefly the WebTango automated evaluation approach [Ivory, 2001; Ivory *et al.*, 2000; Ivory *et al.*, 2001; Ivory and Hearst, 2002a], which we elaborate on in this chapter. We designed WebTango to leverage the benefits of both performance evaluation [Jain, 1991; Sauer and Chandy, 1981] and usability evaluation to evaluate the quality of sites designed primarily to disseminate information (i.e., informational sites). Performance evaluation is used predominately in the assessment of computer systems, and usability evaluation is used for assessing interfaces. In the spirit of measurement techniques in the performance evaluation domain, benchmarking in particular, the methodology entails computing an extensive set of quantitative page-level and site-level measures. These measures can be viewed as a benchmark because they enable objective comparison of web interfaces. Specifically, we use these measures to derive statistical models of highly rated interfaces. As is done with guideline review methods in the usability evaluation domain (see Chapter 4), the models are then used in the automated analysis of web pages and sites. Unlike other guideline review methods, the guidelines are in essence derived from empirical data. Hence, it is also possible to use the models to validate or invalidate many guidelines proposed in the web design literature.

We elaborate on this approach for several reasons: (1) it represents a new methodology for the human-computer interaction field and, at the time of this publication, is still the only approach of its kind; (2) it has broad implications for other evaluation approaches, due to the extensive set of web interface aspects that it assesses and the quantitative thresholds that it educes for these aspects; (3) it demonstrates the application of data mining beyond log file analysis (see Section 4 of Chapter 3); and (4) it enables context-sensitive evaluation of web interfaces.

We begin this chapter with descriptions of two scenarios that motivate our work. Section 2 provides an overview of the 5-step approach that we use to derive, apply, and validate design knowledge from highly rated interfaces; Section 3 describes the tools that we developed to support our approach. We then discuss each step in detail:

- **Step 1:** Section 4 describes the 157 page- and site-level quantitative measures that we developed to assess various aspects that affect web site quality (i.e., usability, accessibility, performance, etc.).

- **Steps 2 and 3:** Section 5 describes our data collection and model building efforts; it describes the evolution of our predictive models (profiles) over a four-year period.

- **Step 4:** Section 6 demonstrates how evaluators can use the profiles to assess and improve web site designs.

- **Step 5:** Section 7 summarizes results from an empirical study, in which novice designers used the profiles to modify web sites and then users evaluated the original and modified sites.

Section 8 discusses briefly how the profiles can be used to validate or invalidate vague or contradictory design guidelines in the literature; Chapter 13 provides a more comprehensive discussion of our analysis of design guidelines. Finally, we summarize future research efforts and conclude the chapter.

1.   Motivating Scenarios

As background for the methodology presented in this chapter, we provide scenarios for both evaluating and designing web interfaces.

1.1   Web Interface Evaluation

Figure 8.1 depicts an analysis scenario: a web designer seeking to determine the quality (i.e., usability, accessibility, performance, etc.) of an interface design. If the site has already been designed and implemented, the designer could use the site as input to an analysis tool. The analysis tool (or benchmark program) would then sample pages within the site and generate a number of quantitative measures pertaining to all aspects of the interface. A key component of benchmarking is the ability to determine how well benchmark results compare to other systems or a best case [Jain, 1991; Sauer and Chandy, 1981]. For this scenario, designs that have been rated favorably by expert reviewers or users could be used for comparison purposes. Hence, the analysis tool could compare the input design's quantitative measures to those for highly rated designs.

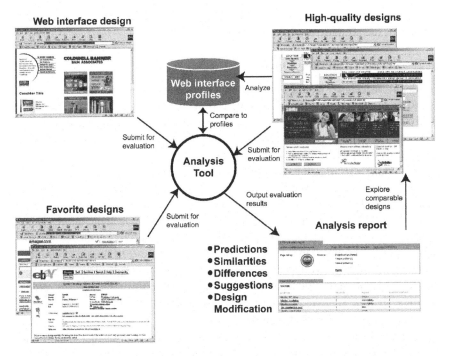

Figure 8.1. A web interface evaluation scenario. The analysis tool compares features of a submitted design to features of highly rated designs. It then provides a detailed analysis report, which the designer can explore to improve her design.

Ideally, the analysis tool goes beyond traditional benchmarking and generates a report containing: (1) an interface quality or usability prediction, (2) links to similar highly rated designs from the comparison sample, (3) differences and similarities to the highly rated designs, and (4) specific suggestions for improvements. The designer could use these results to choose between alternative designs as well as to inform design improvements. The tool could also perform some simple design modifications automatically (e.g., changing font types or sizes or changing color combinations). This analysis process could be iterated as necessary.

Similarly, the designer could use the analysis tool to explore results for other interface designs, such as favorite sites. This process may help to educate the designer on subtle aspects of design that may not be apparent from simply inspecting interfaces.

The WebTango methodology and tools are designed to support many aspects of this web interface evaluation scenario. Currently, recommending design improvements, presenting comparable designs, and automated design modification are not supported; future work will focus on these aspects. All other aspects of the scenario are fully supported.

1.2   Web Interface Design

Ideally, a designer would want to obtain feedback on interface designs earlier in the design process, as opposed to after implementation. If the tool supported analysis of designs represented as images or templates, then it would be possible to support this evaluation. In particular, the tool needs to use image processing techniques to evaluate these design representations.

One could also imagine supporting the designer even earlier in the design process, such as during the design exploration and refinement phases [Newman and Landay, 2000]. Given a large collection of favorably rated sites, the designer could explore this collection to stimulate design ideas similarly to practices employed in the architecture domain [Elliott, 2001]. During the design exploration phase, the designer could look for ways to organize content within health sites as well as navigation schemes, for example. During the design refinement phase, the designer may look for effective page layouts, color palettes, site maps, navigation bars, form designs, etc.

Ideally, characteristics of web pages and sites can be represented in a way to facilitate easily identifying pages and sites to satisfy queries that are similar to the ones above. Task-based search techniques that exploit metadata [Elliott, 2001; English *et al.*, 2001; Hearst, 2000; Yee *et al.*, 2003] should be helpful. Hearst [2000] proposes an approach wherein search interfaces present users with metadata facets for refining search results. Elliott [2001] presents a similar approach for exploring large online collections of architecture images; metadata describes the content of images, including location, architect, style, and kind of building.

Metadata for web interfaces could consist of the quantitative measures developed for the WebTango methodology as well as others that describe, for instance, the size of the site, the type of site, page size, a page's functional type, elements on a page (e.g., navigation bars), as well as site ratings. Many of these measures could be computed automatically by the analysis methodology presented in this chapter and then organized into metadata facets. Scapin *et al.* [2000] presents a useful and relevant framework for organizing web guidelines that includes a taxonomy of index keys (e.g., alignment, buttons, downloading, headings, language, scrolling, navigation structure, and so on); this taxonomy could be used to inform the metadata facets.

2.   Derivation of Design Guidance from Empirical Data

The WebTango methodology entails deriving design guidance (i.e., prevalent design patterns) by examining well-designed web interfaces. More specifically,

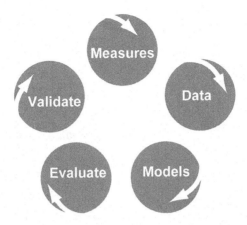

Figure 8.2. WebTango process for deriving, applying, and validating design knowledge from highly rated web interfaces. The entire process (in clockwise order from the top) is completed initially to develop and validate profiles of highly rated interfaces. To assess the quality of a web interface, the Data and Evaluate steps are completed. Figure 8.3 elaborates on the profile development and interface assessment phases.

the idea is to enable designers to compare their designs to the well-designed ones to determine whether their designs exhibit similar properties, and if not, how they differ. The general approach involves the following steps, which Figure 8.2 summarizes. We discuss each of these steps in the remainder of this chapter.

1 Identifying an exhaustive set of quantitative interface measures

2 Computing measures for a large sample of rated interfaces

3 Deriving statistical models from the measures and ratings

4 Using the models to predict ratings for new interfaces

5 Validating model predictions

The analysis methodology consists of two distinct but related phases (Figure 8.3): (1) establishing an interface quality baseline and (2) analyzing interface quality. Both phases share common activities—crawling web sites to download pages and associated elements (Site Crawling) and computing page-level and site-level quantitative measures (Metrics Computation). During the first phase, the page- and site-level measures coupled with expert ratings of sites are analyzed to determine profiles (predictive models) of highly rated interfaces. These profiles encapsulate key quantitative measures, thresholds for these measures, and effective relationships among key measures; thus, they can be considered as an interface quality baseline.

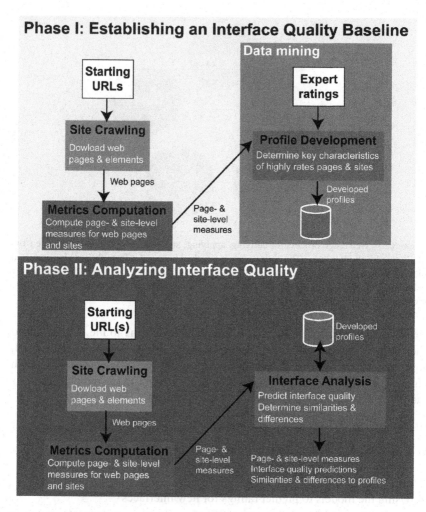

Figure 8.3. Profile development and interface evaluation phases of the WebTango process. All steps in the WebTango process (Figure 8.2) are completed to develop profiles of highly rated interfaces. Only two of the steps are completed to assess the quality of a web interface.

During the second phase, the page- and site-level measures are compared to the developed profiles as a way to assess interface quality. Sites analyzed in the latter phase are usually not the same as the sites that are used to develop profiles. Once profiles are developed, the analysis phase can be used continuously. However, the interface quality baseline phase needs to be repeated periodically (annually or semi-annually) to ensure that profiles reflect current web design practices.

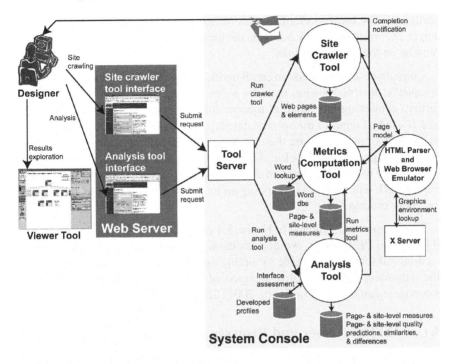

Figure 8.4. WebTango prototype architecture. The tools support the analysis methodology.

Our analysis methodology is consistent with other guideline review methods (discussed in Chapter 4) and benchmarking methods. What distinguishes this analysis approach from other guideline review methods is: (1) the use of quantitative measures, (2) the use of empirical data to develop guidelines, and (3) the use of profiles as a comparison basis.

3. WebTango Prototype Architecture and Tools

We have developed a rudimentary prototype to support profile development and interface evaluation (Figure 8.4). This prototype is available for public use via separate form-fillin interfaces for the site crawling and analysis steps; future work will integrate these interfaces to support the entire process. The interface for each tool routes requests to a server daemon (the *Tool Server*) for processing; the daemon in turn forks new processes to forward requests to the appropriate backend tool (*Site Crawler* or *Analysis Tool*). Both the Site Crawler and *Metrics Computation Tool* interact with the *HTML Parser and Browser Emulator*; this component creates a detailed representation of a web page, including the screen coordinates (x and y location) for each page element, the width and height of each element, the font used, foreground and background color, and other attributes. The browser emulator determines many of the details, such as the height and width of text, by querying the graphics environment via the X Server running on the system console.

Currently, each tool sends an email notification to the client when the request completes; this notification includes a link to an archive file (in gzipped tar format) containing the output of running the tool. The output of running each tool is used as input to the subsequent step. For example, pages downloaded by the Site Crawler Tool are then processed by the Metrics Computation Tool to output page- and site-level measures. The *Viewer Tool* enables designers to interactively explore results from the Analysis and Metrics Computation Tools. Future work will focus on developing an interactive, integrated tool to support the entire process.

The components depicted in Figure 8.4 comprise over 40,000 lines of Java, HTML, and PERL code; we discuss them in detail in the remainder of this section. All tools are available for online use via the WebTango Project's web site (http://webtango.ischool.washington.edu/tools/). More details about each component can be found in [Ivory, 2001, Chapter 4].

3.1   HTML Parser and Browser Emulator

We used the Multivalent Browser (developed as part of the Berkeley Digital Library Project) [Phelps, 1998; Phelps, 2001] as a starting point for the HTML Parser and Browser Emulator depicted in Figure 8.4.[1] The Multivalent Browser enables creators of digital documents to represent their documents at multiple layers of abstraction and to annotate them with behaviors (e.g., actions), highlighting, and edit marks. The browser provides a means for these documents to be distributed and viewed by others. A variety of document formats are supported—OCR output, zip, ASCII, XML, and TeX—in addition to HTML. The browser parses HTML similarly to the Netscape Navigator 4.75 browser's method and supports style sheets. It does not support frame sets, scripts, and other objects, such as applets and Macromedia Flash pages.

We revised extensively (~60% of code changed) the Multivalent Browser code to generate a detailed page model for the Site Crawler and Metrics Computation Tools. Most of the revisions focused on enumerating frames, images, links, and objects that appear in a web page and annotating each node in the page's tree structure with information about how the element is formatted (e.g., bolded, colored, italicized, etc.), whether it is a link (and if so, whether it is an internal or external link), and downloading page elements to determine their sizes. The new parser also performs numerous corrections of HTML errors (e.g., repairing out of order tags and tables without <tr> or <td> tags) while processing web pages.

We configured the new parser and browser emulator to simulate the Netscape Navigator 4.75 browser with default settings (fonts, link colors, menu bar, address bar, toolbar, and status line). At development time, most monitors were 800x600 pixels [DreamInk, 2000; Nielsen, 2000]; thus, we assumed a window size of 800x600 pixels. The current implementation does not support pages that use frame sets, although it does support pages with inline frames; given that Netscape 4.75 does not support inline frames, designers typically provide alternative HTML, which our tools can process. Future work entails using the Mozilla open source parser and browser to support more accurate page rendering, frame sets, and scripts as well as to address performance issues with the current tool.

3.2   Site Crawler Tool

We developed a special web site crawler to address limitations of existing crawlers, such as Wget [GNU Software Foundation, 1999] and HTTrack [Roche, 2001]. Existing crawlers rely on path information to determine the depth of pages, which can be somewhat misleading. They are also not selective in determining pages to download; they download advertisements and Macromedia Flash pages, for instance. Finally, they typically attempt to mirror the directory structure of the remote site or place all images, style sheets, etc. into one directory; this makes it challenging to relocate an individual page and its associated elements. Like existing crawlers, the Site Crawler Tool is multi-threaded. In addition, the tool has the following key features.

- It accesses pages at multiple levels of the site, where level zero is the home page, level one refers to pages one link away from the home page, level two refers to pages one link away from the level one pages, and so on. The standard settings are to download the home page, up to 15 level-one pages, and 45 level-two pages (3 from each of the level-one pages).

- It selects links for crawling such that: they are not advertisements, guest books, Flash pages, login pages, chat rooms, documents, or shopping carts; and they are internal to the site.

- It stores each downloaded page in a directory with all images, style sheets, frames, and objects (e.g., scripts and applets) aggregated and stored in subdirectories. This makes it easy to relocate pages and associated elements.

The Site Crawler Tool replaces links to images, style sheets, and other page elements on the remote server with the corresponding locally stored filenames. It also creates input files for the Metrics Computation Tool.

3.3   Metrics Computation Tool

The Metrics Computation Tool is consistent with other benchmarks for evaluating computer systems: (1) it is portable to other platforms due to its implementation in Java, (2) it produces quantitative measures for comparison, and (3) its results are reproducible (i.e., successive runs of the tool on the same page produce the exact same results). The tool computes 141 page-level and 16 site-level measures; these measures assess many facets of web interfaces, as discussed in Section 4. We developed numerous heuristics for computing these measures, such as detecting headings, good color usage, internal links, and graphical ads. The tool also uses a number of auxiliary databases, such as the MRC psycholinguistic database [Coltheart, 2001] (for determining spelling errors and the number of syllables in words) and other lists of acronyms, abbreviations, medical terms, and common (or stop) words. Currently, the tool only processes English text.

3.4   Analysis Tool

The Analysis Tool encompasses several statistical models for assessing web page and site quality [Ivory, 2001; Ivory and Hearst, 2002a; Ivory and Hearst, 2002b]. Statistical models include decision trees, discriminant classification model functions, and K-means cluster models as discussed in Section 5. For cluster and discriminant classification models, the tool reports the top ten measures that are similar and different from highly rated interfaces; it also provides acceptable measure values. For cluster models, it also reports the distance between measure values on a page and measure values at the cluster centroid; the distance reflects the total standard deviation units of difference across all measures. Currently, the Analysis Tool does not provide the designer with example sites or pages; future work will focus on developing an algorithm to provide examples. Future work will also focus on supporting automated critique or providing explicit suggestions for improvements as well as interactive analysis.

3.5   Viewer Tool

The Metrics Computation and Analysis Tools generate a collection of text files containing quantitative measures and qualitative predictions computed for designer-specified sites. The Viewer Tool facilitates easy viewing of and navigation of this output (Figure 8.5) [Debroy, 2002]. Various components of the viewer parse prediction rationales, look up descriptions of column headings in information files, and present the data in an organized manner. The viewer window is divided into three major areas: (1) a control panel on the left, (2) a viewing panel in the middle, and (3) an information panel on the right. The control panel includes an option to enable users to re-analyze sites. Menus in the information panel allow designers to easily switch from one dataset to another (e.g., a category of measures or a prediction generated by a particular model). In the near future, we will distribute the viewer as a Java jar file along with the Analysis Tool's results.

4. Identification of Web Interface Measures

As depicted in Figure 8.2, the first step of the WebTango process entails identifying an exhaustive set of quantitative measures to assess many aspects of web interfaces. We developed a set of 157 page-level and site-level measures based on an extensive survey of design recommendations from recognized experts and usability studies (e.g., [Flanders and Willis, 1998; Fleming, 1998; Nielsen, 1998; Nielsen, 1999; Nielsen, 2000; Rosenfeld and Morville, 1998; Sano, 1996; Schriver, 1997; Shedroff, 1999; Shneiderman, 1997; Spool *et al.*, 1999]). Our intention was to first quantify features discussed in the literature and then to determine their importance in producing high-quality designs. We begin with a view of a web interface's structure and then present a summary of the 157 measures.

An in-depth discussion of the measures can be found in [Ivory, 2001, Chapter 5]. We also developed an interactive appendix to illustrate all the measures. HTML and PowerPoint versions are available on the WebTango Project's web site (http://webtango.ischool.washington.edu/).

4.1 Web Interface Structure

A web interface is a mix of many elements (text, links, and graphics), formatting of these elements, and other aspects that affect its overall usability, accessibility, and quality. Web interface design entails a complex set of activities for addressing these diverse aspects. To gain insight into web design practices, Newman and Landay [2000] conducted an ethnographic study wherein they observed and interviewed eleven professional web designers. One important finding was that most designers viewed web interface design as being comprised of three components—information design, navigation design, and graphic design.

- *Information design* focuses on determining an information structure (i.e., identifying and grouping content items) and developing category labels to reflect the information structure.

- *Navigation design* focuses on developing navigation mechanisms (e.g., navigation bars and links) to facilitate interaction with the information structure.

- *Graphic design* focuses on visual presentation and layout.

- *Experience design* is an overarching aspect and encompasses all three of these categories, as well as properties that affect the user experience, such

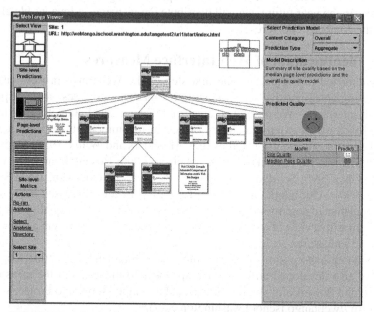

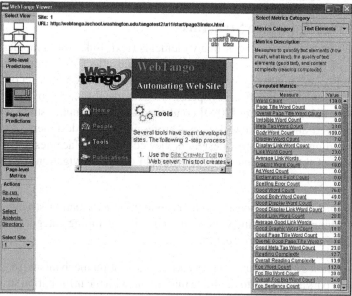

Figure 8.5. WebTango Viewer Tool. The top screen shot depicts site quality results. The bottom screen shot depicts page-level measures.

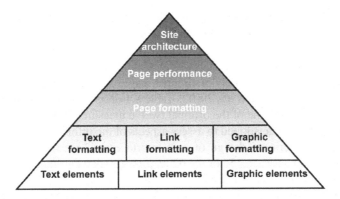

Figure 8.6. Web page and site structure. Text, link, and graphic elements are the building blocks of a web interface. Page- and site-level features use these elements to improve the user's experience.

as download time, the presence of graphical ads, popup windows, etc. [Creative Good, 1999; Shedroff, 2001].

We can further refine information, navigation, graphic, and experience design into the aspects depicted in Figure 8.6. The figure shows that text, link, and graphic elements are the building blocks of web interfaces; all other aspects are based on these. The next level of Figure 8.6 addresses formatting of these building blocks, while the subsequent level addresses page-level formatting. The top two levels address the performance of pages and the architecture of sites, including the consistency, breadth, and depth of pages. The bottom three levels of Figure 8.6 are associated with information, navigation, and graphic design activities, while the top two levels—Page performance and Site architecture— are associated with experience design.

4.2   Web Interface Measures

We conducted an extensive survey of the web design literature, including texts written by recognized experts (e.g., [Fleming, 1998; Nielsen, 2000; Sano, 1996; Spool *et al.*, 1999]) and published user studies (e.g., [Bernard and Mills, 2000; Bernard *et al.*, 2001; Boyarski *et al.*, 1998; Larson and Czerwinski, 1998]) to identify key features that affect the quality, usability, accessibility, performance, and so on of web interfaces [Ivory *et al.*, 2000]. We did not consult HTML style guides, because researchers have shown them to be highly inconsistent [Ratner *et al.*, 1996]. We identified 62 features from the literature, including: the amount of text on a page, fonts, colors, consistency of page layout across the site, use of frames, and others. We then developed 157 quantitative measures to assess many of the 62 features.

Our early metric development work showed that we could use twelve web interface measures—Word Count, Body Text Percentage, Emphasized Body Text Percentage, Text Positioning Count, Text Cluster Count, Link Count, Page Size, Graphic Percentage, Graphics Count, Color Count, Font Count, and Reading Complexity—to accurately distinguish pages from highly rated interfaces [Ivory *et al.*, 2000; Ivory *et al.*, 2001]. Table 8.1 describes the 157 quantitative measures (including nine of the original twelve measures and variations of the other three) that we developed to assess aspects of the information, navigation, graphic, and experience design of web interfaces. These measures provide some support for assessing 56 of the 62 features (90 percent) that are identified as affecting usability and accessibility in the web design literature. Measures developed for our early studies assessed less than 50 percent of these 62 features.

In developing our web interface measures, we adhered to guidelines provided for determining performance metrics. Specifically, we implemented a subset of measures that have the following characteristics.

- **Low variability:** measures are not a ratio of two or more variables; there is one exception to this rule—the average number of words in link text—which was developed to assess a feature reported in the literature.

- **Nonredundancy:** two measures do not convey essentially the same information.

- **Completeness:** measures reflect all aspects of the web interface (i.e., information, navigation, graphic, and experience design).

To validate the implemented measures, we used a sample of fourteen web pages that had widely differing characteristics. We manually computed the actual value of each measure and then compared these values to the automatically computed values. With a few exceptions, all the measures were highly accurate (greater than 84 percent accuracy across the sample). The least accurate measures—text positioning count (number of changes in text alignment from flush left) and text and link text cluster counts (areas highlighted with color, rules, lists, etc.)—require image processing to assess more accurately.

5.   Development of Web Interface Profiles

The second and third steps in the WebTango process entail computing the measures for a sample of rated pages and sites and then employing data mining approaches to develop models that can discriminate key features of high-quality interfaces; these steps correspond to the top part of Figure 8.3. We have completed four model-building efforts and, at the time of publication, are completing our fifth such effort. The studies have shown that it is possible to derive novel types of web design guidelines (statistical models) by dissecting good and poor designs. (Dissecting example designs is a common practice in developing

Table 8.1. Measures for assessing web design quality and usability. (Each category corresponds to a block in Figure 8.6.)

Category	Number of measures	Aspects measured
Text elements	31	Amount of text, type, quality, and complexity. Includes visible and invisible text.
Link elements	6	Number and type of links.
Graphic elements	6	Number and type of images.
Text formatting	24	How body text is emphasized; whether some underlined text is not in text links; how text areas are highlighted; font styles and sizes; number of text colors; number of times text is repositioned.
Link formatting	3	Colors used for links and whether there are text links that are not underlined or colored.
Graphic formatting	7	Minimum, maximum, and average image width and height; page area covered by images.
Page formatting	27	Color use, fonts, page size, use of interactive elements, page style control, and so on. Key measures include evaluating the quality of color combinations (for text and panels) and predicting the functional type of a page.[a]
Page performance	37	Page download speed; page accessibility for people with disabilities; presence of HTML errors; and "scent" strength.[b]
Site architecture	16	Consistency of page elements, element formatting, page formatting and performance, and site size (number of pages or documents).[c]

[a] The decision tree for predicting page type—home, link, content, form, or other—exhibited 84 percent accuracy for 1,770 pages.

[b] Our model predicts download speed with 86 percent accuracy. It considers the number and size of HTML, graphic, script, and object files and tables on the page. We use output from Bobby 3.2 (http://www.cast.org/bobby/) [WatchFire, 2002] runs to report accessibility errors. We report the total number of HTML errors determined by Weblint 1.02 [Bowers, 1996]. To assess scent quality, we report word overlap between the source and destination pages; the source link text and destination page; and the source and destination page titles.

[c] Consistency measures are based on coefficients of variation (standard deviation normalized by the mean) across measures for pages within the site. The site size measures only reflect the portion traversed by the crawler.

design guidelines and patterns [Flanders and Willis, 1998; Heller and Rivers, 1996a; Johnson, 2000; Norman, 1990; Smith and Mosier, 1986; van Duyne *et al.*, 2002].) Furthermore, a preliminary study (see Section 7) suggests that web designers can use such guidelines to improve their sites. In this section, we summarize our four model-building efforts and then contrast models that we built during the last two efforts.

5.1   A Simple Prediction Model

The first study presented a preliminary analysis of a collection of over 400 informational web pages [Ivory *et al.*, 2000]. We labeled web pages as rated (that is, rated favorably by users or experts) and unrated (those that had not been so rated). For each web page, our early metrics computation script computed twelve quantitative measures having to do with page composition, layout, amount of information, and size (e.g., number of words, links, and colors). The analysis involved applying a linear discriminant classifier to the page types (rated and unrated) to assess if the measures could predict the pages' standings within these groups; the predictive accuracy was 63 percent and 6 measures—text cluster count, link count, page size, graphics count, color count, and reading complexity—were associated significantly with rated sites. Analysis of home pages revealed that they had measurably different characteristics than the other pages, suggesting the need for context-sensitive models.

Exploring relationships among measures enabled us to hypothesize about key design aspects of rated pages (e.g., that they used a multi-level heading scheme, with a different color for each heading level, to facilitate scanning [Nielsen, 2000; Schriver, 1997; Spool *et al.*, 1999]); we validated our hypotheses by inspecting random page samples.

5.2   Context-Sensitive Prediction Models

The second study reported an analysis of 1,898 pages from sites evaluated for the Webby Awards 2000 [Ivory *et al.*, 2001; The International Academy of Arts and Sciences, 2000]. For the first stage of the Webby Awards, anyone can submit a web site for review, thus sites vary widely from those that are well-designed to those that are poorly designed. At least three expert judges evaluated each submitted site on six criteria: content, structure and navigation, visual design, functionality, interactivity, and overall experience; the six criteria correlated highly. Web sites were also classified into 27 topical groups (content categories).

We conducted a usability study of 57 evaluated sites to examine the relationship between Webby judges' scores and ratings assigned by participants (non experts) who used sites to complete tasks [Ivory, 2001, Chapter 7]. Although the results suggested some relationship between expert and end user ratings, strong conclusions could not be drawn because the study was conducted at least six months after the judges reviewed the sites. Statistical analysis of judges' ratings revealed that content was the predominate factor in overall ratings and visual design was the least significant factor in most cases [Sinha *et al.*, 2001]. Furthermore, the analysis showed that assessment criteria varied in importance based on the content category, suggesting that the judges considered the genres of sites when they evaluated them.

For the second study, we obtained pages from sites in six categories—community, education, finance, health, living, and services—and computed the same quantitative measures examined in the first study, except for reading complexity. We grouped sites according to their overall score in the Webby standings as follows: *good* (top 33 percent of sites) versus either *not-good* (remaining 67 percent of sites) or *poor* (lowest 33 percent of sites). The analysis involved developing two statistical models to assess if the measures could predict the pages' standings within these groups. The first model used multiple linear regression to distinguish good from not-good sites; the predictive accuracy was 67 percent when content categories (e.g., community and education) were not considered, and even higher on average when the categories were assessed separately. The second model used discriminant classification analysis to compute statistics for good versus poor sites. The predictive accuracy of the second model ranged from 76–83 percent when categories were considered.

5.3   Elaborate Prediction Models

Our third study reported an analysis of 5,346 pages and 333 sites from the Webby Awards 2000 [Ivory and Hearst, 2002a; Ivory and Hearst, 2002b]. The analysis used the 157 quantitative page- and site-level measures, the six content categories, and a page type classifier (for distinguishing among home pages, content pages, link pages, forms, and other pages). Using this extensive set of interface measures, we were able to develop more sophisticated statistical models for distinguishing pages and sites in the *good* (top 33 percent of sites), *average* (middle 34 percent of sites), and *poor* (bottom 33 percent of sites) groups. Specifically, we developed context-sensitive models to predict page and site standings based on the content category and on the functional type of pages. We also developed models to predict standings independent of the design context.

The accuracy of page-level models ranged from 93–96 percent, and the accuracy of site-level models ranged from 68–88 percent; the site-level accuracy was considerably less possibly due to inadequate data. We used K-means clustering to partition the web pages from good sites into three sub-groups (small-page, large-page, and formatted-page). These clusters had significantly different characteristics and provided more context for evaluating web designs.

Another limitation of the site-level models is that they do not take page-level quality into consideration. Thus, it is possible for a site to be classified as good even though all the pages in the site are classified as poor and vice versa. To remedy this situation, we compute the median predictions for pages in the site. We also report an aggregate site-quality prediction by applying some heuristics to the site-level and median page-level predictions. For instance, if the median page-level prediction is average and the site-level prediction is good, then the aggregate site-level quality is reported as average. These additional predictions need to be considered in determining the overall quality of a site.

We incorporated the models developed in this study into the current Analysis Tool prototype (Tables 8.2 and 8.3). The prototype reports predictions (i.e., whether an interface belongs to the good, average, or poor group based on its quantitative measures) along with justifications, such as decision tree rules and how interface measures are similar or different to/from measures for highly rated interfaces. The prototype enables designers to consider the context (e.g., the content type, functional type, page size, and overall site structure) in which pages and sites are designed during assessment. (Badre and Laskowski [2001] have shown context to be an important consideration in web site design.) The Viewer Tool enables designers to interactively explore quality assessments and quantitative measures.

5.4   Expanded Content Category Models

Our fourth study entailed the analysis of 4,833 pages and 570 sites from the Webby Awards 2002 [Ivory, 2003c]. Similarly to the third study, we used the 157 quantitative page- and site-level measures, the six content categories, and the page type classifier. We also incorporated four additional content categories—activism, best practices, print & zines, and travel. To examine how well the approach can be applied to functional sites, we also built models for commerce sites. The accuracy of page-level models ranged as follows: 90–95 percent (overall page quality), 93–96 percent (content category quality), and 80–85 percent (page type quality). These ranges are consistent with the ranges for the 2000 models; the page-type models actually improved in accuracy by five to ten percent. The dataset was not amenable to rebuilding the cluster models that we had built for the 2000 dataset; we believe this difference is attributable to the broader range of content categories represented. The accuracy of site-level models was 89–91 percent for the overall site quality and 82–92 percent for the content category models. We attribute this significant increase in prediction accuracy to the larger dataset that we used (720 versus 333 sites).

Future work will entail incorporating the original and the new prediction models into the Analysis Tool. We are currently developing models from the 2003 Webby Awards. The 2003 dataset contains measures for roughly three times as many pages and sites than those used in previous studies. In addition, it includes data for seven additional content categories—government & law, science, news, politics, spirituality, sports, and youth.

Table 8.2. Profiles used to assess web page quality.

Profile	Model Type	Assessment	Output
Overall page quality	Decision tree	Classifies pages as good, average, or poor, regardless of page type or content category.	• Rule that generated the prediction.
Closest good-page cluster	K-means clustering	Maps pages into small-, large-, or formatted-page clusters.	• Distance between a page and the closest cluster's centroid. • Top 10 measures consistent with the cluster.[a] • Top 10 measures inconsistent with the cluster and acceptable metric ranges.[a]
Page type quality	Discriminant classification	Classifies pages as good, average, or poor, according to page type.	• Top 10 measures consistent with the page type.[a] • Top 10 measures inconsistent with the page type and acceptable metric ranges.[a]
Content category quality	Discriminant classification	Classifies pages as good, average, or poor, according to content category.	• Top 10 measures consistent with the content category.[a] • Top 10 measures inconsistent with the content category and acceptable metric ranges.[a]

[a] Measures are ordered by their importance in distinguishing pages in the three clusters (or classes) as determined from analyses of variances (ANOVAs).

5.5 Evolution of the Web Interface Models

Given that we have used the same quantitative measures for the past two model-building efforts, it is possible to determine the degree to which the old models predict new ratings and vice versa. For example, the 2000 page-level models predicted the ratings of the 2002 pages with 85 percent consistency. The 2000 site-level models predicted the ratings of the 2002 sites with 78 percent consistency; we attribute this lower consistency to the fact that the 2000 site-level models are not as accurate as the page-level models.

Table 8.3.   Profiles used to assess web site quality.

Profile	Model Type	Assessment	Output
Overall site quality	Decision tree	Classifies sites as good, average, or poor, regardless of content category.	• Rule that generated the prediction.
Median overall page quality[a]	Statistical	Classifies sites as good, average, or poor, based on the median page quality (overall page quality model).	–
Aggregate overall site quality[a]	Derived heuristics	Classifies sites as good, average, or poor, based on the median overall page quality and the overall site quality models.	–
Content category quality	Decision tree	Classifies sites as good, average, or poor, according to content category.	• Rule that generated the prediction.
Median content category quality[a]	Statistical	Classifies sites as good, average, or poor, based on the median page quality (content category quality model).	–
Aggregate content category quality[a]	Derived heuristics	Classifies sites as good, average, or poor, based on the median content category quality and the site content category quality models.	–

[a] The median and aggregate models address differences in predictions at the page and site levels.

When we examine model consistency in the opposite direction (i.e., how well do the 2002 models predict 2000 ratings), there is very little consistency among predictions (33–35 percent). One possible interpretation of this discrepancy is that the effective design practices (e.g., use of headings and link clustering) that designers used in 2000 are still being used. However, design practices appear to have evolved. While some practices are still the same, new findings and tools, as well as developed design expertise, has lead to new design practices. Hence, periodically rebuilding the models enables us to capture these evolving design practices. We will examine this hypothesis with the 2003 models and a future empirical study.

6. Application of the Web Interface Profiles

The fourth step in the WebTango process entails using the profiles to assess and improve the quality of other web site designs, which we elaborate on in this section. The intent of this section is three-fold: (1) to demonstrate how the models can be applied systematically to this problem, (2) to illustrate the type of design changes informed by the models and how they vary across models, and (3) to highlight the current limitations of the models. The example assessment closely follows the evaluation scenario depicted in Figure 8.1, which is the overarching goal of the WebTango Project. Currently, interpreting model predictions and determining appropriate design changes is a manual process, though the Viewer Tool provides some support. Future work will focus on automating recommendations for improving designs as well as implementing these recommendations. We will also incorporate mechanisms for identifying comparable high-quality designs.

We begin this section with a summary of the process for assessing web design quality. We then demonstrate use of the 2000 models for assessing and improving two example sites and show how the model output informs design improvements.

6.1 Assessing Web Design Quality

Figures 8.1 and 8.4 depict how a web site designer might use the WebTango method and tools to evaluate a web design. Essentially, the designer submits a partially designed site (HTML representation) to the Analysis Tool, which uses the metrics tool to compute the quantitative measures. It then compares these measures to the profiles of highly rated designs; it can conduct this analysis based on the context—general content category, page size, and page type. The tool reports differences between the submitted design and similar well-designed sites (Tables 8.2 and 8.3). The designer can use the Viewer Tool to explore these results and to inform design improvements. He can repeat the assessment process as necessary.

We describe two example assessments in the remainder of this section. The first example demonstrates the assessment of a single, simplistic page; the second example demonstrates the assessment of a small site with a more complex design. As background to the discussion, we mention briefly results from a small study wherein users evaluated the example pages and sites [Ivory, 2001, Chapter 9]. Three students (two undergraduates and one graduate) used the profiles to refine (manually) three web sites, and the authors modified an additional two sites (described in the two assessment examples). During the study, 13 participants made 15 page-level comparisons and four site-level ratings of the original and modified versions of the sites. Section 7 describes the study in detail.

6.2   Example Assessment #1

Figures 8.7 and 8.8 depict the original and modified versions of an example page from our study (discussed in Section 7). The overall page quality model classifies the original page as poor, mainly because no font smaller than nine point was used and because images (not shown in the figure) at the bottom of the page are formatted in a way that makes the page longer than necessary. Good sites that contain nonessential information in the footer tend to signal this by placing this information in a smaller font size.

The good-page cluster model provides insight about the design's quality. It reports that the page is 23.05 standard deviation units from the large-page cluster centroid. The model also reports several key deviations from the cluster, such as inadequate text and poor text positioning.

We modified the page based on the overall page quality and large-page cluster models. We improved text layout by introducing a second text column and reducing the top navigation area to one line. We also removed horizontal rules to reduce vertical scrolling, as dictated by the large-page cluster model. Ten of the thirteen study participants preferred the modified page to the original one after we made these conservative changes.

6.3   Example Assessment #2

Figures 8.9–8.11 show three pages taken from a small (nine-page) site in the Yahoo Education/Health category. The site provides information about training programs offered to educators, parents, and children on numerous health issues, including leukemia and cerebral palsy. We selected the site because it was not in the training or testing sets that we used for model building. We selected it also because on first glance, it appeared to have good features, such as clear and sharp images and a consistent page layout, but on further inspection it seemed to have some design problems. We focused on answering the following questions.

- Is this a high-quality site? Why or why not?

- Are these high-quality pages? Why or why not?

- What can be done to improve the quality of this site?

The first step was to download a representative set of pages from the site. For this particular site, only eight level-one pages were accessible, and no level-two pages were reachable, for a total of nine downloaded pages. Although there

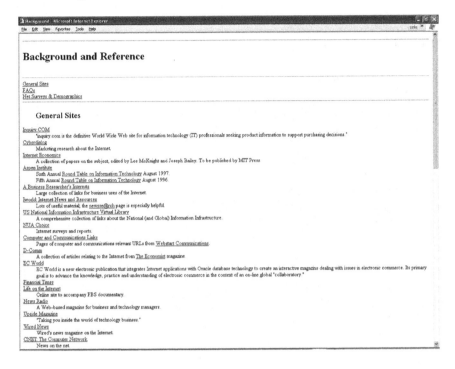

Figure 8.7. Original version of the web page for the first assessment example.

was a page containing links (Figure 8.10), the links were to pages that were external to the site.

The next step was to use the Analysis Tool to compute site- and page-level measures and to apply the models to individual pages and to the site as a whole. Each model encapsulates relationships between key predictor measures and can be used to (1) generate quality predictions and (2) determine how pages and sites are consistent with or deviate from good pages and sites.

In the discussions below, when decision tree rules are used to generate predictions, the consequences are interpreted manually. When cluster models are applied, the score for each measure on an individual page is compared to that of the cluster centroid, and if the measure differs by more than one standard deviation unit from the centroid, the measure is reported as being inconsistent with the cluster. Cluster deviations are also interpreted manually. Although the Viewer Tool provides support for interpreting predictions, it was not developed when the assessment was conducted [Ivory, 2001; Ivory and Hearst, 2002b]. Detailed information about this example assessment is available in [Ivory, 2001, Chapter 8].

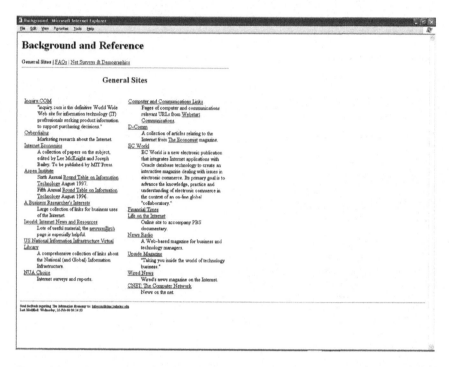

Figure 8.8. Modified version of the web page for the first assessment example. We based our improvements on the overall page quality and closest good-page cluster models described in Table 8.2.

6.3.1 Site-Level Assessment

The example site can be classified in both the health and education content categories, so we ran the site-level decision tree model initially without differentiating by content category. The site-level model predicted that the site is similar to poor sites overall; the median page quality prediction (i.e., median computed over the overall page quality model's predictions for the nine pages; poor) is consistent with the overall site quality model's prediction. The corresponding decision tree rule (top of Figure 8.12) reveals that the site has an unacceptable amount of variation (i.e., inconsistency) in link elements (31 percent), although variation for other site-level measures is acceptable. The combination of the link element variation and the lack of a comparable overall element variation violates patterns discovered on good sites.

The major source of link element variation is the text link count. Eight out of nine pages have from two to four text links; the remaining page has 27 text links, and acts as a links page (see Figure 8.10). The decision tree rule suggests that a link element variation level below 29 percent is typical on good sites.

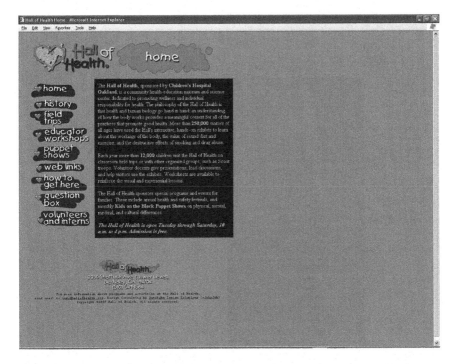

Figure 8.9. Home page taken from the example health education site (http://www.hallofhealth.org/home.html; September 14, 2001).

One interpretation of this finding is that good sites strive to keep the navigation structure consistent among pages and may even distribute links over multiple pages to maintain this consistency. Hence, the rule may indicate the need to similarly redistribute the links on this page.

We also assessed site quality according to the two applicable content categories—health and education. The decision tree for health sites predicted that the site is a poor health site (middle of Figure 8.12). In this case the problem is inadequate text element variation. Most of the pages on the site contain paragraphs of text without headings and use only one font face (serif); this feature may make it harder for users to scan the page to find the information that they need [Nielsen, 2000; Spool *et al.*, 1999]. The median health page quality prediction (poor) is consistent with the health site prediction.

The decision tree for education sites made a prediction contrary to that for sites overall and health sites; it found the site to be consistent with good education sites (bottom of Figure 8.12). Good health and good education sites are similar with respect to graphic formatting variation, but are quite different on

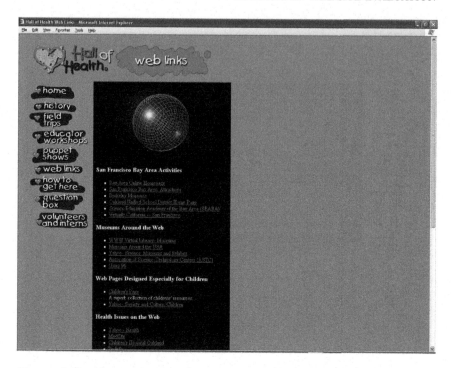

Figure 8.10. Link page taken from the example health education site (http://www.hallofhealth.org/weblinks.html; September 14, 2001).

the other measures, which is the cause for this disparity. However, as will be discussed below, the median education page quality is poor.

6.3.2   Page-Level Assessment

The decision tree model for predicting page quality reports that all nine pages are consistent with poor pages. The home page (Figure 8.9) contains seventeen italicized words in the body text; the model considers pages with more than two italicized words in the body text to be poor pages (see rule at the top of Figure 8.13). Schriver [1997] suggests that italicized text should be avoided, because it is harder to read on computer screens than in printed documents.

We developed a color measure, Minimum Color Count, to track the number of times each color is used on a page and to report the minimum number of times a color is used; this measure detects the use of an accent or sparsely-used color. The model classifies the content page (Figure 8.11) as poor mainly because the minimum number of times a color is used is sixteen and all of the text, including the copyright text at the bottom of the page, is formatted with

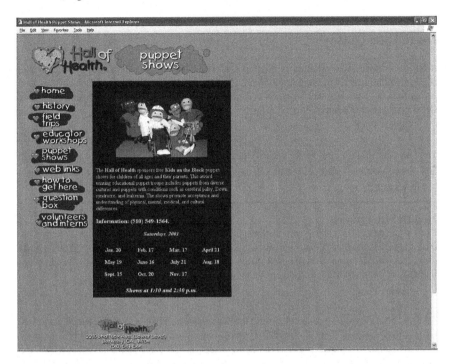

Figure 8.11. Content page taken from the example health education site (http://www.hallofhealth.org/puppetshows.html; September 14, 2001).

a font size greater than 9pt (bottom of Figure 8.13). Good pages tend to have an accent color that they use sparingly, whereas poor pages seem to overuse accent colors. Good pages also tend to use a smaller font size for copyright or footer text, unlike poor pages. Additionally, the example content page contains 34 colored body text words, which is twice the average number found on good pages; in the extreme case, a large number of colored words could result in the uncolored words standing out more so than the colored words. The same prediction and decision tree rule is reported for the link page.

To gain more insight about ways to improve page quality, we used the Analysis Tool to map each page into one of the three clusters of good pages—small-page, large-page, or formatted-page. All pages mapped to the small-page cluster and were far from the cluster centroid (median distance of 10.9 standard deviation units); the page from the dataset that is closest to the center of this cluster has a distance of 4.0 standard deviation units. Pages in the example site deviate on key measures that distinguish pages in this cluster, including the graphic ad, text link, link text cluster, interactive object, and link word counts. Table 8.4 summarizes, for the sample content page, the ten key measures (i.e., measures

Overall Site Quality

if ((Page Performance Variation is missing OR (Page Performance Variation $\leq$ 90.2)) AND (Overall Variation is not missing AND (Overall Variation $\leq$ 14.49)) AND (Link Element Variation is missing OR (Link Element Variation > 29.195)) AND (Overall Element Variation is missing OR (Overall Element Variation $\leq$ 26.07)))

    Class = Poor

This rule classifies the site as poor because the pages have acceptable page performance, overall, and overall element variation, but they have more than 29.2 percent variation in link elements (30.68 percent).

Health Site Quality

if ((Graphic Element Variation is not missing AND (Graphic Element Variation $\leq$ 32.695)) AND (Text Element Variation is missing OR (Text Element Variation > 47.45)) AND (Text Element Variation is missing OR (Text Element Variation $\leq$ 92.25)))

    Class = Poor

This rule classifies the site as poor because the pages have acceptable graphic element variation, but they have between 47.45 percent and 92.25 percent variation in text elements (53.18 percent).

Education Site Quality

if ((Median Page Breadth is missing OR (Median Page Breadth $\leq$ 11.25)) AND (Page Formatting Variation is missing OR (Page Formatting Variation $\leq$ 27.785)) AND (Page Title Variation is missing OR (Page Title Variation $\leq$ 132.495)) AND (Graphic Formatting Variation is not missing AND (Graphic Formatting Variation $\leq$ 16.165)))

    Class = Good

This rule classifies the site as good due to an acceptable combination of measures: the median page breadth (8) is less than twelve; and pages in the site have very little similarity in page titles (37.5 percent), page formatting variation (0 percent), and graphic formatting variation (3.19 percent).

Figure 8.12. Decision tree rules reported for the example health education site. The rules were reported by the overall (top), health (middle), and education (bottom) site quality models.

that play a major role in distinguishing pages in this cluster) that deviate from the cluster centroid; deviations are similar for other pages in the site. Most of these deviations, including two of the top ten measures (text link count and good link word count), can be attributed to the fact that the site provides predominately graphical links instead of textual links for navigation. Table 8.4 also shows deviation on the page height (vertical scrolls), the use of words formatted

Home Page

if ((Italicized Body Word Count is not missing AND (Italicized Body Word Count > 2.5)))
    Class = Poor

This rule classifies the home page as poor because it contains more than two italicized words (17) in the body text.

Link and Content Page

if ((Italicized Body Word Count is missing OR (Italicized Body Word Count ≤ 2.5)) AND (Minimum Font Size is not missing AND (Minimum Font Size > 9.5)) AND (Minimum Graphic Height is missing OR (Minimum Graphic Height ≤ 36)) AND (Minimum Color Use is not missing AND (Minimum Color Use > 14.75)))
    Class = Poor

This rule classifies both the link and content pages as poor because they contain an acceptable number of italicized words in the body text and contain at least one image with a height less than 37 pixels, but all text is formatted with a font size greater than 9pt and all colors are used more than fifteen times. Good pages tend to use a font size that is smaller than 9pt, typically for copyright text, and they use an accent color.

Figure 8.13. Decision tree rules reported for the three example pages. These rules were reported by the overall page quality model.

with sans serif fonts (sans serif word count), and the overall use of fonts (font count—combinations of a font face, size, bolding, and italics).

We also evaluated the quality of these pages using the more context-sensitive page quality models for health and education pages (as opposed to the overall page quality model). The health model predicted that all but two pages were poor health pages, which mirrors the results of the site-level model. However, the education model predicted that all pages were poor education pages, which contradicts the corresponding site-level prediction. In both cases, prediction rationales were similar to the issues mentioned above. The contrast between site- and page-level predictions demonstrates the need to incorporate page-level predictions into the site-level prediction, as previously discussed.

Finally, we evaluated the quality of these pages using the models for each page type—home, link, and content. The page type decision tree model made accurate predictions for six of the nine pages, but inaccurately predicted that three pages were consistent with link pages; visual inspection suggested that these pages were actually content pages. Mispredictions were mainly due to an improper balance of link, body, and display text stemming from an overuse of image links. After correcting the page type predictions, the models classified

Table 8.4. Top ten measures that deviate from the small-page cluster for the example content page.[a]

Measure	Value	Cluster Range
Vertical Scrolls	2	(0.56–2.00)
Text Column Count	5	(0.62–4.36)
All Page Text Terms	129	(138.59–353.24)
Link Count	12	(12.40–41.24)
Text Link Count	2	(4.97–27.98)
Good Link Word Count	3	(7.43–49.67)
Bobby Browser Errors	6	(7.54–14.99)
Font Count	6	(3.64–5.80)
Sans Serif Word Count	0	(13.91–253.57)
Display Word Count	33	(1.13–18.67)

[a] The measures are presented in their order of importance, as determined by analyses of variances (ANOVAs). Each range reflects one standard deviation unit around the metric value at the cluster centroid. The page's measures are 8.33 standard deviation units from the cluster centroid.

all nine pages as poor pages. The page type quality models reported several deviations that were also reported by other models, including the minimum font size, minimum color use, sans serif word count, and text link count.

6.3.3   Summary of Assessment Findings

The models provide some direct insight for resolving design issues associated with some of the measures. For example, decision tree rules reported by the overall page quality model indicate inconsistent measures with a ">" in the threshold (e.g., italicized body word count > 2.5); they also indicate consistent measures with a "<" in the threshold. The Viewer Tool parses decision trees rules and displays consistent and inconsistent measures. The designer could explore ways to reduce measure values below the thresholds, such as removing italics or text coloring, changing font sizes, breaking text into multiple columns, etc. The same guidance holds for the other decision tree models.

Similarly to the decision tree rules, the cluster and discriminant classification models provide ranges for acceptable metric values; they also report the top ten measures that deviate from the underlying models. Some of the model deviations are straightforward to correct, provided the designer understands the model output and relevant measures. Other model deviations are not as straightforward to correct, such as introducing additional links and content or reducing reading complexity. Future work on automating design changes should make it easier to interpret and use the models to improve designs.

Based on the analysis, we derived a list of possible ways to improve the site. The changes below are ordered based on their potential impact (how much they mitigate measures that were reported frequently as being inconsistent). The recommendations only apply to the results generated during the initial application of the models; subsequent model applications revealed further changes that are not discussed here. No recommendations are made to address the accessibility and Weblint errors, because the role of these measures in improving design quality is unclear. Specific changes made as well as the results of the changes are discussed in the next section.

1 Increase the number of text links and corresponding link text (text link, link word, and good link word counts). This change will simultaneously increase the total number of links and internal links (link and internal link count) and decrease link element variation.

2 Use a smaller font size for some text, such as the footer text (minimum font size).

3 Decrease color overuse for page text and introduce an accent color (minimum color count).

4 Minimize or eliminate the use of italicized words in body text (italicized body word count).

5 Minimize text positioning (changes from flush left and columns where text starts; text positioning and column counts).

6 Minimize font combinations (font face, size, bolding, and italics combinations; font count).

7 Reduce the sizes of images (average graphic width, minimum graphic height, and graphic pixels).

8 Improve the page layout to reduce vertical scrolling (vertical scrolls).

9 Use tables with explicit widths to control the page layout (fixed page width use).

10 Vary the text elements and the formatting of text elements on the page (text element variation, good body and display word counts, sans serif word count).

11 Reduce the number of colors used for body text (body color count).

6.3.4   Improving the Site

Although the example site is somewhat aesthetically pleasing and highly consistent across pages within the site, the individual pages and the site as a whole are classified as being of poor quality. We modified the pages to incorporate a subset of the recommendations discussed above.

- To improve the color and text link counts and to simultaneously reduce the link count variation, a link text cluster (i.e., an area of text links shaded with a different background color to make it stand out) was added as a footer at the bottom of each page; the textual links in the cluster mirror the content of the graphical links. It was not necessary to split the link page into multiple pages, because adding the footer decreased the link element variation from 31 to 7 percent.

- To improve text formatting and the text element variation score: headings were used to break up paragraphs; additional font variations were used— Arial font (sans serif) for body text and Trebuchet (serif) for headings; and the font size of the copyright text was reduced to 9pt. The color of headings was also changed to gold for consistency with the models. We implemented all changes via an internal style sheet; the addition of the style sheet also improved the self-containment scores (i.e., degree to which all page elements are rendered solely via the HTML and image files).

- To improve the emphasized body text scores (i.e., bolded, colored, italicized, etc.), italics and colors used within body text were converted to bold, uncolored body text on all pages. Colored, non-italicized body text was also converted to uncolored body text.

- To improve the minimum color usage scores, a color accent was added to the vertical bars between the text links in the footer of each page. A browser-safe color was selected as dictated by a subsequent prediction by the overall page quality model.

- To reduce vertical scrolling, the logo and copyright notice at the bottom of the pages were placed adjacent to each other in one table row. The sizes of images and borders around them were also reduced to improve space utilization. Furthermore, text was wrapped to the left of the images versus images not being inlined with text.

- To further improve the page layout, fixed widths (640 pixels) were used for the main layout table.

Figures 8.14–8.16 depict the revised pages that correspond to the pages in Figures 8.9–8.11; many of the changes are not visible, because they appear at the bottom of the pages. Furthermore, we implemented only a subset of the potential changes.

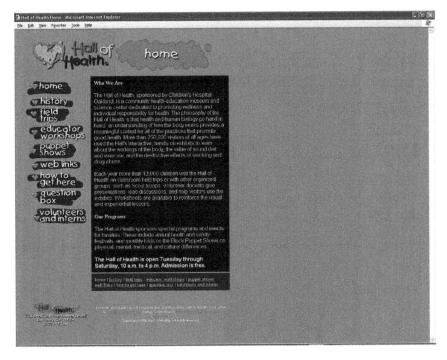

Figure 8.14. Modified home page for the example health education site. Gold headings were added, sans serif fonts were used for body text, colored and italicized body text was removed, and a fixed page width of 640 pixels was used. A footer navigation bar was added to the bottom of the page, an accent color was added to the footer navigation bar, footer elements were reorganized to reduce vertical scrolling, and the font size of footer text was reduced.

6.3.5   Subsequent Assessment

After making these changes, the models classified all pages correctly by functional type, and they rated them as good pages overall as well as good health pages. Figure 8.17 depicts the complex decision tree rule that classified all the pages as good overall. The median distance to the small-page cluster was 4.7 as compared to 10.9 standard deviation units for the original pages. Eight pages were rated as average pages based on their functional type; one was rated as poor. In addition, five of the nine pages were rated as average education pages; the four remaining pages were rated as poor. These differences in predictions demonstrate the potential difficulty of satisfying all the models simultaneously. A clear design objective needs to be chosen prior to making any changes, because the models could reveal a different set of changes to make.

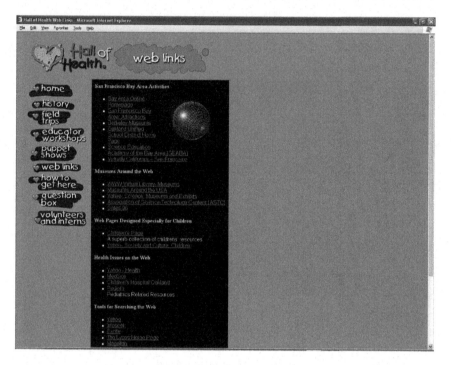

Figure 8.15. Modified link page for the example health education site. Gold headings were added, sans serif fonts were used for body text, colored and italicized body text was removed, the sizes of images were reduced, and a fixed page width of 640 pixels was used. A footer navigation bar was added to the bottom of the page, an accent color was added to the footer navigation bar, footer elements were reorganized to reduce vertical scrolling, and the font size of footer text was reduced; none of these changes are visible in the screen snapshot. See Figure 8.14 or 8.16 for the footer navigation bar.

The site was still classified as a poor site overall, but for a different reason—too much text element variation. The original site had very little variation in text elements (body and display text in particular); adding headings to pages increased the text element variation (75.5 percent) above the acceptable threshold of 51.8 percent. Ensuring that all pages contain similar amounts of display text is probably the simplest way to resolve this issue. Some pages, such as the example link page, have long headings, while other pages have relatively short headings. The site was also classified as a poor health site and a good education site, consistent with classifications before the modifications; the same decision tree rules were reported (see Figure 8.12). The median overall page, education page, and health page quality predictions contradicted the site-level models.

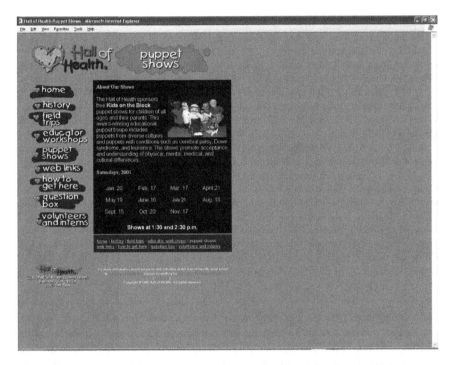

Figure 8.16. Modified content page for the example health education site. Gold headings were added, sans serif fonts were used for body text, colored and italicized body text was removed, the sizes of images were reduced, and a fixed page width of 640 pixels was used. A footer navigation bar was added to the bottom of the page, an accent color was added to the footer navigation bar, footer elements were reorganized to reduce vertical scrolling, and the font size of footer text was reduced.

7. Evaluation of the Web Interface Profiles

The final step in the WebTango process entails validating the web interface profiles. This section presents findings from an empirical study of pages and sites modified based on the 2000 models [Ivory, 2001; Ivory and Hearst, 2002a; Ivory and Hearst, 2002b]; we discussed example modifications in the preceding section. The study examines (1) whether it is possible for others to use the profiles to modify designs and (2) whether the resulting designs are of a higher quality than the original ones. A detailed discussion of the study can be found in [Ivory, 2001, Chapter 9].

7.1 Study Design

We conducted a study to determine whether changes made based on two profiles—the overall page quality and the good cluster models (see Table 8.2)—

if ((Minimum Font Size is missing OR (Minimum Font Size ≤ 9.5)) AND (Graphic Ad Count is missing OR (Graphic Ad Count ≤ 2.5)) AND (Exclaimed Body Word Count is missing OR (Exclaimed Body Word Count ≤ 11.5)) AND (Minimum Graphic Height is missing OR (Minimum Graphic Height ≤ 38.5)) AND (Vertical Scrolls is missing OR (Vertical Scrolls ≤ 3.5)) AND (Bad Panel Color Combinations is missing OR (Bad Panel Color Combinations ≤ 2.5)) AND (Object Count is missing OR (Object Count ≤ 4.5)) AND (Good Meta Tag Word Count is missing OR (Good Meta Tag Word Count ≤ 42.5)) AND (Minimum Color Use is missing OR (Minimum Color Use ≤ 12.5)) AND (Horizontal Scrolls is missing OR (Horizontal Scrolls ≤ 0.5)) AND (Weblint Errors is missing OR (Weblint Errors ≤ 54.5)) AND (Colored Body Word Count is missing OR (Colored Body Word Count > 0.5)) AND (Emphasized Body Word Count is missing OR (Emphasized Body Word Count ≤ 183)) AND (Bolded Body Word Count is missing OR (Bolded Body Word Count ≤ 43.5)) AND (Script Bytes is not missing AND (Script Bytes ≤ 173.5)) AND (Text Positioning Count is missing OR (Text Positioning Count ≤ 9)) AND (Serif Word Count is missing OR (Serif Word Count ≤ 325.5)) AND (Italicized Body Word Count is missing OR (Italicized Body Word Count ≤ 1.5)) AND (Graphic Count is not missing AND (Graphic Count ≤ 15.5)) AND (Minimum Graphic Width is missing OR (Minimum Graphic Width ≤ 97.5)) AND (Bobby Browser Errors is missing OR (Bobby Browser Errors > 6.5)))

Class = Good

This rule classifies a page as a good page because it: uses a smaller font size for some text; has fewer than sixteen images and no graphical ads; uses at least one image with a height smaller than 39 pixels as well as at least one image with a width smaller than 98 pixels; has fewer than 183 total emphasized (i.e., italicized, bolded, colored, etc.) body words, but has fewer than 11.5 exclaimed body words (i.e., body words followed by exclamation points), fewer than 44 bolded body words, fewer than two italicized body words, and at least 1 colored body word; requires fewer than four vertical scrolls and no horizontal scrolls; starts text in nine or fewer vertical positions; uses fewer than 2.5 bad panel color combinations and uses an accent color; uses no scripts, applets, or other objects; uses fewer than 43 good meta tag words and has fewer than 325 words formatted with serif fonts; and has fewer than 55 Weblint errors and more than six Bobby browser errors.

Figure 8.17. Decision tree rule reported for all the modified example pages. This rule was reported by the overall page quality model.

improve design quality (i.e., usability, accessibility, performance, and so on). We randomly selected five study sites from various Yahoo categories, such as finance and education; study sites included the two discussed in Section 6. Two undergraduate students and a graduate student modified three of the study sites, while the authors modified the other two sites. The students had little or no training in web site design and had very little experience with building web sites. Furthermore, they did not have prior experience with the Analysis Tool, the quantitative measures, nor the profiles. They made straightforward changes based directly on the decision tree rules and cluster model results.

Thirteen participants (people who had and did not have web design experience) completed a within-subjects experiment wherein they performed two types of tasks. The first task—page-level analysis—required participants to explore the original and modified versions of a web page and to select the design that they felt exhibited the highest quality; there were a total of fifteen comparisons for pages from three sites. The second task—site-level analysis—required participants to explore a collection of pages from a web site and to rate the quality of the site on a 5-point scale. Participants rated original and modified versions of two sites; there were a total of four site rating tasks. Given that only a subset of pages were modified for each site, it was not feasible to have participants attempt to complete information-seeking tasks during this study.

7.2   Study Results

The page-level analysis focused on testing the hypothesis that pages modified based on the overall page quality and the good cluster models are of a higher quality than the original pages. The remodeling did not entail changing the content on pages, except for redistributing content over multiple pages, adding headings, etc. as dictated by the models. Thus, most of the differences between the original and modified pages were minimal and focused on the page layout and text formatting.

The results showed that modified pages were preferred 57.4 percent of the time, while the original pages were preferred 42.6 percent of the time. The Chi-Square test [Easton and McColl, 1997] revealed this difference to be significant ($\chi^2 = 4.3$, asymptotic significance of .038). Participants preferred the modified pages more so than the original ones in ten of the fifteen comparisons. Their comments about why they preferred the modified pages supported the changes made based on the profiles. In particular, participants felt that the modified pages were easier to read, required less scrolling, were cleaner, used better color schemes, made better use of whitespace, used headings, eliminated italics, and used better fonts.

Comments also revealed that in a few cases, mainly for four pages on the same site, participants responded negatively to changes made based on the profiles. For example, in modifying pages to minimize vertical scrolling, one of the web designers accidentally introduced horizontal scrolling. Participants preferred the original version of the pages, because the width of text was restricted to fit within the browser window (i.e., the page did not require horizontal scrolling). If we excluded responses for pages on this site, then the results for the two remaining sites show that modified pages were preferred 66.9 percent of the time, while the original pages were preferred 33.1 percent of the time; this difference was highly significant ($\chi^2 = 14.9$, asymptotic significance of .000).

The site-level analysis focused on testing the hypothesis that sites with pages modified based on the overall page quality and the good page cluster models are of a higher quality than the original sites. Similarly to the page-level analysis, students used the profiles to modify individual pages in the site. Students relied on the median overall page quality (see Table 8.3) for site level assessments; as the quality of the individual pages improved, so did the median overall page quality. Students did not use the overall site quality model, due to the discrepancy between page- and site-level predictions that existed at the time of the study.

Participants rated the quality of the original sites as 3.0 on average (σ = 1.36); however, they rated the quality of modified sites as 3.5 on average (σ = 1.03). A paired samples t-test [Easton and McColl, 1997] revealed that this difference was significant (p = .025); this means that each participant tended to rate the modified version higher than the original version. Similarly to the page-level analysis, participants' comments provided support for many of the changes made based on the profiles.

7.3   Study Implications

The study demonstrated that it is possible for people, other than the authors, to interpret and apply the models. However, it also demonstrated the need to ensure that errors are not introduced during this process. Both the page- and site-level results were promising, in that they showed that participants responded favorably to design changes that were made based on the models, even though they were conservative for this first study. It is possible that less conservative changes would have resulted in larger differences in page preferences and site ratings. We will re-examine this question with future studies after we have implemented automated recommendations and possibly modifications in some manner.

8.   Analysis of Web Design Guidelines

Another application of the quantitative measures and profiles is to revisit web design recommendations, specifically for recommendations that are contradictory, vague, or not empirically validated. Ideally, quantifying effective design patterns and revealing concrete thresholds (i.e., numerical ranges for measures) will provide the extra guidance that novice or occasional web designers need to build better sites.

We have contrasted thresholds derived from our 2000 and 2002 models for several aspects of web interfaces, including the amount of text, font styles and sizes, and colors. The statistical models revealed quantitative thresholds that validate and, in some cases, invalidate advice in the literature. The design patterns extend beyond individual measures to show, for instance, that the amount of text formatting is proportional to the amount of text on a page (i.e., a change in one aspect may necessitate a change in another). We also found that the guidance varies slightly depending on the design context (e.g., page style) and that fundamental design patterns have not changed radically over recent years.

Chapter 13 elaborates on our analyses of web design guidelines. More detailed discussions can be found in [Ivory, 2001, Chapter 10] and [Ivory, 2003b]. Our examinations demonstrate that the methodology makes it possible to derive web design guidelines directly from empirical data.

9.   Future WebTango Research Directions

Research outlined in this chapter represents an important first step toward enabling non-professional designers to iteratively improve the quality of their web site designs. The methodology and tools are still in their infancy and provide support only for refining an implemented site; thus, there are many ways in which they can be improved. We summarize future research toward this end.

9.1   Advancing Research on Web Design and Evaluation

We will conduct research to facilitate advances in web interface design and evaluation that has broad implications for other automated web site evaluation researchers and for web practitioners. We are designing studies to identify an empirically validated web site design process, which we plan to support with a design tool. We have conducted preliminary studies of several existing automated evaluation tools (see Chapters 11 and 12 in Part III) [Ivory and Chevalier, 2002; Ivory *et al.*, 2003] and will continue examining the efficacy of such tools, including our own. We will also work to develop a corpus of usability-tested sites, as a way to further research on web site design and the validation of automated evaluation methodologies.

9.2   Improving the WebTango Measures

We plan to expand the set of quantitative measures to assess other design aspects, such as the reuse of web interface elements across pages in a site. A major limitation of the current set of measures is that they do not assess content quality. Future work will explore using text analysis techniques to possibly derive other measures of content quality. Another limitation is that the measures do not adequately gauge accessibility for the disabled; we found that the good web pages tended not to be accessible, as determined by the Bobby tool. Future work will examine other ways to measure accessibility, for instance computing the nesting level of tables. (Although tables may help sighted users scan pages, they may impede blind users.)

We are currently exploring the use of image processing techniques to classify design components, to improve the accuracy of existing measures, to enable the development of new ones, and to enable support for non-HTML pages and early design representations. Supporting early design representations also requires adjustments to the profiles, such as ignoring certain measures during analysis.

9.3   Developing a Robust Evaluation Tool

All the WebTango tools need to be reimplemented as part of a robust, open source browser, such as Mozilla; this redevelopment will enable support for framesets, scripts, applets, and other objects, as well as real-time analysis. Real-time analysis is crucial for developing an interactive evaluation tool to support iterative design and evaluation.

Other key components of the interactive evaluation tool include: (1) recommending design improvements based on model predictions, (2) applying recommendations so users can preview the changes, and (3) showing comparable designs for exploration. Some model deviations are easy to correct, such as removing or changing text formatting, using good color combinations, and resizing images; it is possible to automatically modify the HTML code to incorporate these types of changes. Other changes, such as reducing vertical scrolling, adding text columns, improving readability, and adding links are not as straightforward. We consider the automated correction of design deviations to be crucial for improving the current state of the web. Our empirical studies of novice and professional designers demonstrate that designers find it extremely difficult to implement design guidelines, even with automated evaluation tools [Ivory and Chevalier, 2002; Chevalier and Ivory, 2003a; Chevalier and Ivory, 2003b; Ivory *et al.*, 2003]; thus, automating design changes should help tremendously.

More work needs to be done to better understand the profiles before interactive evaluation can be supported. For example, factor analysis or multidimensional scaling techniques [Easton and McColl, 1997] could be used to reduce the number of measures and to gain more insight about relationships among measures. This would enable recommendations and modifications to be based on combinations of measures, rather than individual measures.

9.4   Extending the Methodology and Measures to Other Domains

A natural extension of this work is to enable profiles to be developed to capture effective design practices in other cultures. This would require support for non-English languages, mainly using language-appropriate dictionaries and text analysis algorithms. This may also require changes to the assessment of good color usage, because colors have specific meanings in some cultures.

Another extension of this work would be to develop a quality summary for web pages and sites. This summary would provide a quick overview or characterization that could be used by search engines for ordering search results or possibly in visualizations of clickstreams through sites (e.g., in the WebQuilt tool [Hong *et al.*, 2001]). The summary for search engine ordering may consist of a single rating, while the summary for the latter case may consist of a rating in addition to other details, such as the predicted page type, the closest good page cluster, and download speed. We are conducting an experimental study to examine whether communicating information about page quality, the number of ads, or the number of words can better support users—fully sighted, blind, and low vision—in Internet searching. Study results will inform the incorporation of such information in search interfaces.

Another application of our corpus of analyzed web pages and sites is to enable designers to explore the collection to inform design choices. Ideally, characteristics of web pages and sites could be represented in a way that facilitates easily identifying pages and sites that satisfy some design criteria, such as effective navigation schemes within health sites or good page layouts, color palettes, and site maps. Task-based search techniques that exploit metadata [Elliott, 2001; English *et al.*, 2001; Hearst, 2000; Yee *et al.*, 2003] should be helpful. Metadata for web interfaces could consist of the quantitative measures that we developed as well as others that describe, for instance, the size of the site, the type of site, a page's size, a page's functional type, elements on a page (e.g., navigation bars), as well as site ratings.

Another extension of this work is to use the profiles to derive parameters for a web interface simulator, similar to those discussed in Chapter 7. Monte Carlo simulation [Law and Kelton, 1991] could be used as a way to automate web site evaluation by mimicking users' information-seeking behavior and estimating navigation time, errors, etc. Similarly to the guideline threshold derivation, profiles could be used to derive simulation model parameters, such as thinking and reading times for pages. The cluster models could be used to derive timing estimates for these activities based on the average number of links, words, and other measures that reflect page complexity. User studies would be conducted to validate the baselines before incorporating them into the simulator.

We are also exploring the development of design and evaluation methodologies for the early design stages. Specifically, we are examining the use of machine learning techniques, such as self-organizing maps [Kohonen, 1997], to support designers. For example, we plan to study whether it is possible to use self-organizing maps to represent the space of high-quality designs and, furthermore, to assist designers with making design choices that will produce a high-quality design.

10.   Discussion

This chapter presented an automated analysis methodology that is consistent with measurement approaches used in the performance evaluation domain and guideline review approaches used in the usability evaluation domain. Unlike other web assessment techniques, this approach uses quantitative measures and empirical data to develop guidelines for comparison purposes.

Even though we have demonstrated that it is possible to find correlations between values for measures and expert ratings, we make no claim about the profiles representing causal links. It is possible that the highly rated sites are highly rated for reasons other than what is assessed with the measures, such as the quality of the content on the site. The current models and tools cannot improve on poor content. However, the empirical studies provided preliminary evidence that they can provide insight on how to take good content that is poorly presented and improve its presentation, thus improving users' experience in accessing that content. And, because it is possible to empirically find commonalities among the presentation elements of the highly rated sites, this finding provides strong evidence that the presentational aspects of highly rated sites that differ from those of poorly rated sites are in fact important for good design.

Although the tools are robust, they suffer from several limitations. Currently, the crawling and analysis tools are separate processes and could benefit from being consolidated. Another limitation is that the tools are somewhat compute intensive and do not enable real-time assessment. The major limitation of this approach is that the quantitative measures do not capture users' subjective preferences. For example, one study has shown that perceived download speed is more important than actual download speed [Scanlon and Schroeder, 2000a]. Although we can measure actual download speed, it may not be possible to assess perceived speed. Nonetheless, the methodology can be viewed as a reverse engineering of design decisions that were presumably informed by user input.

Notes

1 The Multivalent Browser code was provided courtesy of Tom Phelps.

Chapter 9

PROMISING RESEARCH DIRECTIONS

Automated web site evaluation methods have many potential benefits, including reducing the costs of non-automated methods, aiding in comparisons between alternative designs, and improving consistency in evaluation results. However, we do not think that the methods have as much influence on web site designs as they could have. For instance, our survey of 169 web practioners revealed that only fifteen percent of them report that they always use such tools in their work practices (see Chapters 1 and 10).

In this chapter, we discuss research directions to widen the influence of these methods. We then discuss ways to expand and improve several promising approaches.

1. Increasing the Influence of Automated Evaluation Methods

We think that, for several reasons, the existing automated evaluation methods have marginal influence on web site designs:

1 There is little evidence about the efficacy of these methods, specifically whether they: (1) from a designer's perspective, result in sites that are better than sites produced without them; and (2) from a user's perspective, result in sites that are more usable and accessible. Chapter 12 describes a study that we conducted to assess the efficacy of three methods.

2 They do not provide support for the entire web site design process. Most approaches require a site to be implemented so that it can be evaluated. Furthermore, there is very little integration of approaches.

3 They do not consider the context (e.g., type of site or page) in which sites are designed. The WebTango approach (discussed in Chapter 8) is one exception.

4 They make assumptions about web site users that may reflect one or more types of users, but not the diverse set of web users.

We suggest ways to address these limitations in the following sections.

1.1   Methodology Validation

To address the efficacy issue, there needs to be a concerted effort, among automated evaluation researchers, to validate methodologies. More specifically, researchers could benefit from having access to a corpus of evaluated sites. (The CIFter study [NIST Visualization and Usability Group, 2001] is a related effort, wherein multiple testing teams evaluated a web site; the objective was to have evaluation results reported in the common industry format.) The corpus should consist of at least one hundred sites, where each has been tested by users with diverse abilities. Extensive testing data should be captured (e.g., log files, task completion times, and subjective ratings). This data needs to be analyzed to catalog usability issues and to represent them in a manner that facilitates verifying whether a method detects the issue or not.

Researchers can use this corpus to assess how well their approaches detect documented usability, accessibility, and other issues. Similarly to other bench-marking efforts, researchers can report standard quantitative measures (e.g., percentage of problems found or types of problems found) for their method-ologies. Reported measures for all methods should be disseminated broadly so that potential users and researchers can consult them.

1.2   Design Process Support

Newman and Landay's ethnographic study of professional web site designers [2000] and other literature sources [De Troyer and Leune, 1998; Ford and Boyarski, 1997; Fuccella, 1997; Heller and Rivers, 1996b; Nielsen, 2000; Sano, 1996; Shneiderman, 1997; van Duyne *et al.*, 2002] describe several stages in the web design process (see Figure 9.1). Site requirements are identified during the discovery phase; requirements need to address many issues, such as who the intended users are, what tasks they need to accomplish, what constraints need to be met, and so on. Several design alternatives may be explored during the design exploration phase. However, one design idea is chosen and improved upon during the design refinement phase. Site implementation typically occurs during the production phase; design templates or style guides may be developed initially to guide the implementation effort. The implemented site is tested and repaired if necessary during the quality assurance phase; afterwards, it is released for broad use. Once the site is released, it undergoes continuous

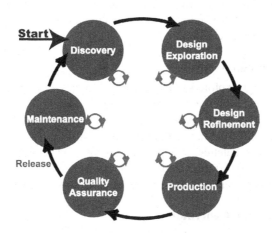

Figure 9.1. Web site design and development process. This figure is a repetition of Figure 1.1.

maintenance (e.g., updating content). Iteration may occur during each of these phases, as depicted in Figure 9.1.

Existing automated evaluation tools and HTML authoring tools support web designers in the later stages of design—production, quality assurance, release, and ongoing assessment—when changes are less likely to be made [Nielsen, 1993]. Furthermore, current support is inadequate and could be extended as follows.

1.2.1 Web Design Environment

A design environment that can provide designers, especially novice designers, with a cognitive model of the design process, give them guidance and feedback on their design processes, and assist them with producing the site that they designed will increase the likelihood that designers will produce sites that are usable and accessible. The environment should enable designers to plug in design or evaluation tools throughout the design and development process, as needed. The AWUSA [Tiedtke *et al.*, 2002] framework (discussed in Chapter 3) integrates multiple assessment techniques (task-based log file analysis, guideline review, and web usage mining); it provides some guidance on addressing the plug-in challenge.

The Project Management Administration Web Site (PAWS) [Griffiths *et al.*, 2002] is one tool aimed in this direction. Griffiths *et al.* designed the tool to support novice designers (multimedia students) in following a software-engineering–based design process; however, this process was not validated via empirical studies. PAWS provides a hyper-linked version of the process with descriptions of each step; students can associate documents with each step. PAWS does not provide process feedback, and students reported that the interface had inadequate usability.

1.2.2   Web Design Archive

During the design exploration and refinement stages, designers could employ an archive of sites, which exhibit usability and accessibility principles. For instance, they can identify pages and sites that satisfy one or more design criteria, such as effective navigation schemes within health sites or effective page layouts, color palettes, and site map designs. The archive of sites that we analyze for the WebTango method (discussed in Chapter 8), as well as the proposed corpus of evaluated sites, could be used for this purpose.

1.2.3   Web Design Generator

Similarly to automated graphical interface generators [Balbo, 1995; Mackinlay, 1986; Sears, 1995], web site generators can be developed to support designers during the design refinement stage. For instance, an informational site builder could simply require a designer to specify the site's content (in some raw format) and then generate an initial design. Ideally, the design tool would: (1) break content into logical units, (2) structure these units for readability, (3) determine an effective navigation structure, and (4) construct pages based on effective design practices.

Form-based site generators (e.g., autowebmaker [autowebmaker, 2003], easiwebmaker [Easiwebmaker, 2003], Yahoo! Geo-Cities [Yahoo! Inc., 2003], and Terra Lycos Tripod [Lycos, Inc., 2003]) are a step in this direction. They hide coding details from designers and simultaneously restrict their creativity, by limiting control over the design itself; in exchange, designers can easily build sites that ideally reflect effective design practices. Designers are still responsible for determining how to organize content and structure navigation on the site.

It is also possible to develop a web design generator that focuses more so on graphical design, similarly to the graphical interface generators. For example, the approach could generate some initial designs, based on information gathered from the discovery stage. Damask [Lin and Landay, 2002] is a similar system that provides design patterns (sketches that van Duyne *et al.* [2002] identified) so that designers can incorporate them into their sketches.

Recent work is examining the application of layout techniques to web pages [Allen *et al.*, 1999; Reichenberger *et al.*, 1995]. Web layout approaches entail the use of rhetorical structure theory [Mann and Thompson, 1987] to identify rhetorical relations among web page elements and to use these rhetorical relations to inform the page layout. Automated web page layout is still an evolving research area, and the tools are mostly under development.

1.2.4 Web Design Simulator

During design exploration, designers could use a simulator to provide objective measures for evaluating alternative designs. The simulator would consider the effects of page and site design elements and employ user models representing a diverse set of users and devices, unlike existing simulators.

Another alternative is to support the designer in making design choices that will increase the likelihood that the implemented site will be usable and accessible. For instance, we plan to use machine learning techniques, such as self-organizing maps [Kohonen, 1997], to represent the space of high-quality designs. We will use image processing and classification techniques to represent the high-fidelity designs at lower-fidelity representations (e.g., schematics or sketches) so that throughout the design process, we can automatically determine if the designer's design is consistent with other high-quality designs (i.e., is the designer following a path that will likely produce a usable and accessible site).

1.3 Design Context Consideration

Badre and Laskowski [2001] have shown context to be an important consideration in web site design, yet existing methodologies, with the exception of the WebTango prototype, do not consider the context in which sites are designed. The WebTango prototype considers contextual information (e.g., the content type, functional type, page size, and overall site structure) during assessment. However, it also demonstrates that evaluations may differ, depending on the context, and that designers may need guidance to help them to resolve such discrepancies. Nonetheless, the WebTango approach provides an example of and is an important first step toward context consideration. More research is needed in this area.

1.4 User Diversity Consideration

Existing automated (and many non-automated) evaluation approaches typically assess web sites based on one user model, for instance a sighted user accessing a site via a computer with a 56.6K modem and a 15-inch monitor [DreamInk, 2000] or a blind user accessing the site via a computer with a 56.6K modem and screen reader [WatchFire, 2002]. Research needs to be conducted to develop a set of user models to represent a diverse set of web site users [Computer Science and Telecommunications Board, 1997], including users with disabilities (visual, hearing, physical, cognitive, and learning [Architectural and Transportation Barriers Compliance Board, 2000; Coyne and Nielsen, 2001; DO-IT, 2002a; DO-IT, 2002b; DO-IT, 2002c; DO-IT, 2002d; Nielsen, 2001; World Wide Web Consortium, 1999]) and users of varying ages [Cardoso *et al.*, 2002; Ellis and Kurniawan, 2000; Mead *et al.*, 1997]. These models would

Table 9.1. Synopsis of automated analysis support for usability testing methods. (This table is a repetition of Table 3.1.)

Method Class:	Testing
Automation Type:	Analysis
Method Type:	Log File Analysis—analyze usage data (18 methods)

Evaluation Method	Effort
Use of task models (AWUSA, QUIP, WebQuilt, KALDI, WebRemUSINE)	IFM[a]
Statistical analysis (traffic- and time-based)	IF
On-line analytical processing ([Büchner and Mulvenna, 1998], WebLogMiner)	IF
Usage mining (AWUSA, LumberJack, M*i*DAS, SpeedTracer, WUM, WEBMINER, WebLogMiner)	IFM[a]
Visualization (pattern-, behavior-, usage-, and evolution-based)	IF

[a] Methods may or may not require a model.

specify limitations, access devices, and other constraints. Ideally, automated evaluation tools would assess designs based these user models.

2.   Expanding Existing Automated Evaluation Methods

We have studied numerous methods that support automated web site evaluation. Based on the methods surveyed, research to further develop log file analysis, guideline review, analytical modeling, and simulation techniques could result in several promising techniques, as discussed in more detail in this section.

2.1   Log File Analysis Approaches

The survey showed log file analysis to be a viable methodology for automated analysis of usage data. Table 9.1 summarizes current approaches to log file analysis. These approaches could be expanded and improved in the following two ways:

- Generating synthetic usage data for analysis;

- Augmenting task-based approaches with guidelines to support automated critique.

Generating synthetic usage data for analysis. The main limitation of log file analysis is that it still requires formal or informal interface use to employ. One way to expand the use and benefits of this methodology is to leverage a small amount of test data to generate a larger set of plausible usage data. This is even more important for web interfaces, because server logs do not capture a complete record of user interactions. There are two simulation approaches that support this generation, one using a genetic algorithm [Kasik and George, 1996] and the other using information scent modeling [Chi *et al.*, 2000] (see Chapter 7). The genetic algorithm approach determines user behavior during deviation points in an expert user script (task sequence), while the information scent model selects navigation paths by considering word overlap between links and web pages. Both of these approaches generate plausible usage traces with limited formal or informal interface use. These techniques also provide valuable insight on how to leverage real usage data from usability tests or informal use. For example, real data could also serve as input scripts for genetic algorithms; the evaluator could add deviation points to these.

Augmenting task-based approaches with guidelines to support automated critique. Given a wider sampling of usage data, using task models during log file analysis is a promising research area to pursue. Task-based approaches that follow the WebRemUSINE (Web Remote USer Interface Evaluator) [Paganelli and Paternò, 2002] model in particular (i.e., compare a task model expressed in terms of temporal relationships to usage traces) provide the most support, among the methods surveyed. WebRemUSINE outputs information to help the evaluator understand user behavior, preferences, and errors. Additionally, WebRemUSINE already reports substantial analysis data, which could be compared to usability guidelines to support automated critique.

An alternative task-based approach is to analyze navigation behavior to automatically identify patterns indicative of potential problems. Although web usage mining (discussed in Section 4 of Chapter 3) entails analysis of navigation behavior, the current aim is not to identify distinctive patterns that are indicative of problems (e.g., hub-and-spoke navigation). Identifying navigation patterns in log files is still largely a manual process, and designers could benefit from automation support.

2.2 Guideline Review Approaches

Although there are many guideline review methods for analyzing and critiquing web interfaces (see Tables 9.2 and 9.3), existing approaches only cover a small fraction of usability aspects [Brajnik, 2000] and have not been validated empirically. Chapter 8 presented an approach for developing web design guidelines directly from empirical data. More research is needed to expand the web design aspects that are evaluated and to validate the methodologies. The previously discussed corpus of evaluated sites would address the latter issue. The use of image processing and other techniques could enable tools to assess broader design aspects. For example, an automated version of the Page Layout Change approach [Farkas, 2003] could analyze the consistency of layouts across pages in a site.

Table 9.2. Synopsis of automated analysis support for inspection methods.[a] (This table is a repetition of Table 4.1.)

Method Class:	Inspection
Automation Type:	Analysis
Method Type:	Guideline Review—expert checks guideline conformance (10 methods)

Evaluation Method	Effort
Analyze the structure of pages and site (HyperAT, Gentler, Rating Game, WebTango)	
Use guidelines for analysis (AWUSA, Dr. HTML, KWARESMI, WebSAT, WebTango)	
Analyze the scanning path of a page (Design Advisor)	
Analyze visual consistency across pages (Page Layout Change)	

[a] The effort level for all methods is minimal, which is denoted by the missing entries in the Effort column.

Table 9.3. Synopsis of automated critique support for inspection methods.[a] (This table is a repetition of Table 4.2.)

Method Class:	Inspection
Automation Type:	Critique
Method Type:	Guideline Review—expert checks guideline conformance (15 methods)

Evaluation Method	Effort
Use coding standards for critique (Dr. Watson, HTML Validator, CSS Validator, Weblint)	
Use guidelines for critique (508 Suite, AccessEnble, AccVerify/AccRepair, ALTifier, A-Prompt, Bobby, Dr. Watson, EvalWeb, InFocus, LIFT, PageScreamer, WAVE)	

Method Class:	Inspection
Automation Type:	Critique
Method Type:	Cognitive Walkthrough—expert simulates user's problem solving (1 method)

Evaluation Method	Effort
Use text similarity measures for critique (CWW)	

[a] The effort level for all methods is minimal, which is denoted by the missing entries in the Effort column.

2.3   Analytical Modeling Approaches

As previously discussed, analytical modeling approaches for web interfaces still remain to be developed. It may not be possible to develop new approaches

Table 9.4. Synopsis of automated analysis support for simulation methods. (This table is a repetition of Table 7.1.)

Method Class:	Simulation
Automation Type:	Analysis
Method Type:	Information Processor Modeling—mimic user interaction (1 method)

Evaluation Method	Effort
Employ a GOMS-like model to analyze navigation (Site Profile)	M

Method Class:	Simulation
Automation Type:	Analysis
Method Type:	Information Scent Modeling—mimic web site navigation (3 methods)

Evaluation Method	Effort
Employ an information-scent model to analyze navigation (Bloodhound, CoLiDeS, [Miller and Remington, 2002])	M

using a paradigm that requires explicit task hierarchies (e.g., GOMS analysis [John and Kieras, 1996]). However, a variation of Cognitive Task Analysis (CTA) [May and Barnard, 1994] may be appropriate for web interfaces, provided more effort is spent to fully develop the methodology. To use the approach, the evaluator provides interface parameters to an underlying model for analysis versus developing a new model to assess each interface. The approach is consistent with analytical modeling techniques employed outside of HCI, such as in the performance evaluation of computer systems [Jain, 1991]. One of the drawbacks of CTA is the need to describe the interface to the system. Integrating this approach into a web site design environment should make it more tenable.

2.4 Simulation Approaches

Table 9.4 summarizes current approaches to simulation analysis. Simulation, in general, is a promising research area to pursue for automated analysis, especially for evaluating alternative designs in the early design stages. It is possible to use several simulation techniques employed in the performance analysis of computer systems, in particular Monte Carlo simulation [Jain, 1991], to enable designers to perform what-if analyses with web site designs.

Monte Carlo simulations enable an evaluator to model a system probabilistically (i.e., sampling from a probability distribution is used to determine what event occurs next). Monte Carlo simulation could contribute substantially to automated analysis by eliminating the need for explicit task hierarchies or user models. Most simulations in this domain rely on a single user model, typically an expert user. Monte Carlo simulation would enable designers to perform what-if analysis and study design alternatives with many user models. The Bloodhound methodology [Card *et al.*, 2001; Chi *et al.*, 2000; Chi *et al.*, 2001; Chi *et al.*, 2003], which entails simulating web site navigation, is a close approximation to Monte Carlo simulation.

3.   Discussion

Automated evaluation has many potential benefits, including reducing the costs of non-automated methods, aiding in comparisons between alternative designs, and improving evaluation consistency. However, existing approaches are not influencing web site designs as much as they could. More research is needed to validate and integrate methods, to support evaluation during the early design stages, and to incorporate design context and diverse user abilities into assessments. Furthermore, research to enhance analytical modeling, simulation, guideline review, and log file analysis techniques could result in several promising automated evaluation techniques.

III

PRACTITIONER'S PERSPECTIVE

Chapter 10

AUTOMATED EVALUATION TOOLS

In Part II, we discussed research efforts aimed at developing or refining automated evaluation methodologies for evaluating web interfaces. Some of these efforts have produced commercial or research software (e.g., WatchFire Bobby [WatchFire, 2002], the HTML Validation Service[1] [World Wide Web Consortium, 2001c], the Web Static Analyzer Tool [Scholtz and Laskowski, 1998], and many others) that practitioners can use to evaluate web site usability, accessibility, coding, performance, and so on. In the remainder of this book (Part III), we examine the use of automated evaluation tools, and we discuss the role and the efficacy of existing tools.

In this chapter, we begin by providing background information that is pertinent to our discussion. Specifically, we describe how the automated evaluation methodologies (discussed in Part II) have been instantiated as automated evaluation tools. Section 2 describes the structure of automated evaluation tools, summarizes five types of evaluation tools (e.g., guideline review and log file analysis), and then provides details about each. In Section 3, we present results from a survey of 169 practitioners wherein we asked them about their use of automated evaluation tools. We conclude this chapter with a discussion of the current role of these tools. We refer the reader to Appendix A for an exhaustive list of methodologies and tools that are discussed in this chapter, as well as throughout Part II.

The remaining chapters in Part III focus on the automated evaluation tools that practitioners use and other applications of them. Chapter 11 compares the evaluation results reported across tools for a single web page. Chapter 12 reports the results of a study wherein designers used several tools to modify sites and diverse users tested the original and modified sites to determine whether modifications improved the usability and accessibility of sites. Chapter 13 demonstrates how one automated evaluation tool—the WebTango prototype (discussed in Chapter 8) [Ivory and Hearst, 2002a]—can be used to provide concrete thresholds for web design guidelines. We conclude the book with a discussion of ways in which automated evaluation tools can be improved.

1.   Evaluation Approaches

Evaluation is an important part of the web site design and development process [Nielsen, 2000; van Duyne *et al.*, 2002], and there are many ways to conduct an evaluation [Dix *et al.*, 1998; Nielsen, 1993]. Chapter 2 provided an overview of the five major evaluation approaches (method classes), which we repeat below.

- **Testing:** an evaluator observes participants interacting with an interface (i.e., completing tasks) to determine usability problems.

- **Inspection:** an evaluator uses a set of criteria or heuristics to identify potential usability problems in an interface.

- **Inquiry:** participants provide feedback on an interface via interviews, surveys, etc.

- **Analytical Modeling:** an evaluator employs user and interface models to generate usability predictions.

- **Simulation:** an evaluator employs user and interface models to mimic a user interacting with an interface and report the results of this interaction (e.g., simulated activities, errors, and other quantitative measures).

Each of these approaches requires the evaluator to follow a process to successfully complete the assessment. An evaluation process can entail many activities, depending on the method employed. Common activities include:

- **Capture**: collecting usability data, such as task completion time, errors, guideline violations, and subjective ratings;

- **Analysis**: interpreting usability data to identify problems; and

- **Critique**: suggesting solutions or improvements to mitigate problems.

Within each method class, there is software support (tools) to automate or semi-automate some aspects of the capture, analysis, or critique activities: *capture tools* automatically record usage data, *analysis tools* automatically identify potential problems, and *critique tools* automatically identify potential problems and suggest improvements. In this chapter and subsequent ones, we will examine the automated analysis and critique tools that have been developed. These tools assist practitioners with applying the various evaluation approaches (i.e., testing, inspection, inquiry, analytical modeling, or simulation) in the assessment of web sites.

Automated evaluation tools offer several potential advantages over non-automated evaluation, including increased consistency in the errors uncovered and in the features evaluated. However, it is important to note that automation is considered to be a useful *complement* and *addition* to standard evaluation techniques like heuristic evaluation and usability testing—not a substitute. Different techniques uncover different kinds of problems, and subjective measures such as user satisfaction are unlikely to be predictable by automated methods.

2. Overview of Automated Evaluation Tools

Automated evaluation tools are designed similarly, and we discuss their common anatomy in this section. We characterize the types of assessments that analysis and critique tools support and then discuss each type of assessment.

2.1 Tool Anatomy

Given that the automated evaluation tools are based on similar automated evaluation methodologies (see Part II), there is a lot of similarity across tools. Figure 10.1 depicts the anatomy of most tools. They have internal assumptions about web site users (e.g., computer or Internet experience, reading level, and other abilities), their tasks (e.g., browsing or searching for information), and the technology that they use (e.g., web browsers, Internet connections, and assistive technology). For example, the tools may assume that the users are sighted, browsing for information, and accessing the site via a computer with a 56.6K modem and a 15-inch monitor. As another example, the tools may assume that site users are blind, searching for information, and accessing the site via a computer with a 56.6K modem and screen reader. It is important to note that these assumptions may not match the user characteristics that influenced the design of the site. All tools have evaluation criteria (e.g., server response time or guidelines) that they use to evaluate a site, and they typically present evaluation results in report format (graphical or textual).

2.2 Analysis and Critique Tools

There are over fifty automated analysis and critique tools available for evaluating the usability, accessibility, etc. of web sites. We can characterize these tools by the five types of assessments that they supported at publication time.

Check server performance. Performance measurement tools monitor the consistency, availability, and performance of a web server or stress the server to determine the amount of traffic that it can accommodate.

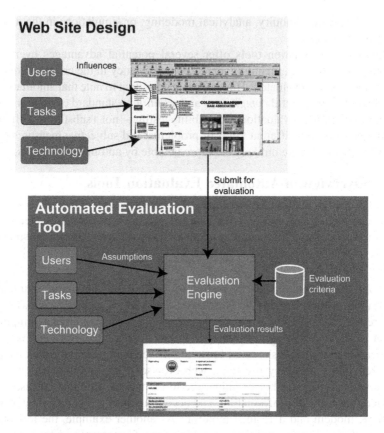

Figure 10.1. Anatomy of an automated evaluation tool. The top part of the figure shows that a web site design is influenced by the intended users, their tasks, and assumptions about the technology that they will use to access the site. The site is submitted to an evaluation tool for assessment. The tool has internal assumptions about the users, tasks, and technology used on the site; these assumptions may or may not match the intended site users. The tool uses these assumptions and its evaluation criteria to evaluate the site and then outputs assessment results, typically in report format.

Analyze site usage data. Log file analysis tools analyze log file data to identify potential problems in usage patterns (e.g., pages that are not being visited, broken links, or server errors).

Check guideline conformance. Guideline review tools detect and flag a web page's or site's deviation from design criteria (e.g., W3C HTML coding standards [World Wide Web Consortium, 2001c], Section 508 guidelines [Center for Information Technology Accommodation, 2002], or W3C Content Accessibility Guidelines [World Wide Web Consortium, 1999]).

Analyze navigation text. Textual analysis tools identify potential navigation problems on web pages that are attributable to confusing headings or link text.

Simulate hypothetical users navigating a site. Information-seeking simulation tools mimic the browsing process of users and output computed measures and actions (e.g., navigation time and navigation paths).

There are automated analysis tools to support all of these assessment types, except for textual analysis. Automated critique tools only support the guideline review and textual analysis assessment types. We provide an overview of each of the five assessment types and the available tools in the remainder of this section; Tables 10.1 and 10.2 depict the tools that we will discuss. Chapters 11 and 12 elaborate on a subset of the tools. Ivory [2003a] presents a comprehensive discussion of these tools and example tool assessments.

2.2.1   Performance Measurement Tools

Web server unavailability or inadequate performance negatively affects web site usability [Wilson, 1999; Zona Research, Inc., 1999; Zurier, 1999]. Chapter 3 discusses the performance measurement and monitoring methodologies that were developed to address this problem. Numerous tools and services monitor web server availability (e.g., [AlertSite, 2002; Bacheldor, 1999; BMC Software, 2002; Exodus, 2002; Freshwater Software, 2002; Keynote Systems, Inc., 2002]) and measure web server performance (e.g., [Keynote Systems, Inc., 2003; Paessler GmbH, 2003; WebPartner, 2002]).

Performance monitoring tools, such as Keynote's Red Alert [Keynote Systems, Inc., 2002], send a request to a web server periodically (e.g., every 5 or 15 minutes) to determine if the server is responsive. If the server is non-responsive, then the tool may attempt to diagnose the source of the failure (e.g., network or server problems) and send an email or phone message about the problem to the webmaster. It is also possible to monitor individual pages in the site like purchase pages or scripts to ensure that they are functioning properly.

Early performance monitoring tools assessed server performance from one or more geographical locations. More recent tools like BMC Software's SiteAngel [BMC Software, 2002] and Freshwater Software's SiteSeer [Freshwater Software, 2002] can collect performance measures from multiple geographical locations, under various access conditions. Given the importance of web server performance and availability, most commercial web servers include tools to assess server availability and performance. One example is the Resource Analyzer [IBM, Inc., 2002] that accompanies IBM WebSphere.

Performance measurement approaches, such as Keynote LoadPro [Keynote Systems, Inc., 2003], WebPartner Stress Testing [WebPartner, 2002], and Paessler Webserver Stress Tool [Paessler GmbH, 2003], send hypothetical user re-

Table 10.1.   Automated web site evaluation tools (Table 1 of 2).

| Assessment Type | Automation Type | |
Tool Name	Analysis	Critique
Performance Measurement		
AlertSite Web Site Monitoring	√	
BMC Software SiteAngel	√	
Exodus Monitoring & Management Services	√	
Freshwater Software SiteSeer	√	
Keynote LoadPro	√	
Keynote Red Alert	√	
Paessler Webserver Stress Tool	√	
WebPartner Stress Testing	√	
WebSphere Resource Analyzer	√	
Log File Analysis		
AWUSA	√	
LumberJack	√	
NetGenesis	√	
NetTracker	√	
QUIP	√	
ScentViz	√	
SpeedTracer	√	
Starfield	√	
WebLogMiner	√	
WEBMINER	√	
WebQuilt	√	
WebRemUSINE	√	
WebTrends	√	
WUM	√	

quests to the web server to determine how much traffic it can handle and its response time under heavy loads. The tools report timing measures like the average wait time across simulated users or the time it takes to return the first requested byte (latency). Nielsen [1994] suggests that response times over ten seconds are unacceptable.

Both performance monitoring and measurement approaches allow practitioners to pinpoint performance bottlenecks, such as slow server response time, that may negatively affect the usability of a web site. They do not require any additional effort to use, once the site has been implemented. However, they focus on server and network performance and provide little insight on the usability of the site itself. Furthermore, they cannot assess users' satisfaction.

Table 10.2.   Automated web site evaluation tools (Table 2 of 2).

Assessment Type	Automation Type	
Tool Name	Analysis	Critique
Guideline Review		
508 Accessibility Suite		√
AccessEnable		√
AccVerify/AccRepair		√
A-Prompt		√
Bobby		√
Dr. Watson		√
InFocus		√
LIFT		√
PageScreamer		√
W3C CSS Validation Service		√
W3C HTML Validation Service		√
WAVE		√
Weblint		√
WebSAT	√	
WebTango	√	
Textual Analysis		
CWW		√
Information-seeking Simulator		
Bloodhound	√	
CoLiDeS	√	
Site Profile	√	

2.2.2   Log File Analysis Tools

Log files are generated during informal web site use or during formal usability testing sessions. Given that web servers automatically log client requests [Drott, 1998; Fuller and de Graaff, 1996; Hochheiser and Shneiderman, 2001; Sullivan, 1997], there are numerous log file analysisLog file analysis approaches (see Chapter 3). Practitioners need to be aware that log file analysis is only as accurate as the log files themselves. There are three approaches to generating log files: server-side logging, proxy-based logging, and client-side logging.

Server-side logging.   Web servers automatically log all requests that they receive. These log files do not capture user interactions that occur only on the client side (e.g., use of within-page anchor links, the back button, or cached pages) and their validity is questionable due to caching by proxy servers and web browsers [Etgen and Cantor, 1999; Scholtz and Laskowski, 1998]. Furthermore, server logs may not reflect usability, especially because these logs are often difficult to interpret [Schwartz, 2000] and users' tasks may not be discernible [Byrne *et al.*, 1999; Schwartz, 2000].

Proxy-based logging. A special proxy server intercepts all web server requests, logs the requests, and subsequently routes the requests to the web server [Hong *et al.*, 2001]. All web page links are redirected to the proxy server, which eliminates the need for users to manually configure their browsers to route requests to the proxy. This approach captures more accurate site usage details (e.g., use of the back button) than server-side logging, makes it possible to run usability tests on any web site (e.g., for competitive analysis), and makes it possible to track study participants accurately, because extra information can be encoded in the study URL. It does not capture many client-side details, such as the use of page elements or window resizing, but it does simplify instrumenting a site for logging, because this instrumentation is done automatically.

Client-side logging. An instrumented browser or web site records all user activity within the browser [Etgen and Cantor, 1999; Scholtz and Laskowski, 1998]. Client-side logs capture the most accurate and comprehensive usage data, because all browser events can be recorded. Hence, such logging may provide more insight about usability.

There are a number of analysis tools to process log files generated by one of the three approaches, provided the logs are in a format that the tools can recognize. Task-based log file analysis tools, such as QUIP (Quantitative User Interface Profiling) [Helfrich and Landay, 1999], WebQuilt [Hong *et al.*, 2001], WebRemUSINE (Web Remote USer Interface Evaluator) [Paganelli and Paternò, 2002], and AWUSA (Automated Website USability Analysis) [Tiedtke *et al.*, 2002], analyze discrepancies between the practitioner's anticipation of the user's task model and what a user actually does while using the site. Each tool enables the practitioner to specify how a user is likely to complete tasks.

Statistical log file analysis tools, such as WebTrends [NetIQ, 2002], NetGenesis [CustomerCentric Solutions, 2002], and NetTracker [Sane Solutions, LLC, 2002], produce quantitative measures like the number of pages viewed by each visitor and the amount of time that users spent on pages. The tools typically present results in graphical and report formats (i.e., static tables and charts). The practitioner must interpret these results to identify potential problems.

OLAP (On-Line analytical Processing) [Büchner and Mulvenna, 1998; Dyreson, 1997; Zaïane *et al.*, 1998] and data mining [Cooley *et al.*, 1997; Etzioni, 1996; Kosala and Blockeel, 2000; Spiliopoulou *et al.*, 1999; Spiliopoulou, 2000; Zaïane *et al.*, 1998] tools make it possible to identify frequent navigation patterns in log files. OLAP tools, such as WebLogMiner [Zaïane *et al.*, 1998], enable practitioners to explore relationships among various dimensions (e.g., the time of web site use, the amount of bytes transferred, and the user's IP address) to make inferences about how users access a site and may enable them to identify areas of the site that need to be improved. Web usage mining tools, such as SpeedTracer [Wu *et al.*, 1997], WEBMINER [Cooley *et al.*, 1997; Cooley *et al.*, 1999], Web Utilization Miner (WUM) [Spiliopoulou and Faulstich, 1998; Spiliopoulou, 2000], and LumberJack [Chi *et al.*, 2002; Heer and Chi, 2002b], enable practitioners to apply data mining techniques (e.g., deriving association rules or decision trees) to identify common usage patterns.

There are also visualization tools, which enable practitioners to filter, manipulate, and render log file data in a way that ideally facilitates analysis. Starfield visualization [Hochheiser and Shneiderman, 2001] is one example that enables evaluators to interactively explore web server log data to gain an understanding of the human factors issues related to visitation patterns. This approach combines the simultaneous display of a large number of individual data points (e.g., URLs requested versus time of requests) in an interface that supports zooming, filtering, and dynamic querying [Ahlberg and Shneiderman, 1994]. Visualizations provide a high-level view of usage patterns (e.g., usage frequency, correlated references, bandwidth usage, HTTP errors, and patterns of repeated visits over time) that the practitioner must explore to identify usability problems.

Some visualizations contrast users' task completion steps to the practitioner's task completion steps (i.e., task-based analysis) or summarize web site navigation. For example, ScentViz [Chi, 2002] incorporates several visualizations into an environment for supporting interactive log file analysis. Section 4.4 of Chapter 3 discusses visualization approaches and provides examples.

2.2.3 Guideline Review Tools

Section 508 guidelines [Center for Information Technology Accommodation, 2002], which required Federal agencies to make their electronic and information technology, including web sites, accessible to people with disabilities, contributed to the development of over 30 guideline review tools (discussed in Chapter 4). For instance, the World Wide Web Consortium's guidelines on evaluating web sites for accessibility [World Wide Web Consortium, 2001a] recommend that practitioners use two of three guideline review tools (Bobby [WatchFire, 2002], WAVE [Pennsylvania's Initiative on Assistive Technology, 2001], or A-Prompt [Adaptive Technology Research Center, 2002]) to identify and correct potential accessibility problems during the design process.

Many of these tools analyze the HTML coding to ensure that it conforms to accessibility or usability guidelines. With few exceptions, they focus on enabling access, rather than improving user experiences. For instance, we have shown that the tools do not adequately address a broad range of user abilities (see Chapter 11) [Ivory *et al.*, 2003]. Other tools, such as the W3C HTML Validation Service [World Wide Web Consortium, 2001c], the W3C

CSS Validation Service [World Wide Web Consortium, 2002b], Dr. Watson [Addy & Associates, 2000], and Weblint [Bowers, 1996], analyze the HTML and CSS coding to determine whether it conforms to W3C standards.

Fundamentally, most tools check for conformance to Section 508 guidelines or W3C Content Accessibility Guidelines and then generate a report that provides some guidance for repairing pages. Only a few tools provide assistance with making changes. For example, the LIFT tools [UsableNet, 2002a; UsableNet, 2002b], 508 Accessibility Suite[2] [Macromedia, 2001], AccVerify/AccRepair [HiSoftware, 2002a; HiSoftware, 2002b], and A-Prompt [Adaptive Technology Research Center, 2002] provide wizards to walk practitioners through code modifications. AccessEnable [RetroAccess, 2002] is a web-based tool that can make some changes to pages automatically; the developer can then download the modified pages. PageScreamer [Crunchy Technologies, 2002] and InFocus [SSB Technologies, 2002] are desktop applications that can also make changes.

Most evaluation tools are either web-based (e.g., AccessEnable and WebSAT [National Institute of Standards and Technology, 2001]) or desktop applications (e.g., AccVerify/AccRepair and Bobby). LIFT, the 508 Accessibility Suite, and AccVerify/AccRepair plug into other applications, such as Dreamweaver, FrontPage, or WinRunner.

Given the predominance of guideline review tools, we discuss them extensively throughout Part III. We discuss how they are being used in practice, compare evaluation results across tools, and report on their efficacy, based on an experimental study. We also demonstrate how one guideline review tool—the WebTango prototype (discussed in Chapter 8)—can be used to derive concrete thresholds for design guidelines presented in the literature.

2.2.4 Textual Analysis Tools

Cognitive Walkthrough for the Web (CWW) [Blackmon *et al.*, 2002; Blackmon *et al.*, 2003] is an automated critique approach that can identify potential navigation problems and provide guidance for correcting them. The approach entails the use of Latent Semantic Analysis [Landauer and Dumais, 1997] to contrast web page text (headings or links) to a specified information-seeking goal (100–200 word narrative and correct link selection on the page). The LSA system computes several similarity measures for the two text inputs, based on the semantic space that the practitioner specifies (e.g., for grade nine reading ability). The authors provide LSA thresholds for three navigation problems: confusable heading or link text, unfamiliar heading or link text, and goal-specific competing heading or link text. Empirical studies have demonstrated that modifying page text to fit within these thresholds improves usability. This tool is under development.

2.2.5   Information-Seeking Simulation Tools

Chapter 7 describes the two simulation approaches that are used to simulate information-seeking on web sites—information processor modeling and information scent modeling. WebCriteria's Site Profile [Web Criteria, 1999] is an example of the first approach, though the tool is no longer available for use. The tool used an idealistic web user model (called Max [Lynch *et al.*, 1999]) to simulate a user's information-seeking behavior and to estimate several metrics, such as page load and optimal navigation times. Given a starting point in the site, a path, and a target page, Max "followed" the path from the starting point to the target page and logged measurement data. These measurements were used to compute an accessibility metric, which is then used to generate a report. The usefulness of the approach was questionable [Brajnik, 2000; Pirolli, 2000].

Several simulators, based on the information scent modeling approach, are being developed. These simulators consider the common keywords (information scent) between users' information-seeking needs and the content on linked pages. Bloodhound [Card *et al.*, 2001; Chi *et al.*, 2000; Chi *et al.*, 2001; Chi *et al.*, 2003] is an example tool. It creates a model of an existing site that embeds information about the similarity of content among pages, server log data, and linking structure. The practitioner uses the simulator to either predict the likelihood that users will find information on a site or predict the information needs reflected by certain navigation patterns. Several studies of simulated and actual navigation patterns showed that the simulated patterns correspond with users' patterns in at least a third of the cases. Bloodhound does not account for the effects of various web page attributes, such as the amount of text or layout of links, on navigation behavior.

Comprehension-based Linked model of Deliberate Search (CoLiDeS) [Blackmon *et al.*, 2002; Kitajima *et al.*, 2000; Blackmon *et al.*, 2003] is a similar theoretical model of the use of information scent during the information-seeking process. Unlike Bloodhound, CoLiDeS considers web page objects (e.g., images and text areas) in its simulation. It models web page processing as a two-phase process. First, the user segments or parses the page into subregions and generates a brief description of each, based on her knowledge of page layout conventions, page titles, headings, and other cues. The user then attends to the subregion whose description is perceived as most similar to the information-seeking need. Blackmon *et al.* [2003] showed that their methodology could predict potential problems with confusing headings and link text. The Cognitive Walkthrough for the Web approach (discussed in the preceding section) is based on the CoLiDeS model.

3.   Use of Automated Evaluation Tools

Given that there are over 50 automated evaluation tools that can check web server performance, analyze log files, check guideline conformance, analyze navigation text, or simulate web site navigation, we were interested in how many of these tools are being used, how often they are being used, and how satisfied practitioners are with the tools. As discussed in Chapter 1, we conducted a survey of web practitioners in August of 2002 [Ivory and Chevalier, 2002; Ivory *et al.*, 2003]. Survey respondents included 169 practitioners (web designers, information architects/designers, usability analysts/human factors, and others) who had a role in developing sites for use by broad user communities.

We asked the practitioners about their work practices related to creating usable and accessible sites, including their use of automated evaluation tools. Only 15 percent of respondents reported that they always used automated evaluation tools. Another 67 percent reported that they used the tools sometimes. We asked the practitioners about the design stages in which they use the automated evaluation tools; 54 percent reported using them throughout the design process as compared to using them early in the design process (6 percent) or after finishing the site (21 percent). Given that the tools only enable evaluation after web pages are implemented, we can interpret practitioners' use of tools "throughout the design process" to mean that they use them throughout the production stage.

We asked the practitioners whether or not they had used 25 automated evaluation tools (Figure 10.2). Many practitioners reported using the WatchFire Bobby[3] [WatchFire, 2002] and the W3C HTML Validator guideline review tools (47 percent and 43 percent, respectively). Other frequently used tools include: WebTrends (22 percent), the Dreamweaver 508 Accessibility Suite (16 percent) [Macromedia, 2001], AnyBrowser (11 percent) [AnyBrowser.com, 2002], WAVE (9 percent) [Pennsylvania's Initiative on Assistive Technology, 2001], and LIFT for Dreamweaver (9 percent) [UsableNet, 2002b]. With the exception of WebTrends, the most frequently used tools support guideline review, which is most likely because these tools do not require informal or formal web site use to apply.

We asked the practitioners, who had reported using automated evaluation tools, to identify both the best and the worst tools they had used. They identified Bobby most often as the best tool (27 percent) and as the worst tool (9 percent). Many practitioners stated that they selected Bobby as the best tool, because it was the only one they knew of or had used. They also thought that it provided more comprehensive information than the other tools, liked the multiple guidelines that it evaluates, and thought that it was relatively easy to use and pass; however, they also mentioned that it was not easy enough to use and that it did not provide enough information. Many practitioners stated that they

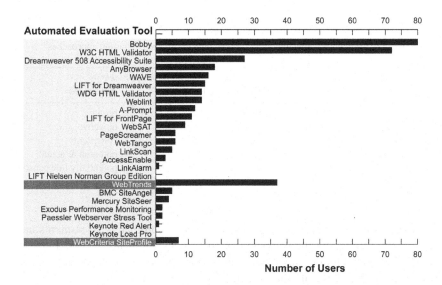

Figure 10.2. Reported use of automated evaluation tools by 169 surveyed practitioners. The shading on the left depicts the types of tools (from top to bottom): guideline review, log file analysis, performance measurement, and information-seeking simulator.

selected Bobby as the worst tool, because it was not easy to use, they disagreed with its guidelines, and it did not provide enough information on how to fix problems.

Finally, we asked the practitioners to provide subjective ratings of automated evaluation tools, in general. Practitioners had mixed opinions about the automated evaluation tools that they had used. At least half of them thought that the tools were helpful in creating usable and accessible sites and in learning about effective design practices. However, the majority of them did not think that using the tools produced better sites than those produced without using tools. They did not think that the tools had adequate functionality or support or that they were easy to use. Their comments suggest that it is helpful for them to have another way to check their designs, after making changes in particular, but the tools are too difficult and too limited to use.

4. Role of Automated Evaluation Tools

Although there are a large number of automated evaluation tools, they are underutilized and considered inadequate, and as such are not having a major influence on web site usability and accessibility. Part of the inadequacy in existing automated evaluation tools can be attributed to some key differences between the tools and the non-automated evaluation approaches. Automated tools can only evaluate the site after it has been implemented (production, qual-

Table 10.3. Differences between non-automated and automated evaluation approaches.

	Evaluation Approach	
Aspect	Non-automated	Automated
Site coverage	narrow	broad
Assessment type	subjective & objective	objective
Assessment consistency	varies	consistent
Identified problems	actual	potential & actual
Usage cost	expensive	potentially inexpensive
Usage stage	all	late stages

ity assurance, and maintenance phases), but non-automated assessments can be applied throughout the web site design and development process. Furthermore, automated tools cannot assess user satisfaction. Table 10.3 summarizes differences along several other dimensions.

Given the current state of automated evaluation tools, their primary role appears to be that of helping practitioners to learn about effective design practices as they code web pages (guideline review) and to identify and correct known problems (e.g., poor server performance, broken links, and bad HTML code). We demonstrate in the remaining chapters that the tools are not as effective as they could be. More work is needed so that the tools can help practitioners to *apply* effective design practices. Chapter 14 discusses ways to improve the tools.

5.   Discussion

There are several potential advantages of automated evaluation tools, in general: (1) identifying potential problems before a site goes live, (2) broadening site evaluation, (3) reducing usability testing costs, and (4) ideally enabling comparisons of alternative designs and choosing the best design. Although there are a large number of tools, they are underutilized and considered inadequate. Their primary role appears to be that of helping practitioners to learn about effective design practices as they code web pages and to identify and correct known problems. More research is needed to improve the usefulness of these tools; we discuss several improvements in Chapter 14.

Notes

1 We use the terms W3C HTML Validation Service, W3C HTML Validator, and W3C Validator interchangeably throughout this book.
2 We use the terms 508 Accessibility Suite and 508 Suite interchangeably throughout this book.

3 Researchers at the Center for Applied Special Technology originally developed Bobby; WatchFire acquired it in July 2002.

Chapter 11

COMPARISON OF GUIDELINE REVIEW TOOLS

Guideline review tools detect and flag a web page's or site's deviation from design criteria (e.g., W3C HTML coding standards [World Wide Web Consortium, 2001c], Section 508 guidelines [Center for Information Technology Accommodation, 2002], or W3C Content Accessibility Guidelines [World Wide Web Consortium, 1999]). A few tools can assist practitioners with making recommended changes or can modify designs automatically. Section 3 of Chapter 10 showed that, among the automated evaluation tools, practitioners were most likely to use guideline review tools, yet they were not satisfied with the tools that they had used.

To gain insight into the current state of guideline review tools, we compare existing tools from two perspectives in this chapter. (The next chapter reports on an experiment that we conducted with three of the tools.) We begin this chapter with a characterization of the user abilities (e.g., use of keyboard and mouse devices and visual, cognitive, and hearing abilities) that practitioners need to consider when designing web sites. Section 2 discusses several approaches for supporting these user abilities, and Section 3 contrasts guideline review tools with respect to the user abilities that they support in their assessments. We conclude with a comparison of evaluation results for ten guideline review tools; we summarize our findings from running the tools on a single web page. Although the comparisons show the range of support provided by existing tools, they also demonstrate that there is very little consistency in evaluations across tools. Nonetheless, our analyses can help practitioners to identify and employ tools that are most appropriate for their web site design contexts.

1.   Characterization of User Abilities

The Web is intended to enable broader access to information and services than was previously available. However, web site usability and accessibility continues to be a pressing problem. Although numerous assistive devices, such as screen readers and special keyboards, facilitate web site use, these strategies may not improve a user's ability to find information, purchase products, and complete other tasks on sites. For example, sites may not have links to help those who use screen readers to skip over navigation bars, or sites may not enable users to increase the font size of text so that they can read it.

Understanding diverse user abilities is important so that we can better support them in web site designs. We use the following categories to characterize user abilities; a detailed discussion can be found in [World Wide Web Consortium, 2001b].

Mouse Use: Users may be able to use a mouse or they may have partial (limited) or no ability to use one. Mouse use may be reduced for physiological reasons. For instance, a motor impairment or blindness may make it difficult to use a mouse.

Keyboard Use: Similarly to mouse use, users may (fully or partially) or may not be able to use a keyboard. We separate keyboard and mouse use because computers are controlled almost exclusively by these two devices, they are required by different aspects of web browsing interfaces, and they depend on motor skills in different ways.

Vision: Users may not have visual impairments that impede their ability to view web pages visually. However, some users have limited visual ability (due to color blindness, low vision, or other impairments) or no visual ability.

Hearing: Similarly to visual abilities, users may (fully or partially) or may not be able to hear sounds on web pages.

Cognition: We consider two aspects of cognition—attention and comprehension. Users may be able to fully or partially attend to web pages. For instance, attention deficits may impede users' attention. Similarly, users may be able to fully or partially comprehend information on web pages; learning and memory impairments may impede users' comprehension.

These diverse user abilities need to be accommodated within web site designs, if possible. We discuss design-level support approaches in the next section.

2.   Supporting Diverse User Abilities

An abundance of design recommendations and guidelines (e.g., [Comber, 1995; Computer Science and Telecommunications Board, 1997; Detweiler and

Omanson, 1996; Flanders and Willis, 1998; Levine, 1996; National Cancer Institute, 2001; Nielsen, 2000; Spool *et al.*, 1999; World Wide Web Consortium, 1999]) are available to help practitioners to build usable and accessible sites. The current trend seems to be to develop new guidelines to address aspects that are unaddressed by existing guidelines, but there are some fundamental problems with the existing ones, including: (1) guidelines are often difficult to understand and to apply [Borges *et al.*, 1998; Chevalier and Ivory, 2003b; de Souza and Bevan, 1990; Scapin *et al.*, 2000]; (2) the needs for different types of users may conflict, and there is little guidance on how to address these conflicts; and (3) practitioners may not be able to address all guidelines at authoring time.

Automated tools were developed to help practitioners to interpret and to apply guidelines, as well as to help users to modify sites dynamically to accommodate their needs [Ivory *et al.*, 2003]. There are over 20 guideline review tools, such as WatchFire Bobby [WatchFire, 2002], UsableNet LIFT [UsableNet, 2002b], and the W3C HTML Validator [World Wide Web Consortium, 2001c], for evaluating web site usability, accessibility, coding, etc. [Ivory and Hearst, 2001; Ivory *et al.*, 2003; World Wide Web Consortium, 2002a]. These tools analyze the HTML code of web pages to determine if it conforms to a set of guidelines, which is referred to as guideline review. A small subset of tools, the LIFT tools in particular, also assist practitioners with modifying the HTML code to conform to guidelines. This chapter and the next examines these tools.

In addition to guideline review tools, there are numerous automated tools for filtering and transforming web sites (e.g., [Huang and Sundaresan, 2000; Kaasinen *et al.*, 2000; Mankoff *et al.*, 2002]) so that they accommodate various user abilities. For example, tools may facilitate web site use by people with motor impairments [Mankoff *et al.*, 2002] or visual impairments [Huang and Sundaresan, 2000]. Ivory *et al.* [2003] present a detailed discussion of automated transformation tools.

3. Evaluating Whether Web Sites Support Diverse User Abilities

Most guideline review tools check whether sites conform to the Section 508 guidelines, the W3C Content Accessibility Guidelines [World Wide Web Consortium, 1999], or both. There is a lot of similarity between these two sets of guidelines, because the Section 508 guidelines are based on the W3C guidelines. (See [Thatcher, 2002] for a side-by-side comparison.) Overall, the tools evaluate whether most user abilities (discussed in Section 1) are supported in web site designs, but they emphasize enabling access, rather than improving user experiences.

To address the limitations of W3C and Section 508 guidelines, Coyne and Nielsen [2001] proposed an additional 75 guidelines derived from studies of users with vision and mobility impairments. Example guidelines include: min-

Table 11.1. Diminished user abilities addressed by guideline review tools.[a]

Tool	Mouse Use		Keyboard Use		Vision		Hearing		Cognition	
	P	N	P	N	P[b]	N	P	N	PA	PC[c]
508 Suite					√					
A-Prompt					√					
AccessEnable					√		√	√		
AccVerify/AccRepair					√					
ALTifier					√					
Bobby	√	√			√	√			√	√
Doctor HTML						√				√
LIFT (all versions)	√	√								
LIFT-NNG	√	√			√	√				√
PageScreamer						√				
W3C HTML Validator					√					
WAVE	√	√				√			√	
Weblint						√				
WebSAT					√	√			√	√
WebTango					√				√	√

[a] P columns denote partial ability. N columns denote no ability. The PA and PC columns denote partial attention and partial comprehension, respectively.
[b] Partial vision includes low vision and color blindness.
[c] Partial comprehension includes learning and memory impairments.

imize the use of graphics or small font sizes for text, avoid pop-up windows, separate browser windows, or cascading menus, and minimize the number of links on a page. These guidelines are embedded in the LIFT tool - Nielsen Norman Group Edition (LIFT-NNG) [UsableNet, 2002a].

Table 11.1 provides a synopsis of the range of user abilities that existing guideline review tools support.[1] We only characterize the diminished or limited user abilities in the table; Appendix A provides a summary for all the tools listed in the table. Depending on the intended site users, the table can help practitioners to determine the evaluation tools that are most appropriate to use.

Overall, many tools address limited visual abilities, a few address other non-visual impairments, and no tools address limited keyboard use. Bobby [WatchFire, 2002] addresses nearly all the user abilities depicted in the table; LIFT-NNG [UsableNet, 2002a], WebSAT [National Institute of Standards and Technology, 2001], and WAVE [Pennsylvania's Initiative on Assistive Technology, 2001] also provide broader coverage of user abilities than all the other tools, except for Bobby. We describe the types of evaluations that the tools conduct and the limitations of their assessments in the remainder of this section.

3.1 Mouse Use

A few tools check to see if web pages enable alternative forms of input (e.g., keyboard or Braille device use) to address the needs of users with some or no ability to use a mouse. For example, Bobby [WatchFire, 2002] and WAVE [Pennsylvania's Initiative on Assistive Technology, 2001] look for keyboard shortcuts for forms and links or for equivalent ways to handle events like mouse roll-overs. However, the tools do not analyze the shortcuts to see if they are meaningful, consistent with common interface shortcuts, or conflict with each other (e.g., the same shortcut may be specified for more than one action). Bobby and WAVE also check for an explicit tabbing order on pages, but there is no analysis of the tabbing order, for instance to see if it is logical. LIFT-NNG [UsableNet, 2002a] checks for the use of cascading menus, which the developers determined to be problematic for users with disabilities [Coyne and Nielsen, 2001].

3.2 Keyboard Use

To accommodate limited keyboard use, the guideline review tools could check to see if web pages enable speech input, rather than physical input (keyboard, Braille device, or mouse input). Although the tools check for the ability to output speech (e.g., checks for the presence of alternative text for images, labels for form elements, and so on), they currently do not assess the ability for users to employ speech-based navigation, wherein they send voice commands to control browsers [Christian *et al.*, 2000]. Additionally, these tools do not consider the needs of users for whom keyboard input is limited or slow. For example, a text entry area for entering a zip code could be simplified by replacing it with 5 menus each containing the digits 0 through 9. Note that a user with normal keyboard use may find the series of menus more cumbersome than simply typing the zip code. This difference in user preferences shows that authoring-time solutions may not always be appropriate, and thus that automated transformation tools are a necessary component of true universal access [Ivory *et al.*, 2003].

3.3 Vision

Nearly all guidelines embedded in the existing tools address the needs of users with little or no vision. Most checks entail looking for the existence of page and frame titles, alternative text for images and other objects, headings for tables, and labels for form elements so that screen readers can process this information [Adaptive Technology Research Center, 2002; Bowers, 1996; Crunchy Technologies, 2002; National Institute of Standards and Technology, 2001; Pennsylvania's Initiative on Assistive Technology, 2001; RetroAccess, 2002; UsableNet, 2002a; Vorburger, 1999; WatchFire, 2002]. Several tools provide wizards to help developers to correct such violations (e.g., [Adaptive Technology Research Center, 2002; HiSoftware, 2002a; Macromedia, 2001; UsableNet, 2002a]), and other tools, such as the ALTifier [Vorburger, 1999] and A-Prompt [Adaptive Technology Research Center, 2002], suggest alternative text based on the page context and other heuristics. LIFT-NNG also checks for the presence of table summaries. None of the tools, however, can assess whether alternative text, titles, labels, headings, or table summaries are meaningful.

Bobby, AccessEnable, and LIFT-NNG check whether pages enable users to skip repetitive navigation links. However, the tools do not check whether skip links actually take the user to the appropriate areas on web pages. LIFT-NNG also checks to see if the page launches separate browser windows, which can impede navigation.

AccessEnable, Doctor HTML, A-Prompt, and WAVE conduct rudimentary analyses of table and form structure. For example, A-Prompt depicts the linear reading order for table contents, and WAVE depicts the linear reading order for the entire page. Developers have to manually evaluate the reading order to determine if it is logical or efficient; automated tools do not support this type of analysis.

The tools perform several checks to address the needs of users with partial vision, such as analyzing color usage [Ivory and Hearst, 2002a; National Institute of Standards and Technology, 2001], font and image sizes [Ivory and Hearst, 2002a; UsableNet, 2002a], and checking for the separation of content from presentation via style sheets [Ivory and Hearst, 2002a; RetroAccess, 2002; Watch-Fire, 2002; World Wide Web Consortium, 2002b]. For example, the W3C CSS Validation Service [World Wide Web Consortium, 2002b] enables developers to see if their style sheets conform to W3C CSS coding standards. As another example, Bobby checks to see if pages use relative positioning (i.e., widths and heights expressed as percentages) rather than absolute positioning (i.e., widths and heights expressed as pixels), which facilitates screen magnification.

The WebTango prototype [Ivory and Hearst, 2002a], which we discussed in Chapter 8, analyzes the quality of text and background color combinations, using Murch's [1985] study of color combination preferences as a basis; it reports the number of good, neutral, and poor color combinations along with the specific combinations used. It also reports on the sizes used for images and text; these sizes are compared to statistical models derived from an analysis of over 5300 web pages [Ivory and Hearst, 2002b]. Similarly, it reports ranges for the number of links, number of words within each text link, and the number of graphics. It also reports on the use of text and link clustering and text alignment, which may be helpful to users with partial vision. The WebTango prototype is a rudimentary research system, and is not currently robust enough for wide use.

LIFT-NNG checks for small text, too many outgoing links, too short text links or button labels, too small buttons, and too many graphics. Accompanying discussions of guideline violations provide some crude thresholds for these aspects. The tool also checks to see if form fields are stacked in vertical columns and whether there is whitespace between vertically aligned text links.

3.4 Hearing

Both the W3C and Section 508 guidelines require text equivalents for audio, video, or other multimedia formats. In addition, they require synchronization of these text equivalents with their sources. Most of the tools check for alternative text for objects, which screen readers can read to a vision-impaired user (see preceding discussion). However, there are no checks to see if this alternative text is easily available to a hearing-impaired user. Furthermore, the tools cannot check whether text equivalents or alternative text are consistent with their sources. AccessEnable seems to be the only tool that can flag whether there is some synchronization between the text equivalents and their sources, though it is not clear how this assessment is accomplished, because synchronization is difficult to check automatically.

3.5 Cognition

W3C and Section 508 guidelines address animation, which can cause problems for users with attention deficits. Bobby, WebSAT, and the 508 Accessibility Suite check for animated images or scrolling text. The WebTango prototype also quantifies the use of animated images and provides ranges based on an analysis of over 5300 web pages. None of the tools can assess whether there are ways to stop animations.

To address the needs of users with comprehension impairments, the guidelines suggest that pages should be well-structured and consistent within a site. For example, Bobby, the LIFT tools, and others check that pages and frames have titles, which can help to orient users. WAVE checks for the use of structural tags, such as headings and lists, to determine if they are used properly. As another example, the WebTango prototype quantifies and provides ranges for the amount of text, links, images, and other elements, as a way to address potential cognitive overload. It also assesses download speed, consistency, the use of link and text clustering, and reading complexity, all of which may impede web site use by users with comprehension impairments. Similarly, Doctor HTML checks for spelling errors and analyzes images (e.g., image size and number of colors). WebSAT also reports the total size of graphics.

LIFT-NNG, WebSAT, and the WebTango prototype evaluate other text, link, and image formatting that may impede web site use. For example, WebSAT reports whether web pages use non-default link colors, less than 2–5 words in text links, line breaks before or after links, horizontal rules, or separate browser windows. WebSAT also reports a ratio of links to words, which may provide some indication of text density. LIFT-NNG reports on the use of small text, too short text links or button labels (less than six characters), too many outgoing links (more than twenty) or images, long cascading menus, separate browser windows, and inadequate space between vertically aligned text links.

Guideline review tools assess many aspects that could have negative effects on comprehension, but the key aspect that is missing is an analysis of the content itself. None of the tools provide concrete insight about the content's quality, cohesion, appropriateness, readability, and so on. Although the tools may be able to improve the presentation of good content, they cannot improve on poor content.

4.   Comparison of Tool Assessments

The preceding section compared the diminished user abilities that are considered in assessments by existing guideline review tools. Although multiple tools may address a specific impairment, there may be differences in how they assess support for the impairment. To better understand these differences, we used ten guideline review tools to evaluate a single web page. Specifically, we examined the consistency of assessments across tools. In addition, we characterized the strengths and weaknesses of the tools with respect to their ease of use, their evaluation accuracy, and the usefulness of their reported results.

4.1   Methodology

We selected the following guideline review tools to evaluate the web page depicted in Figure 11.1.

- 508 Accessibility Suite 1.0.1 [Macromedia, 2001]

- A-Prompt 1.0.6 [Adaptive Technology Research Center, 2002]

- AccessEnable (unknown version) [RetroAccess, 2002]

- AccVerify/AccRepair 5.1 [HiSoftware, 2002b; HiSoftware, 2002a]

- Bobby 4.0 [WatchFire, 2002]

- Doctor HTML 5.0 [Imageware, Inc., 2001]

- LIFT-NNG 0.94 [UsableNet, 2002a]

- W3C HTML Validator (September 19, 2001 version) [World Wide Web Consortium, 2001c]

- WAVE 3.0 beta [Pennsylvania's Initiative on Assistive Technology, 2001]

- WebTango 1.0 [Ivory and Hearst, 2002a]

With the exception of the WebTango prototype, all tools were either available commercially or commercially viable (i.e., robust applications). Based on the synopsis in Table 11.1, the tools evaluated similar usability and accessibility aspects. The HTML Validator is the only tool that focuses exclusively on HTML coding, rather than on usability and accessibility issues.

We initially ran the tools on the web page in the Fall of 2002 and then updated the assessments in May of 2003. We analyzed the reports generated by each tool to determine the total number of errors, number of unique errors, and the number of false errors (i.e., an issue was inaccurately identified as an error). Some tools report alerts for issues that are relevant in general, but not detected on the page; we aggregate the total and unique number of alerts with the total and unique number of errors. We coded the guideline violations so that we could compare the reported errors across tools. In addition, we associated the guideline violations with relevant W3C Content Accessibility Guidelines, Section 508 guidelines, and the user abilities summarized in Table 11.1.

4.2 Results

We summarize our experiences with the tools, specifically their ease of use. We present analysis results across the ten tools and then for individual tools.

4.2.1 Ease of Use

The tools were straightforward to use, at least for the evaluations. A-Prompt was somewhat challenging to use, because it requires the practitioner to specify a file directory and then characterize each table as a layout or data table, before assessments can be completed. Most reports were also straightforward to read, but there were some exceptions, for instance the WAVE report (Figure 11.2). The WAVE tool annotates web pages with icons to indicate guideline violations. There are numerous unintuitive icons, and we had to repeatedly consult the documentation to determine the meaning of each violation. WAVE also indicates the linear reading order on web pages; we initially confused these indicators with the guideline violation indicators.

We found it difficult to explore results or to make repairs with A-Prompt, LIFT-NNG, and the 508 Accessibility Suite. Each tool presents a list of terse violations within a small window (see the window in the middle of Figure 11.3); the LIFT-NNG presents the same guideline violations repeatedly (one for each occurrence). After selecting an error from the list, the tools provide additional details and repair functionality. The repair functionality is accessed from yet another window. Figure 11.3 depicts the cumbersome task flow for evaluating and repairing a web page using the LIFT-NNG tool from within Macromedia Dreamweaver.

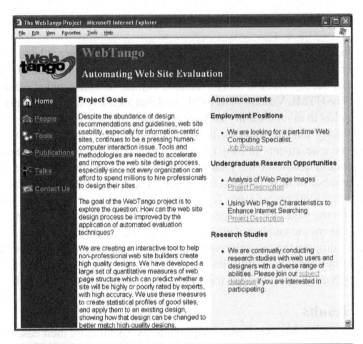

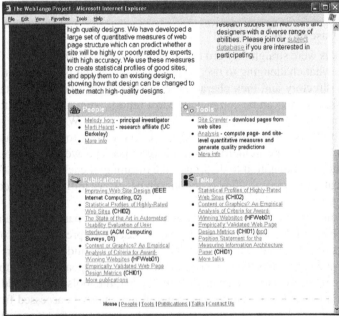

Figure 11.1. Web page used for the comparison of guideline review tools. The page covers two vertical screens and does not conform to all accessibility and usability guidelines. The page uses tables and style sheets to control layout and formatting; it does not use scripts, applets, animated images, or other implementation technology.

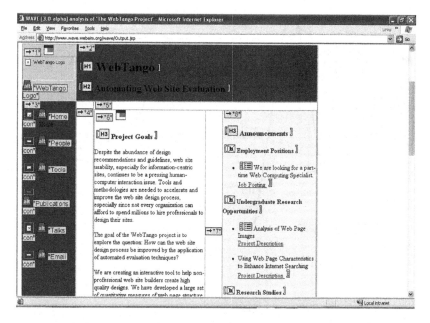

Figure 11.2. Evaluation report produced by WAVE. WAVE overlays guideline violations on the actual web page. It uses numerous icons to flag potential issues and also depicts the page reading order (arrows with numbers).

4.2.2 Errors Reported Across Tools

Our analysis of the reported guideline violations revealed that they represent 45 unique errors (e.g., avoid small text, identify the language of the text, and group related elements when possible). We linked the violations to W3C or Section 508 guidelines (35 and 9 violations, respectively); only 7 violations linked to both a W3C and Section 508 guideline. We analyzed the web site design to determine whether each violation was an accurate assessment. Although we did not conduct an empirical study to confirm the validity or invalidity of violations, only 21 violations (47 percent) seemed to be valid. Inaccurate assessments were reported for issues that could not be evaluated automatically or were not automated by the tools; example violations include: "avoid using shrunk-down pictures of other pages," "do not use the same link phrase more than once when the links point to different URLs," and "flicker is distracting and may be dangerous to some users."

Figure 11.4 shows that most of the guideline violations relate to vision, coding, cognition, and general accessibility and usability issues; the latter category comprises guidelines that are not targeted at a specific user ability, rather they relate to usability and accessibility, in general. Figure 11.5 shows that most guideline violations are considered to be priority two (i.e., moderate [World

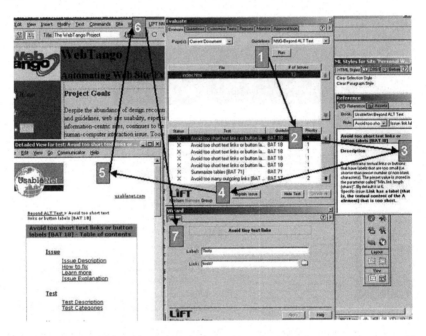

Figure 11.3.   Screen snapshot of the LIFT-NNG tool within Macromedia Dreamweaver. The numbers depict the task flow for a practitioner who wants to evaluate a page (step 1), explore the report (steps 2–3), explore extra guideline information (steps 4–5), and then use the repair wizard to make appropriate modifications (steps 6–7).

Wide Web Consortium, 2001c]); violations include: "avoid deprecated features of W3C technologies" (coding), "avoid using shrunk-down pictures of other pages" (general usability), and "check that the foreground and background colors contrast sufficiently with each other" (vision).

Figure 11.6 shows the number of tools that reported each of the 45 guideline violations. Guidelines were reported by only one tool in most cases (62 percent), which suggests that there is very little consistency in reported errors across tools. Frequently reported errors include: "provide an alternative, HTML-based means of accessing the same functionality" (five tools); "if this is a data table (not used for layout only), identify headers for the table rows and columns" (four tools); and "if style sheets are ignored or unsupported, are pages still readable and usable" (three tools). Only the latter violation seemed to be valid for the web page.

The inconsistency that we found in reported violations is similar to inconsistencies discovered in usability evaluations. As an example, two comparative usability testing studies (CUE-1 [Molich *et al.*, 1998] and CUE-2 [Molich *et al.*, 1999]) demonstrated less than a one percent overlap in findings among four

Aspects Assessed by Tools

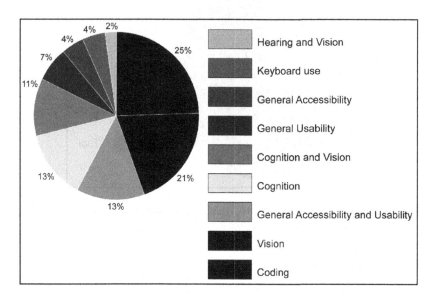

Figure 11.4. Aspects evaluated across tools. The pie chart shows the percentage represented by each category in counterclockwise order from the top. We associated the 45 guidelines with the user abilities summarized in Table 11.1, if possible. In some cases, a guideline referred to multiple abilities, which we reflect in the graph. We do not distinguish the degrees (e.g., full or partial) of user abilities that the tools assessed.

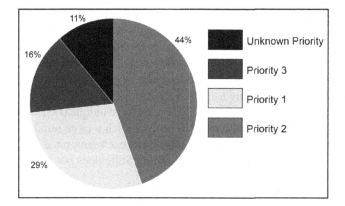

Figure 11.5. Priorities associated with guideline violations. The pie chart shows the percentage represented by each category in counterclockwise order from the top. We used the priorities associated with the W3C and Section 508 guidelines to determine most priorities.

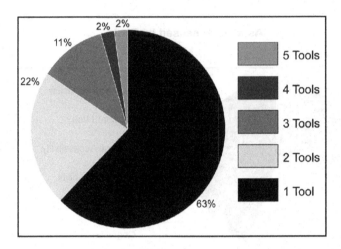

Figure 11.6.   Errors reported across tools. The pie chart shows the percentage represented by each category in counterclockwise order from the top.

and nine independent usability testing teams when they evaluated the same two user interfaces.[2] The lack of systematicity or predictability in the findings of automated evaluation tools is surprising, especially because they evaluate seemingly similar aspects.

4.2.3   Errors Reported by Each Tool

Figure 11.7 contrasts the number of violations reported by each of the tools. Some violations were reported as actual errors, while some were reported as alerts (i.e., issues that the practitioner should be aware of, though the tools did not actually detect a problem in the web page); we aggregated the number of alerts and violations and present the total in the figure. The tools reported an average of eleven violations, seven of which (62 percent) were valid, on average.

Bobby and the 508 Accessibility Suite both reported over 100 errors, which is at least five times as many as those reported by the other eight tools. However, only 18–20 percent of the reported errors were unique (i.e., not repeated). Although it could be overwhelming to process such a large number of errors, Bobby simplifies this process by only presenting each error once, along with its number of occurrences. The 508 Accessibility Suite does not aggregate errors in this manner.

Table 11.7 shows that the remaining tools reported a smaller number of errors, of which, larger percentages were unique, valid, and assessed automatically versus requiring practitioner inspection. AccVerify is an exception to this trend; it only reports two violations, both were invalid and not assessed automatically. Surprisingly, even though the tools support automated assessment, for tools like

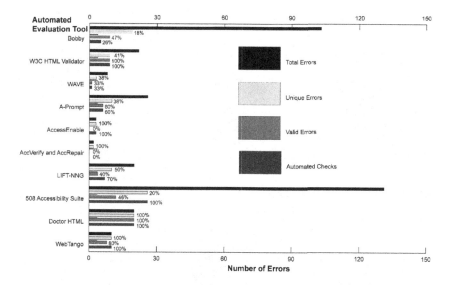

Figure 11.7. Errors reported by each tool. We show, from top to bottom, the total number of violations (errors and alerts), the number of violations that are unique (i.e., not repeated), the number of unique violations that are valid for the web page (Valid Errors), and the number of unique violations that are assessed automatically (Automated Checks) for each tool. Percentages next to the bars for unique errors reflect the ratio of the number of unique errors to the total number of errors. Percentages next to the bars for valid errors reflect the ratio of valid errors to the number of unique errors. Similarly, percentages next to the bars for automated checks reflect the ratio of errors that are assessed automatically to the number of unique errors.

Bobby and WAVE, only a few violations are checked automatically. Essentially, the tools flag a number of issues, which the practitioner has to investigate to determine if they are valid and address as necessary.

Figures 11.8 and 11.9 contrast the aspects that each tool assessed. Bobby, A-Prompt, and the 508 Accessibility Suite provided the most holistic evaluations (i.e., addressed multiple user abilities and other issues), and they reported the most violations overall. The remaining tools only assessed at most three aspects, and substantial percentages of the reported errors addressed coding issues, rather than specific user abilities or general usability or accessibility.

5. Discussion

Existing guideline review tools appear to address some user abilities in their assessments. However, the emphasis of these tools seems to be heavily on supporting blind users and users with comprehension impairments, at least to some degree. The tools currently provide little or no assessment support for users who are not able to use a keyboard or have hearing impairments. The

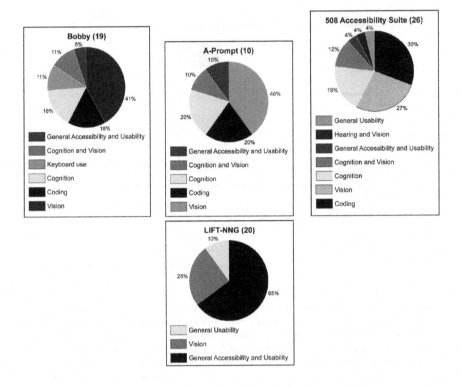

Figure 11.8.   Aspects evaluated by each tool (Figure 1 of 2). The number in parentheses at the top of each chart reflects the number of unique errors reported. Pie charts show the percentage represented by each category in counterclockwise order from the top. We associated the errors with the user abilities summarized in Table 11.1, if possible. In some cases, an error referred to multiple abilities, which we reflect in the graphs. We do not distinguish the degrees (e.g., full or partial) of user abilities that the tools assessed.

tools do not appear to be robust enough to handle non-HTML implementations of web sites, such as implementations in Macromedia Flash, dynamic HTML, and other technologies. Furthermore, one of the major limitations of these tools is that they do not analyze content, even though content is considered the most important aspect of a web site (see [Sinha *et al.*, 2001] for an analysis).

   With few exceptions, all the tools were easy to use and their reports were straightforward to read. Our comparison of the assessments that the ten guideline review tools generated for the same web page (Figure 11.1) showed that there was little consistency in evaluations across the tools, even though most tools are based on the common W3C and Section 508 guidelines. We also discovered that tools, such as Bobby and WAVE, simply flag errors for which the practitioner needs to determine if they are valid and, if necessary, to address

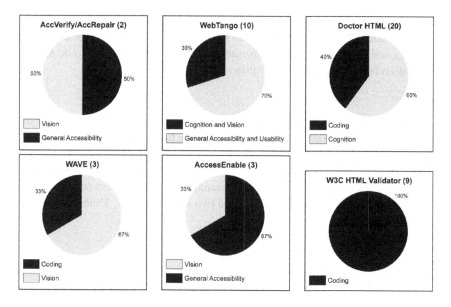

Figure 11.9. Aspects evaluated by each tool (Figure 2 of 2). The number in parentheses at the top of each chart reflects the number of unique errors reported. Pie charts show the percentage represented by each category in counterclockwise order from the top. We associated the errors with the user abilities summarized in Table 11.1, if possible. In some cases, an error referred to multiple abilities, which we reflect in the graphs. We do not distinguish the degrees (e.g., full or partial) of user abilities that the tools assessed.

them accordingly. Nonetheless, we found that Bobby, A-Prompt, and the 508 Accessibility Suite cover broader user abilities in their assessments than the other seven tools.

Even if the tools support a range of user abilities, their effectiveness is unclear. Our survey of practitioners in Chapter 10 revealed that they have mixed feelings about the tools, and our evaluation of three popular tools in Chapter 12 reveals some tool limitations. Furthermore, our analysis in this chapter shows that there is little consistency in evaluation results across tools for the same web page. It also showed that less than half of the reported errors were valid. We attribute these issues to the fact that the tools use separate evaluation engines (even for the same guidelines), rather than employ a common evaluation core. We discuss ways to address this limitation and others in Chapter 14.

Although some issues can be evaluated and addressed at design time, others cannot (e.g. accommodating users for whom keyboard input is limited or slow) [Ivory *et al.*, 2003]. Thus, integrating automated transformation and evaluation tools may be a viable solution. For example, if a transformation tool could dynamically collapse navigation levels and only expose one level at a time, then this transformation may improve web site use by vision-impaired, cognition-impaired, and other users. On the other hand, it is still necessary to evaluate the usability and accessibility of transformed pages; thus, there needs to be a tight integration between automated evaluation and transformation tools.

Notes

1 Guideline review tools are discussed as they existed at the time of our analysis (September 30, 2002). It is realized that these tools are constantly evolving and possibly incorporating changes that might affect the findings. Apologies are offered in advance for any discrepancies due to more recent tool versions.
2 The first study involved four professional teams, while the second study involved seven professional teams and two student teams. Details were not provided about study participants.

Chapter 12

EMPIRICAL STUDY OF GUIDELINE REVIEW TOOLS

Our analysis of automated evaluation tools in Chapter 11 revealed that the tools do not cover the full range of user abilities. There was also very little consistency in their assessments for the same web page. But how do the tools perform in practice for the user abilities and other aspects that they do support?

As far as we know, there is little evidence about the efficacy of the existing automated web site evaluation tools, guideline review tools in particular. There have been studies of a few tools. For example, we showed that for the WebTango prototype (Chapter 8), participants preferred web pages that were modified to conform to our statistical models of highly rated web designs over the original ones and that participants rated sites that were modified based on our models higher than the original ones; differences were significant in both cases. As another example, UsableNet's LIFT - Nielsen Norman Group Edition [UsableNet, 2002a] assesses a site's conformance to guidelines that were developed from studies involving users with and without visual and mobility impairments [Coyne and Nielsen, 2001]. The premise is that the empirically derived guidelines are inherently effective.

In this chapter, we present data on the performance of automated evaluation tools. We conducted a study of three guideline review tools—WatchFire Bobby, UsableNet LIFT, and the W3C HTML Validator [Ivory and Chevalier, 2002; Ivory et al., 2003]. Although the first two tools explicitly address accessibility and usability aspects, the latter tool does not. However, the premise is that conforming to standard coding practices may eliminate usability and accessibility issues that invalid HTML code may cause, such as overlapped or nested lists [Paciello and Paciello, 2000]. The study consisted of two phases: (1) designers used the tools to modify subsections of five web sites and (2) users with diverse abilities used the original and a selection of modified sites to

145

complete information-seeking tasks. We organize our discussion around these two studies.

1.   Designers' Usage of the Bobby, LIFT, and HTML Validator Tools

We conducted a study with nine experienced designers, wherein each designer modified subsections of five sites—www.section508.gov, www.govbenefits.gov, spam.abuse.net, www.irs.gov, and www.usatoday.com. Designers made modifications with the intent of improving each site's universal accessibility (i.e., both the usability or "the extent to which a product can be used by specified users, to achieve specified goals, with effectiveness, efficiency and satisfaction, in a specified context of use" [International Organisation for Standardisation, 1998] and the accessibility or "usability of a product, service, environment or facility by people with the widest range of capabilities" [International Organisation for Standardisation, 2002]). Designers completed modifications with or without the assistance of one or more automated evaluation tools (WatchFire Bobby, UsableNet LIFT, or W3C HTML Validator). Our objective was to examine designers' usage of these frequently used tools and to assess whether using the tools was beneficial to them.

1.1   Study Design

We asked nine designers, who had at least two years of design experience, to participate in a 5x5 between-subjects experiment, wherein each designer modified subsections of five web sites. They modified each site in one of five evaluation conditions. Designers completed the first site modification without the assistance of an automated evaluation tool (manual). Designers completed the second through fourth site modifications using one automated evaluation tool (Bobby, Validator, or LIFT). Designers completed the fifth and final site modification using all three tools (combo). We counterbalanced both the order of site modifications and the usage of individual tools.

Designers completed the following tasks for each site and evaluation condition:

1 Explore the site to become familiar with the subsection. We provided designers with a usage scenario (Table 12.1) and disabled links within the subsection to other site areas or to external sites.

2 Evaluate the universal accessibility of the site subsection. Designers used a five-point scale (very low to very high) for these ratings. We did not specify how designers were to make these judgments; in some cases, designers inspected both the rendered pages and the HTML code.

Table 12.1. Description of the five study sites.^a

Site	Id	#Pages	Subsection	Scenario
Section 508	1	8	About 508	Making a company's site EEOC compliant
GovBenefits	2	8	GovBenefits Program List	Finding funding sources for a clinical geriatrics professor
Spam Abuse^b	3	6	Help for Users	Complaining about rude spam emails
IRS	4	7	Accessibility	Finding a Braille version of the 2001 Education Credits form
USA Today	5	6	FAQ	Getting the crossword puzzle to work in AOL

^a For each site, we include an identifier (Id), the number of pages in the subsection (#Pages), the name of the subsection, and the usage scenario.
^b Three pages on the Spam Abuse site were ASCII text, rather than HTML pages.

3 Modify the site subsection to improve its universal accessibility. In conditions without an automated evaluation tool, designers enumerated a list of problems and used their own expertise to guide modifications. Otherwise, they could only address problems identified by the tool. Designers had twenty minutes to modify the first four sites and forty minutes for the final site (combo condition). They made modifications using either the Microsoft FrontPage or the Macromedia Dreamweaver authoring environments on PCs running Microsoft XP.

4 Evaluate the universal accessibility of the modified site subsection (same rating scale used in step 2).

5 Evaluate the automated evaluation tool (conditions with one tool).

Designers completed a debriefing questionnaire about their experiences while using the tools. We asked them to think aloud throughout the study session, and we videotaped sessions and captured screen activity. Table 12.1 summarizes the site subsections that designers rated and modified. Site contents were of general interest to a broad user community, with three of the sites—1, 2, and 4—being government sites. Site designs ranged from a simplistic design with few graphics (site 1) to a text- and graphics-intensive design (site 5).

1.2   Study Tools

WatchFire Bobby [WatchFire, 2002], UsableNet LIFT [UsableNet, 2002b], and the W3C HTML Validator [World Wide Web Consortium, 2001c] tools represent the state-of-the-art in automated web site evaluation tools (see preceding chapter). They are among the most frequently used tools (see Chapter 10), offer different functionality, and enable subsequent evaluation of site changes (i.e., design iteration).

Designers used the desktop version of WatchFire Bobby 4.0, which determines if web pages conform to the W3C or Section 508 guidelines and provides guidance for correcting problems. Example guidelines include: "provide alternative text for all images" and "explicitly associate form controls and their labels with the LABEL element." Figure 12.1 depicts an example Bobby report and a web page overlay.

The W3C HTML Validator (September 19, 2001 version) is a web-based tool that determines if web pages conform to coding standards and provides guidance for correcting violations. Example guidelines include: "end tag for element 'A' which is not open" and "element 'TABLE' not allowed here."

UsableNet LIFT determines if web pages conform to accessibility and usability guidelines (e.g., W3C and Section 508), provides guidance for correcting problems, and in some cases, provides support for repairing the HTML code for images, tables, and forms. Unlike with Bobby and the Validator, designers used versions of the LIFT tool embedded within FrontPage or Dreamweaver. The developers claim that the Dreamweaver version, LIFT Nielsen Norman Group Edition 0.94 (LIFT-NNG), contains the same core guidelines as the FrontPage 1.1.1 version (LIFT-FP), as well as additional guidelines derived from usability studies involving participants with and without visual and mobility impairments [Coyne and Nielsen, 2001]. Example guidelines include: "use 'skip links' so that users can skip links or navigational elements" (both versions) and "avoid too many outgoing links (LIFT-NNG)." Figure 12.2 depicts a typical task flow for evaluating and repairing a web page.

1.3   Study Results

We examine whether the three tools enabled more comprehensive evaluations or enhanced designers' throughput, based on quantitative measures. We then summarize subjective evaluations of the tools' effectiveness.

1.3.1   Evaluation Coverage

Our analysis of the number of problems identified in conditions with and without automated tools revealed that, as expected, the automated tools identified significantly more potential problems than the designers identified, especially when considering the total number of errors identified within each site (Figure 12.3). (However, we show in the next section that designers made more design changes when they did not use an automated evaluation tool.) The numbers do not show that the tools, excluding Bobby, mostly report the same errors (once for each occurrence). Our analysis of page-level errors, as opposed to site-level errors, revealed that there was not much difference in the number

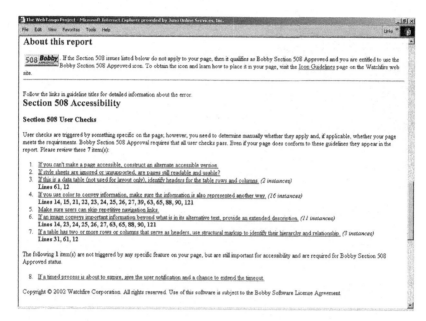

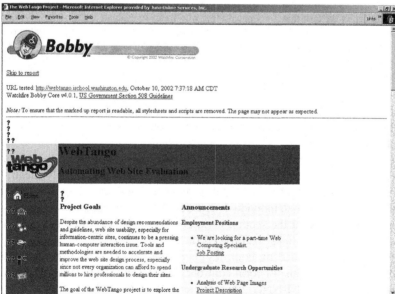

Figure 12.1. Report (top) and web page overlay (bottom) that Bobby generated. Bobby checked for Section 508 conformance, and flagged areas for manual review with a '?.'

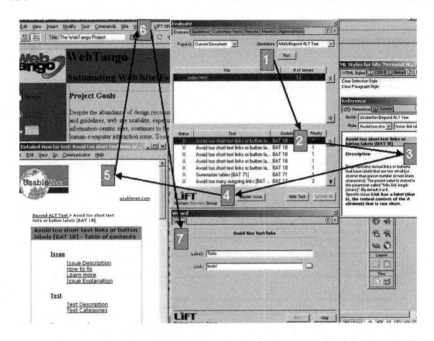

Figure 12.2. Screen snapshot of the LIFT-NNG tool within Macromedia Dreamweaver. The numbers depict the task flow for a practitioner who wants to evaluate a page (step 1), explore the report (steps 2–3), explore extra guideline information (steps 4–5), and then use the repair wizard to make appropriate modifications (steps 6–7). This figure is a repetition of Figure 11.3.

of Bobby- and designer-reported problems at the page-level, possibly because Bobby summarizes the number of unique problems along with the number of occurrences.

Figure 12.4 depicts the types of problems that the designers and tools identified—accessibility, usability, or other issues. Designers primarily identified higher-level accessibility and usability problems that were applicable to the entire site, rather than to individual pages, such as "spell things more clearly...," "...make clearer what the section is describing and where the links will go," and "...multicolored links (bad for vision impairment)...." There were only a few problems identified by both designers and one or more tool, including: add attributes or labels for form controls (Bobby and LIFT tools), reduce the number of links (LIFT-NNG), increase text size (LIFT-NNG), add or remove ALT text (Bobby and LIFT tools), and add skip links (LIFT tools). Designers did not enumerate any problems that the Validator identified (primarily other types of coding errors), but they repaired HTML tags when they modified sites in the manual condition.

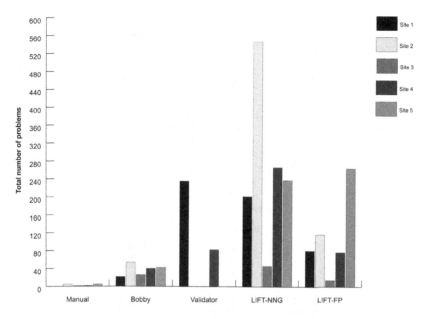

Figure 12.3. Total number of problems identified for each site subsection. No designer modified site 1 in the manual condition, which is the reason why there were no problems identified. We aggregated the Bobby priority 1, 2, and 3 errors. The Validator failed on sites 2, 3, and 5.

1.3.2 Designer Throughput

Although the automated tools identified more problems than the designers identified, study results suggest that they did not enhance the designers' throughput (i.e., their ability to resolve identified design problems within a short amount of time). Figure 12.5 shows that designers made significantly more changes in the manual condition than in the tool conditions ($p < 0.05$). Designers modified a median of three pages on each site in the manual condition, two pages in both LIFT conditions, one page in the Validator condition, and no pages in the Bobby condition; differences were significant ($p < 0.05$). Analyses of variances (ANOVAs) did not show significant effects due to prior tool usage or design experience.

Surprisingly, designers only modified a total of three pages in the Bobby condition. Participants' comments suggest that they did not think that any modifications were needed, based on the reported problems; this impression is somewhat evident from the proportion of designers who reported that they had completed site modifications and were satisfied with them in the Bobby condition (Figure 12.6). Recall from Section 4 of Chapter 11, Bobby requires the designer to manually inspect their designs to determine whether guideline

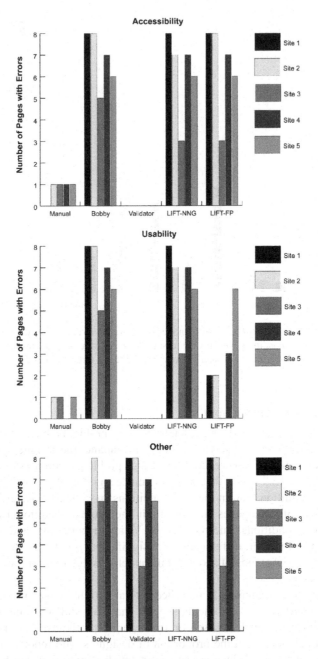

Figure 12.4. Types of problems identified for each site subsection. We depict the number of pages for which accessibility (top), usability (middle), or other (bottom) errors were identified within each site subsection. Designers enumerated problems that typically applied to the entire site in the manual condition, which is not reflected in the charts. No designer modified site 1 in the manual condition. The Validator reported a failure error for all pages on sites 2, 3, and 5.

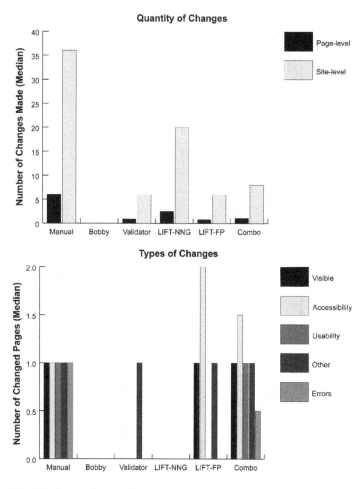

Figure 12.5. Median number (top) and types (bottom) of changes made. For each site subsection, we computed the mean number of changes made on individual pages and the total number of changes made at the site-level. We then computed the median of these measures across the five sites, which we depict in the top chart. Similarly, we classified the changes that the designers made to sites as addressing usability, accessibility, and other issues; we also noted whether changes were visible or introduced errors. We depict the median number of pages with these types of changes in the bottom figure. ANOVAs revealed that all differences in the number of changes (top chart) are significant ($p < 0.05$). ANOVAs also revealed that the accessibility and error differences (bottom chart) are significant ($p < 0.05$).

violations are valid, in most cases. Hence, less experienced designers may incorrectly assess whether or not a violation is valid.

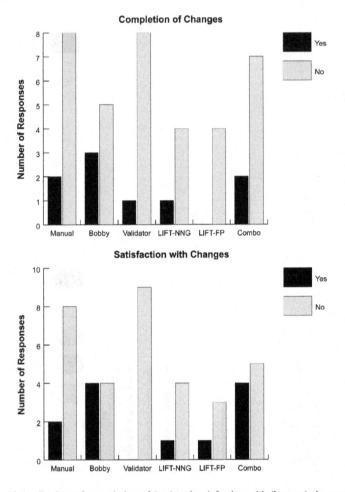

Figure 12.6. Designers' completion of (top) and satisfaction with (bottom) site modifications.

It is even more surprising that designers made significantly more modifications in the manual condition than in the LIFT conditions, because the LIFT tool can assist designers with making some repairs, such as changing ALT text or image dimensions. There were no significant differences in the number of problems that tools reported before and after modifications.

Figure 12.5 (chart on the bottom) shows that designers made more holistic changes in the manual condition than in the other tool conditions, except for in the combo condition. Figure 12.3 showed that the Bobby and LIFT tools identified a range of design issues, which addressed usability and accessibility. However, designers were not able to resolve these issues within the alloted time.

Designers' modifications in the manual condition addressed usability, accessibility, and other problems fairly equally. Figure 12.5 also shows that designers introduced more errors while making modifications in the manual condition than in the individual tool conditions; designers also introduced errors in the combo condition. In the latter condition, the tools did not detect the introduced errors.

Our analysis of the changes made across designers for the same site and the same condition revealed that designers made similar types of changes more often in the manual condition than in the tool conditions. There was typically one page within each site for which multiple designers made one or more similar changes. Results suggest that the tools may or may not result in deterministic changes, because designers could interpret reported problems or solutions quite differently.

1.3.3   Tool Effectiveness

We asked designers to rate the universal accessibility of sites both before and after modifications. A related-samples test [Easton and McColl, 1997] revealed that there were no significant differences in these ratings, possibly because designers often did not have enough time to complete modifications (Figure 12.6, top chart) or thought that sites needed to be redesigned (Figure 12.6, bottom chart).

For each tool, designers' responded that they strongly disagreed to strongly agreed with nine statements, including: assessments were accurate and relevant, the tool was easy to use, the tool was extremely helpful in improving universal accessibility, and the tool helped them to learn about effective design practices. There were significant differences in responses to the latter two statements. Responses suggest that Bobby was the most helpful and that the Validator was the least helpful. Similarly, responses suggest that Bobby and LIFT-NNG helped designers to learn about effective practices.

On the debriefing questionnaire, 50 percent of designers identified Bobby as the most effective tool, and 63 percent identified the Validator as the least effective tool. Surprisingly, 56 percent of designers reported that neither using all three tools nor using one tool was the best usage scenario. Several designers commented about the need to rely on designers' expertise or usability analysis (e.g., "...there are usually embedded corporate reasons for placement of objects...needs to be taken into consideration").

2.   Users' Usage of Modified Sites

The preceding study demonstrated that although the automated evaluation tools identified more errors than the designers identified without using them, designers made more design changes in the condition without tools. To determine if the changes resulted in measurably different site experiences, we

selected modified versions of each of the five sites for usability testing by users
with and without disabilities.

2.1   Study Design

We designed a 6x5 between-subjects experiment to determine if there would
be any differences in user performance or in subjective ratings for the original
and modified versions of the sites (Table 12.2). We also wanted to understand
the types of changes that produced significant differences. We asked 22 users
to participate in a ninety-minute or two-hour study session,[1] wherein we gave
them a scenario for each site and then asked them to browse the site to find
specific information (see Table 12.1). We counterbalanced both the site order
and the site version (i.e., modification condition); participants completed tasks
on only one version of each site.

Participants' ages ranged from 18 to 55; an equal number of males and females participated. Participants had very diverse ethnic backgrounds, and the
majority were native English speakers, had a college or post-graduate education, were intermediate computer and Internet users, and typically spent ten or
more hours on-line a week. Thirteen participants had a visual (6), hearing (1),
moderate mobility (3), learning (1), physical (5), or other (1) disability. Three
participants had multiple disabilities.

Participants mainly used Netscape Navigator to complete study tasks. Blind
participants experienced incompatibility problems between the JAWS screen
reader software and Netscape Navigator, thus they needed to use Internet Ex-
plorer instead. Two participants with mobility disabilities used the keyboard
exclusively. For participants with visual and physical disabilities, testers read
the study tasks aloud and assisted participants with completing the post-task
questionnaires. For 89 percent of the tasks, participants had never used the
sites.

2.2   Study Results

When we analyzed data across all the sites, ANOVAs showed no significant
differences in the participants' task completion success, their task completion
times, or their subjective ratings based on the site versions (i.e., modification
conditions) as well as on whether participants had disabilities or not. However,
our analysis of data for individual sites revealed a few significant differences
in results for sites 2, 3, and 5. It is interesting to note that the modifications
that designers made to these sites in the manual condition improved user performance, yet this was not the case for the modifications that designers made
in the tool conditions.

Site 2: Participants spent more time completing tasks on the LIFT-NNG ver-
    sion of site 2 than the original one (median of 286 seconds versus 163). The

Table 12.2. Total number of participants who evaluated each site version.[a,b]

Condition	Site 1	2	3	4	5
Original	6 (4)	4 (2)	5 (4)	4 (2)	4 (2)
Manual	–	5 (3)	4 (2)	8 (4)	5 (4)
Bobby	–	–	–	5 (4)	3 (1)
Validator	5 (4)	–	8 (4)	–	5 (3)
LIFT-NNG	7 (3)	5 (3)	–	–	5 (3)
Combo	4 (2)	8 (5)	5 (3)	5 (3)	–

[a] The number to the left of each parenthesis denotes the total number of participants, and the number in the parenthesis denotes those participants who had disabilities.
[b] The – indicates site versions that were not tested.

designer modified all pages in the LIFT-NNG version, but the modifications addressed coding issues (e.g., fixing tags and adding a document type definition) instead of usability and accessibility issues. The designer also introduced an error on the first page, which affected its layout.

Site 3: Participants rated the manual version of site 3 higher than the original one (3.25 versus 1.4 on a five-point scale). The designer made extensive visible modifications to four of the six pages in the manual version. Most of the changes addressed usability issues: wrapping long text links in the navigation bar and adding vertical space between them, increasing the font size for links, formatting headings so that they appear more distinctly, adding vertical space between links in a bulleted list, and removing an acronym scheme to reduce potential cognitive overload. The designer did not introduce errors on any pages.

Site 5: No participant was able to complete the task on the Validator version of site 5, but 80 percent of participants completed tasks on the manual version. (Only 25 percent of participants completed tasks on the original version.) The designer only modified one page in the Validator version; changes consisted of adding alternative text to indicate advertisements. There was a blind user in this condition, and the user did not complete the task. The designer modified three pages in the manual version; changes addressed usability and accessibility issues, such as moving relevant links to a prominent position at the top of the page, adding headings to the table of contents for a FAQ, increasing font size, and adding vertical space around links. Unlike the Validator version, the manual version had visible errors on two pages.

Participants only spent a median of 91 seconds completing tasks on the

LIFT-NNG version of site 5 versus 186 seconds on the manual version. However, twice as many participants (80 percent) completed the task on the manual version, which explains the extra time. The designer only modified alternative text to indicate spacer images on pages in the LIFT-NNG version. Due to the busy nature of the initial page, participants typically gave up on completing the task. As discussed above, the designer of the manual version made considerable changes to reduce page complexity and consequently, cognitive overload.

3.   Discussion

Within the narrow parameters of our study, results suggest that the three automated evaluation tools were not effective in helping designers to improve web site usability and accessibility. However, we consider our results to be preliminary. Perhaps if we used less mature sites, studied novice or expert designers, or gave designers more time to learn the tools, to understand the guidelines, and to modify sites, then the outcome may be different. Nonetheless, our findings have implications for both researchers and web practitioners. Clearly, more research needs to be done to validate the guidelines embedded in automated evaluation tools and to make them more usable. Fundamentally, our results suggest that the guidelines do not examine higher-level issues that limit web site use, such as page complexity or whether text is legible with the color combinations used. This assessment was also suggested by our analysis in Section 3 of Chapter 11.

Although it should be evident that web practitioners cannot rely on the automated evaluation tools alone to improve sites, study results show this to be the case. Our studies suggest that the guidelines embedded in the tools, or perhaps the way designers interpret them, may not necessarily improve the usability and accessibility of web sites, at least not more so than when experienced designers rely on their own expertise. Results do suggest that the tools play an important role in educating web practitioners about effective design practices.

Notes

1 The two-hour sessions were to allow extra time for participants with disabilities to complete the study.

Chapter 13

ANALYSIS OF WEB DESIGN GUIDELINES

There are numerous design guidelines and study results to provide guidance on the way to design web sites so that they are usable and accessible. However, practitioners experience difficulty in applying guidelines, at least in the format in which they are typically presented; they are often discussed vaguely and sometimes conflict with one another. For instance, there is a wide gap between the recommendation "make the site consistent" and its application. Automated evaluation tools, guideline review tools in particular, were developed to assist practitioners with conforming to design guidelines. However, we have demonstrated throughout Part III that the tools have not evolved to the point where they adequately simplify this process. How might we help practitioners to better adhere to guidelines in the interim?

In this chapter, we demonstrate how the WebTango automated evaluation framework (discussed in Chapter 8) makes it possible to derive concrete thresholds (i.e., numerical ranges) for prescriptive web design guidelines. Ideally, quantifying effective design patterns and revealing concrete thresholds will provide the extra guidance that web practitioners need to build better sites. We begin this chapter with a brief synopsis of the WebTango methodology; we refer the reader to Chapter 8 for a comprehensive discussion of the methodology, in particular the quantitative measures that we discuss in this chapter. We then describe how we use the methodology to derive concrete thresholds for prescriptive guidelines. Section 3 uses the derived thresholds to examine guidelines for several aspects of web site designs, including the amount of text and links, the number of fonts, colors, and graphics, and consistency across pages. In some cases, our derived thresholds validate or invalidate guidelines presented in the literature.

1.   The WebTango Methodology

Using the WebTango appproach, we can derive statistical models of effective design practices from empirical data [Ivory, 2001]. The methodology entails computing 157 highly accurate, quantitative page-level and site-level measures. The measures assess many aspects of web interfaces, including the amount of text on a page, color usage, and consistency. We use these measures along with ratings from Internet professionals (Webby Awards judges [The International Academy of Arts and Sciences, 2000]) to build statistical models or profiles of high quality web interfaces. Our models have been able to predict, with over 90 percent accuracy in most cases, whether or not the measures and relationships among them on individual pages or the site overall are consistent with design patterns that are used on highly or poorly rated pages and sites. We use these models in the automated analysis of web sites.

Another application of the quantitative measures and profiles is to revisit web design recommendations, specifically for recommendations that are contradictory, vague, or not validated empirically. Ideally, quantifying effective design patterns and revealing concrete thresholds (i.e., numerical ranges for measures) will provide the extra guidance that practitioners need to build better sites. We contrast thresholds derived from our 2000 and 2002 models in this chapter. Detailed discussions of our analyses of web design guidelines can be found in [Ivory, 2001, Chapter 10] and [Ivory, 2003b].

2.   Analysis Procedure

As discussed in Section 5 of Chapter 8, we have developed a number of statistical models (profiles) for predicting the quality of web pages and sites (see Tables 8.2 and 8.3). (We use the term *quality* to refer to the rating categories that we derived from the Webby judges' ratings; sites that were rated in the top 33 percent form the *good* category, in the middle 34 percent form the *average* category, and in the bottom 33 percent form the *poor* category.) Each model encompasses key relationships among the measures that have a significant role in the predictions. They enable us to determine how a web interface's measures are similar to or different from common design patterns that we found for high quality interfaces. For example, we can use the mean and standard deviation for the number of words on highly rated pages to determine a concrete range that can inform other designs.

We contrast thresholds derived from our 2000 and 2002 models and show that fundamental design patterns have not changed radically over recent years. Our analysis uses the 2000 cluster (small-page, large-page, and formatted-page) and the 2002 overall page quality models. The cluster models provide more context than the latter quality model, because they elicit thresholds based on the type of page being designed (e.g., a small web page).

3.   Analysis Results

We examine guidelines for seven aspects of web interfaces, including the amount of text, fonts, colors, and consistency, and provide quantitative thresholds for these aspects; [Ivory, 2001, Chapter 10] discusses additional aspects like accessibility and download speed. In addition to providing a quantitative range for each aspect, we discuss design patterns that we discovered by inspecting correlations between measures for the aspect and other complementary measures. For example, we show that headings are introduced in proportion to the amount of text on a page. The highlighted design patterns demonstrate how practitioners might apply the derived thresholds to improve the usability and accessibility of their designs. Finally, we discuss how the derived thresholds validate and, in some cases, invalidate guidelines.

3.1   Amount of Text on a Page

The literature contains contradictory heuristics about the ideal amount of text for a web page. Some texts say that users prefer all relevant content to appear on one page [Landesman and Schroeder, 2000], while other texts suggest that content should be broken up into smaller units across multiple pages [Flanders and Willis, 1998; Nielsen, 2000]. Furthermore, there is no concrete guidance on how much text is enough or too much.

Table 13.1 depicts ranges for the total number of words on a page (word count). Contrary to the design heuristics, ranges suggest that pages with both a small and a large amount of text is acceptable. However, our profile analysis revealed that text formatting needs to be proportional to the amount of text on a page [Ivory, 2001]. Table 13.1 shows that headings (display word count), text clustering (text cluster count), as well as the number of columns where text starts on pages (text column count) varies for the three clusters. Ranges are all significantly different across clusters as determined by analyses of variance (ANOVAs). Ranges for the overall page quality (i.e., across page types) are consistent with the cluster models and illustrate the use of proportional text formatting as well.

3.2   Length and Quality of Link Text

Nielsen [2000] suggests that web designers use 2–4 words in text links; however, Sawyer and Schroeder [2000] suggest that they use links with 7–12 "useful" words (i.e., words that provide hints about the content on a destination page). Our average link words measure suggests that text links on good pages contain from two to three words. Furthermore, the average good link words measure suggests that one to three of these words are not common words or the word 'click,' thus they are potentially useful. Ranges for each of the three good page clusters are very similar. Hence, the data suggests that link text on good

Table 13.1.   Word count and other text element and formatting ranges for good pages.[a]

Measure	Good Page Cluster			Overall Page
	Small-Page	Large-Page	Formatted-Page	
Word Count	72–371	710–1008	218–517	61–627
Display Word Count	1–18	20–38	14–32	0–28
Text Column Count	0–4	1–5	6–10	0–7
Text Cluster Count	0–2	1–4	2–4	0–3

[a] Thresholds are from the 2000 good page cluster models and the 2002 overall page quality model.

pages is consistent with Nielsen's heuristic. There is one caveat to this finding: Our tool does not distinguish between links within the body text or outside of the body text (e.g., in a navigation bar) and there could be differences for the two types of links.

3.3   Number and Type of Links on a Page

There is an ongoing debate in the literature about the appropriate number and types of links to use on web pages. Table 13.2 provides ranges for the link, text link, redundant link, and link graphic counts on pages. The table also depicts ranges for link text cluster counts (i.e., regions on web pages wherein links are grouped together in lists, colored, or bordered regions) and shows that the number of link text clusters are somewhat proportional to the number of links on pages. For example, pages in the formatted-page cluster appear to have the most links as well as the most link text clusters, most likely because they contain one or more navigation bars on them.

The table shows that redundant or repeated links are used on good pages [Flanders and Willis, 1998; Kim and Yoo, 2000; Sano, 1996; Spool *et al.*, 2000] and graphical links are not avoided as suggested in the literature [Sawyer and Schroeder, 2000; Scanlon and Schroeder, 2000b; Spool *et al.*, 1999]; it is possible that the graphical links have text in them, which is not currently detected by our metrics tool. Given the ranges for redundant links along with the ranges for text and graphical links, it appears that links are repeated in both text and image formats [Flanders and Willis, 1998; Sano, 1996; Sawyer and Schroeder, 2000]. However, the measures do not currently reveal how often redundant links correspond to those that are also graphical links. Table 13.2 shows that good pages tend not to use within-page links (page link count), which is suggested in the literature [Nielsen, 2000; Sawyer and Schroeder, 2000; Spool *et al.*, 1999].

Table 13.2.   Link element and text formatting ranges for good pages.[a]

| | Good Page Cluster | | | Overall |
Measure	Small-Page	Large-Page	Formatted-Page	Page
Link Count	12–41	35–64	54–82	10–56
Text Link Count	5–28	24–47	35–58	2–37
Link Graphic Count	5–14	5–14	12–21	2–21
Redundant Link Count	1–9	4–12	9–16	0–12
Page Link Count[b]	–	–	–	0–1
Link Text Cluster Count	0–1	0–1	1–3	0–3

[a] Thresholds are from the 2000 good page cluster models and the 2002 overall page quality model.
[b] The page link count is not used in the good cluster models, which we indicate with a "–."

3.4   Use of Non-Animated and Animated Graphical Ads

Most texts suggest that graphical ads should be minimized or avoided [Flanders and Willis, 1998; Klee and Schroeder, 2000; Nielsen, 2000; Spool *et al.*, 1999], but one study suggests that ads increase credibility [Kim and Fogg, 1999]. Our measures of the number of graphical ads (animated and non-animated) suggest that good pages are likely to contain no more than two graphical ads. Pages in the 2002 dataset used graphical ads to a lesser degree than pages in the 2000 dataset; the latter pages contained one graphical ad on average. Good pages in both datasets tend to have zero or one animated graphical ad, which suggests that animation is used sparingly.

3.5   Font Styles and Sizes

A number of empirical studies (e.g., [Bernard and Mills, 2000; Bernard *et al.*, 2001; Schriver, 1997]) have examined the use of serif and sans serif fonts, as well as appropriate font sizes. Our analysis revealed that sans serif is the predominant font style used on good pages (Table 13.3); studies have shown these fonts to be more readable than serif fonts online [Bernard and Mills, 2000; Schriver, 1997]. The 2002 dataset suggests that serif fonts and font style variations (i.e., combinations of font face, size, bolding, and italics) in general, are being used to a lesser degree than in the past (2–7 combinations on a page). Similarly, slightly larger font sizes are used (9–12 pts on average, with a minimum font size of 8–10 pts).

3.6   Unique Colors and Color Combinations

The literature offers various recommendations on using a small number of colors [Flanders and Willis, 1998; Murch, 1985], browser-safe colors [Kaiser, 1998], default link colors [Nielsen, 2000; Spool *et al.*, 1999], color combina-

Table 13.3. Font style and size ranges for good pages.[a,b]

Measure	Good Page Cluster Small-Page	Large-Page	Formatted-Page	Overall Page
Font Style[c]	–	–	–	Sans Serif
Font Count	3–5	5–7	5–8	2–7
Sans Serif Font Count	–	–	–	0–1
Serif Font Count	–	–	–	0–1
Average Font Size	10–11pt	10–11pt	9–10pt	9–12pt
Minimum Font Size	8–9pt	8–9pt	8–9pt	8–10pt

[a] Thresholds are from the 2000 good page cluster models and the 2002 overall page quality model.
[b] Not all of the font-related measures are used in the cluster models, which we indicate wiht a "–."
[c] The font style measure reflects the predominant font face (serif, sans serif, or undetermined) used on a page.

tions with adequate contrast [Flanders and Willis, 1998; Murch, 1985; Nielsen, 2000], and so on. We have developed over twelve measures related to color usage (Table 13.4). Our analysis revealed that good pages tend to use from one to three colors for body text (body color count) as well as one to two colors for headings (display color count); it appears that the number of heading colors is proportional to the amount of text or formatting on pages. Although it is not clear whether different colors are used for body and heading text on these pages, unique color counts (5–11) suggest that this may be the case. The 2002 dataset reflects a small decrease in the number of different colors used for text, which is more consistent with guidance in the literature [Flanders and Willis, 1998; Murch, 1985]. We also found that good pages tend to use good text color combinations more so than neutral and bad text color combinations; we use results from Murch's study of color combinations [Murch, 1985] to determine the quality of color combinations (i.e., good, neutral, or bad).

Two to four colors are used for links, and the default browser colors (red, blue, and purple) are not always used; these ranges suggest that good pages do not closely follow the guidance in the literature. Ranges for the total number of unique colors (5–11) show that good pages do not adhere to the guidance of using no more than six discriminable colors [Murch, 1985]. Furthermore, they do not strictly use browser-safe colors (only 3–6 of the 5–11 unique colors) as recommended by the literature.

3.7   Consistency Across Pages

Some texts advocate consistent use of design elements across web pages [Flanders and Willis, 1998; Fleming, 1998; Mahajan and Shneiderman, 1997], while other texts claim that such elements become invisible [Sano, 1996; Sawyer

Table 13.4. Color and color combination ranges for good pages.[a,b]

Measure	Good Page Cluster			Overall Page
	Small-Page	Large-Page	Formatted-Page	
Body Color Count	–	–	–	0–3
Display Color Count	0–1	1–2	0–2	0–2
Link Color Count	–	–	–	2–4
Standard Link Color Count	0–1	0–1	0–2	0–2
Color Count	5–8	6–9	9–12	5–11
Browser-Safe Color Count	–	–		3–6
Good Text Color Combinations	1–3	2–4	4–6	1–5
Neutral Text Color Combinations	–	–	–	0–2
Bad Text Color Combinations	–	–	–	0–1
Good Panel Color Combinations	0–0	0–0	0–1	0–1
Neutral Panel Color Combinations	–	–	–	0–1
Bad Panel Color Combinations	0–1	0–1	1–2	0–2

[a] Thresholds are from the 2000 good page cluster models and the 2002 overall page quality model.
[b] Not all of the color-related measures are used in the cluster models, which we indicate with a "–."

et al., 2000]. The literature also suggests that page titles (i.e., title tags) should be varied [Nielsen, 2000]. We derived twelve measures to reflect the percent of variation for groups of related page-level measures [Ivory, 2001]; a large variation percentage reflects less consistency and vice versa. Our analysis suggests that page layouts vary more so in the 2002 dataset (5–55 percent) than in the 2000 dataset (0–22 percent); thus, it appears that the trend is to introduce more variation into page layouts as opposed to keeping them consistent. This trend is somewhat disturbing, because at least one study has shown that performance improves with consistent interfaces [Mahajan and Shneiderman, 1997]. The link element and formatting variation measures suggest that navigation elements are fairly consistent across pages on good sites. Finally, the page title variation suggests that titles vary considerably on good sites (19–139 percent).

4. Discussion

We summarized design patterns derived from our analysis of page- and site-level quantitative measures for sites rated highly in the review stage of the

2000 and 2002 Webby Awards. The design patterns extend beyond individual measures to show, for instance, that the amount of text formatting is proportional to the amount of text on a page (i.e., a change in one aspect may necessitate a change in another). We also demonstrated that the guidance varies slightly depending on the design context (e.g., page style). The derived patterns should provide some concrete guidance for improving web site designs. In some cases, such as the number and types of links and graphical ads, what is done in practice contradicts the literature; perhaps these areas need to be examined with further empirical studies. For the most part, design patterns were fairly consistent across the two years.

Chapter 14

PROMISING TOOL DEVELOPMENT DIRECTIONS

Automated web site evaluation tools are instantiations of the various methodologies that were developed to broaden site coverage during assessments, to improve consistency in evaluation results, and to decrease the costs of non-automated methods. Although there are well over 40 tools, predominately for guideline review, existing tools are not being used as an integral part of web site design practices, nor are they currently perceived as being highly beneficial. Our analysis and empirical study of guideline review tools showed that there is very little consistency in results across tools, even when the tools evaluate similar aspects, and that their effectiveness in improving web site designs remains to be documented.

How might tool developers go about improving the state-of-the-art in automated web site evaluation tools? We discuss several improvements in this chapter. We also conclude with a discussion of the benefits of tools as they existed at publication time.

1. Limitations of Automated Evaluation Tools

Automated evaluation tools have the same underlying issues as the automated evaluation methodologies from which they stem: (1) their efficacy needs to be validated; (2) they need to support the entire web site design process, rather than the late development stages; (3) they need to consider the design context; and (4) they need to consider diverse web site users. Chapter 9 addresses these fundamental issues at the methodological level. In this chapter, we address issues that need to be addressed at the tool level:

1 The tools do not address high-level design issues, such as page complexity or whether text is legible with the color combinations used. Furthermore, most tools evaluate aspects independently, rather than considering, for example,

167

that increasing font size may require a subsequent reduction in the amount of text on a page.

2 The tools themselves have inadequate usability. Furthermore, their presentations of guideline violations or recommendations need to be improved.

3 The tools need to be more robust. For instance, they need to ensure that errors are not introduced during the evaluation process.

We suggest ways to address these limitations in the following sections. Given the predominance of guideline review tools, our discussion is mostly applicable to these types of tools.

2. Evaluation Approaches

Guideline review tools, with the exception of the WebTango prototype (Chapter 8), evaluate web pages and sites by detecting violations of each embedded guideline. In practice, guidelines are related and often conflict with each other, but the tools do not account for interrelatedness or contradictions among guidelines in their assessments, results presentations, or recommendations.

One way to resolve this issue is to associate additional metadata with the guidelines so that this information can be exploited during the evaluation process. For example, Scapin *et al.* [2000] present a useful and relevant framework for organizing web guidelines that includes a taxonomy of index keys (e.g., alignment, buttons, downloading, headings, language, scrolling, navigation structure, and so on); this taxonomy could be used to associate metadata with the guidelines embedded in automated evaluation tools. If multiple guidelines address the same issue, then the tool could at least organize its results and recommendations based on the group of related guidelines.

Classifying guidelines should also make it possible to determine relationships or potential conflicts among then. We could construct a layer on top of the guidelines to reflect these relationships. For instance, we could create a matrix wherein each guideline was represented in a row and a column. Each cell in the matrix could contain a symbol to indicate the relationship between two guidelines (e.g., '+1': positive correlation; '-1': negative correlation; '-100': conflict; or '0': no relationship). Ideally, the tools could use this additional metadata layer to determine whether interrelationships are respected or whether guideline conflicts exist.

Another application of this additional guideline layer is to identify larger groups of guidelines that address high-level issues, such as page complexity or text formatting. Similarly to clustering techniques that are used to determine optimal ways to group information on web sites [Martin, 1999], we could apply a clustering algorithm to the matrix (after transforming it for analysis) to determine groups of related guidelines. These groups could be used to guide assessments, results presentation, and recommendation formulation.

3. Tool Usability

Suggested modifications to the application and reporting of guideline violations should improve tool usability as well. One of the common complaints that practitioners made about the tools in our surveys (see Chapters 1 and 12) and empirical studies is that the tools had inadequate usability. For example, we depicted the cumbersome process that evaluators had to follow to evaluate and repair a web page using one of the LIFT tools (Figures 11.3 and 12.2). A user-centered design process needs to be followed so that more beneficial tools can be developed for practitioners [Rosson *et al.*, 1988; Rosson *et al.*, 1987; Singh and Green, 1988].

Streamlining task flows is necessary, but not sufficient for improving tool usability. Guidelines are often presented in long lists that practitioners have to wade through. Furthermore, guidelines are sometimes vague or require a human factors background to understand. Thus, practitioners experience difficulties interpreting them, which in turn interferes with their ability to implement appropriate changes. Improving guideline presentation is one way to address these issues. Another way is to incorporate automated design changes. Tools like A-Prompt [Adaptive Technology Research Center, 2002], ALTifier [Vorburger, 1999], and LIFT [UsableNet, 2002b] assist practitioners with making limited changes to ALT text, form labels, and table headings. Other types of changes, for instance, clustering links, breaking text up into smaller reading blocks, changing font styles, or changing color combinations, could be handled automatically or semi-automatically as well. Enabling practitioners to preview recommended changes could improve their understanding of guidelines.

Practitioners stated that they need to have more control than they currently have over how and which guidelines are applied. Although most tools allow practitioners to select a set of guidelines to apply, very few enable them to add guidelines or to disable individual guidelines. Furthermore, they do not assist the practitioner with determining which guidelines are most appropriate to her design context. Researchers on the KWARESMI project [Beirekdar *et al.*, 2002a; Beirekdar *et al.*, 2002b; Beirekdar *et al.*, 2003] are developing a standard guideline definition language and framework that practitioners can use to control the application of guidelines, provided that they can specify them correctly. More research and development effort is needed in this area.

4. Tool Robustness

Existing tools are not robust with respect to the types of sites they can evaluate. Most tools are limited to processing static HTML, rather than Macromedia

Flash or other technologies. Image processing and other artificial intelligence techniques are needed to broaden the scope of automated evaluation tools. The tools also need to ensure that practitioners do not introduce errors in the evaluation and repair process. In our empirical study of the Bobby, Validator, and LIFT tools (preceding chapter), there were several cases wherein designers introduced errors and the tools did not detect them.

A final related issue is the lack of consistency in assessments across tools, even when they assess similar guidelines, as discussed in Chapter 11. There needs to be an effort within the automated evaluation tool community to standardize assessments, reporting, and recommendations when tools evaluate the W3C or Section 508 guidelines. This standardization should also help practitioners to select the most appropriate tools to satisfy their evaluation needs. The guideline definition language [Beirekdar *et al.*, 2002a; Beirekdar *et al.*, 2002b; Beirekdar *et al.*, 2003] that KWARESMI's researchers are developing should enable tool developers to reuse the same guidelines and, ideally, employ the same evaluation engine.

5.   Discussion

Automated evaluation tools are potentially beneficial in the web site design process. However, existing tools are limited and difficult to use, which impedes practitioner adoption. More work is needed to design tools to better support practitioners and to improve the usefulness, usability, and robustness of tools.

In their current state, automated evaluation tools play an important role in helping practitioners to learn about effective design practices. Practitioners report that it is helpful to be able to use the tools, in particular after making design changes. The tools reduce the amount of effort that practitioners need to expend to manually check for issues that can be assessed automatically and consistently, so that they can focus on higher-level issues. We also demonstrated how the WebTango prototype clarifies web design guidelines for practitioners by providing concrete thresholds for design aspects. Our analyses and studies of automated evaluation tools should help practitioners to make well-informed decisions about the tools that they incorporate into their work practices.

Appendix A
Web Site Evaluation Methodologies and Tools

In the following list, we summarize the automated and non-automated web site evaluation methodologies and tools that we discussed in this book. (Some methods are for evaluating non-web interfaces; we indicate these methods with a '†.') We provide the abbreviated and full names, references, brief descriptions of their automation support, and the corresponding taxonomy characterizations. We refer the reader to the index for additional discussions.

- 508 Accessibility Suite [Macromedia, 2001]: critique of usability or accessibility (inspection—guideline review; automated critique)

- AccessEnable [RetroAccess, 2002]: critique of usability or accessibility (inspection—guideline review; automated critique)

- AccVerify/AccRepair [HiSoftware, 2002a; HiSoftware, 2002b]: critique of usability or accessibility (inspection—guideline review; automated critique)

- AlertSite Web Site Monitoring [AlertSite, 2002]: monitor web server availability (usability testing—performance measurement; automated analysis)

- ALTifier [Vorburger, 1999]: critique of usability or accessibility (inspection—guideline review; automated critique)

- Anemone [Dodge, 2001; Fry, 2000]: evolution-based visualization and animation of log files (usability testing—log file analysis; automated analysis)

- A-Prompt [Adaptive Technology Research Center, 2002]: critique of usability or accessibility (inspection—guideline review; automated critique)

- AWUSA (Automated Website USability Analysis) [Tiedtke et al., 2002]: task-based analysis, statistical analysis, and mining of log files (usability testing—log file analysis; automated analysis); analysis of usability or accessibility (inspection—guideline review; automated analysis)

- Büchner and Mulvenna [1998]: on-line analytical processing of log files (usability testing—log file analysis; automated analysis)

- Bloodhound [Card et al., 2001; Chi et al., 2000; Chi et al., 2001; Chi et al., 2003]: employ an information-scent model to generate navigation paths (simulation—information scent modeling; automated capture); employ an information-scent model to analyze navigation (simulation—information scent modeling; automated analysis)

171

- BMC Software SiteAngel [BMC Software, 2002]: monitor web server availability (usability testing—performance measurement; automated analysis)

- Bobby [WatchFire, 2002]: critique of usability or accessibility (inspection—guideline review; automated critique)

- CMN-GOMS† (Card, Moran, and Newell GOMS) [Card *et al.*, 1983]: analysis of task structure (analytical modeling—GOMS analysis; non automated)

- CoLiDeS (Comprehension-based Linked model of Deliberate Search) [Blackmon *et al.*, 2002; Blackmon *et al.*, 2003; Kitajima *et al.*, 2000]: employ an information-scent model to analyze navigation (simulation—information scent modeling; automated analysis)

- CPM-GOMS† (Critical Path Method GOMS) [John and Kieras, 1996]: analysis of task structure (analytical modeling—GOMS analysis; non automated)

- CTA (Cognitive Task Analysis) [May and Barnard, 1994]: predict usability problems (analytical modeling—cognitive task analysis; automated analysis)

- CWW (Cognitive Walkthrough for the Web) [Blackmon *et al.*, 2002; Blackmon *et al.*, 2003]: use text similarity measures for critique (inspection—guideline review; automated critique)

- Design Advisor [Faraday, 2000]: analyze the scanning path of a page (inspection—guideline review; automated analysis)

- Disk Tree [Chi, 2002]: usage-based visualization of log files (usability testing—log file analysis; automated analysis)

- Doctor HTML [Imageware, Inc., 2001]: analysis of usability or accessibility (inspection—guideline review; automated analysis)

- Dome Tree [Chi *et al.*, 2000; Chi, 2002]: usage-based visualization of log files (usability testing—log file analysis; automated analysis)

- Dr. Watson [Addy & Associates, 2000]: critique of HTML coding and usability or accessibility (inspection—guideline review; automated critique)

- Enviz Insight [Enviz, Inc., 2001]: capture of online questionnaire data (inquiry—questionnaires; automated capture)

- EvalWeb [Scapin *et al.*, 2000]: critique of usability or accessibility (inspection—guideline review; automated critique)

- Exodus Monitoring & Management Services [Exodus, 2002]: monitor web server availability (usability testing—performance measurement; automated analysis)

- Experience Recorder [NetRaker, 2000]: capture of screen snapshots (inquiry—screen snapshots; automated capture)

- Freshwater Software SiteSeer [Freshwater Software, 2002]: monitor web server availability (usability testing—performance measurement; automated analysis)

- Gentler [Thimbleby, 1997]: structural analysis of web pages and sites (inspection—guideline review; automated analysis)

- GOMS† (Goals, Operators, Methods, and Selection rules) [John and Kieras, 1996]: analysis of task structure (analytical modeling—GOMS analysis; non automated)

- HyperAT [Theng and Marsden, 1998]: statistical analysis of log files (usability testing—log file analysis; automated analysis); structural analysis of web pages and sites (inspection—guideline review; automated analysis)

- InFocus [SSB Technologies, 2002]: critique of usability or accessibility (inspection—guideline review; automated critique)

- Interacting Cognitive Subsystems† [Barnard, 1987; Barnard and Teasdale, 1991]: employ a computational cognitive architecture for interface analysis (simulation—information processor modeling; automated analysis)

- KALDI (Keyboard/mouse Action Logger and Display Instrument) [Al-Qaimari and McRostie, 1999]: log system-level events (usability testing—performance measurement; automated capture); task-based analysis of log files (usability testing—log file analysis; automated analysis); employ same- and different-time different-place testing (usability-testing—remote testing; automated capture)

- Kasik and George† [Kasik and George, 1996]: employ a genetic algorithm model to generate interface usage data (simulation—genetic algorithm modeling; automated capture)

- Keynote LoadPro [Keynote Systems, Inc., 2003]: measure web server performance (usability testing—performance measurement; automated analysis)

- Keynote Red Alert [Keynote Systems, Inc., 2002]: monitor web server availability (usability testing—performance measurement; automated analysis)

- KLM† (Keystrokel-Level Model) [John and Kieras, 1996]: analysis of task structure (analytical modeling—GOMS analysis; non automated)

- KWARESMI (Knowledge-based Web Automatic REconfigurable evaluation with guidelineS optiMIzation) [Beirekdar et al., 2002a; Beirekdar et al., 2002b; Beirekdar et al., 2003]: analysis of usability or accessibility (inspection—guideline review; automated analysis)

- LIFT [UsableNet, 2000; UsableNet, 2002a; UsableNet, 2002b]: critique of usability or accessibility (inspection—guideline review; automated critique)

- LIFT-FP (LIFT for FrontPage) [UsableNet, 2002b]: critique of usability or accessibility (inspection—guideline review; automated critique)

- LIFT-NNG (LIFT - Nielsen Norman Group Edition) [UsableNet, 2002a]: critique of usability or accessibility (inspection—guideline review; automated critique)

- LumberJack [Chi et al., 2002; Heer and Chi, 2002b]: unsupervised mining of log files (usability testing—log file analysis; automated analysis)

- MiDAS [Büchner et al., 1999; Spiliopoulou, 2000]: supervised mining of log files (usability testing—log file analysis; automated analysis)

- Miller and Remington [Miller and Remington, 2000; Miller and Remington, 2002]: employ an information-scent model to analyze navigation (simulation—information scent modeling; automated analysis)

- MIR (Metaphorical Information Representation) [Kizhakke, 2000]: usage-based visualization of log files (usability testing—log file analysis; automated analysis)

- NetGenesis [CustomerCentric Solutions, 2002]: statistical analysis of log files (usability testing—log file analysis; automated analysis)

- NetRaker [NetRaker, 2000]: capture of online questionnaire data (inquiry—questionnaires; automated capture)

- NetTracker [Sane Solutions, LLC, 2002]: statistical analysis of log files (usability testing—log file analysis; automated analysis)

- NGOMSL† (Natural GOMS Language) [John and Kieras, 1996]: analysis of task structure (analytical modeling—GOMS analysis; non automated)

- Noldus [Noldus Information Technology, 2003]: capture of screen snapshots (inquiry— screen snapshots; automated capture)

- Paessler Webserver Stress Tool [Paessler GmbH, 2003]: measure web server performance (usability testing—performance measurement; automated analysis)

- Page Layout Change [Farkas, 2003]: analyze visual consistency across pages (inspection— guideline review; automated analysis)

- PageScreamer [Crunchy Technologies, 2002]: critique of usability or accessibility (inspection—guideline review; automated critique)

- Psychology OnLine [UWEC, 2003]: capture of online questionnaire data (inquiry—questionnaires; automated capture)

- QUIP (Quantitative User Interface Profiling) [Helfrich and Landay, 1999]: task-based analysis of log files (usability testing—log file analysis; automated analysis)

- Rating Game [Stein, 1997]: structural analysis of web pages (inspection—guideline review; automated analysis)

- ScentViz [Chi, 2002]: usage- and evolution-based visualization of log files (usability testing—log file analysis; automated analysis)

- Site Profile [Lynch *et al.*, 1999; Web Criteria, 1999]: employ a GOMS-like model to analyze navigation (simulation—information processor modeling; automated analysis)

- SpeedTracer [Wu *et al.*, 1997]: unsupervised mining of log files (usability testing—log file analysis; automated analysis)

- Starfield [Hochheiser and Shneiderman, 2001]: pattern-based visualization of log files (usability testing—log file analysis; automated analysis)

- Time Tube [Chi, 2002]: evolution-based visualization of log files (usability testing—log file analysis; automated analysis)

- USINE[†] (USer Interface Evaluator) [Lecerof and Paternò, 1998]: log client-side activities (usability testing—performance measurement; automated capture); task-based analysis of log files (usability testing—log file analysis; automated analysis)

- VISVIP [Cugini and Scholtz, 1999]: usage-based visualization and animation of log files (usability testing—log file analysis; automated analysis)

- Vividence [Vividence Corporation, 2002]: capture of online questionnaire data (inquiry— questionnaires; automated capture)

- W3C CSS Validation Service (CSS Validator) [World Wide Web Consortium, 2002b]: critique of CSS coding (inspection—guideline review; automated critique)

- W3C HTML Validation Service (HTML Validator) [World Wide Web Consortium, 2001c]: critique of HTML coding (inspection—guideline review; automated critique)

- WAVE [Pennsylvania's Initiative on Assistive Technology, 2001]: critique of usability or accessibility (inspection—guideline review; automated critique)

- WBG (Web Behavior Graph) [Card *et al.*, 2001]: behavior-based visualization of log files (usability testing—log file analysis; automated analysis)

- Weblint [Bowers, 1996]: critique of HTML coding (inspection—guideline review; automated critique)

- WebLogMiner [Zaïane *et al.*, 1998]: on-line analytical processing of log files (usability testing—log file analysis; automated analysis); mining of log files (usability testing—log file analysis; automated analysis)

- WEBMINER [Cooley *et al.*, 1997; Cooley *et al.*, 1999]: unsupervised mining of log files (usability testing—log file analysis; automated analysis)

- WebPartner Stress Testing [WebPartner, 2002]: measure web server performance (usability testing—performance measurement; automated analysis)

- WebQuilt [Hong *et al.*, 2001]: log Web proxy requests (usability testing—performance measurement; automated capture); task-based analysis of log files (usability testing—log file analysis; automated analysis); employ different-time different-place testing (usability-testing—remote testing; automated capture)

- WebRemUSINE (Web Remote USer Interface Evaluator) [Paganelli and Paternò, 2002]: log client-side activities (usability testing—performance measurement; automated capture); task-based analysis of log files (usability testing—log file analysis; automated analysis); employ different-time different-place testing (usability-testing—remote testing; automated capture)

- WebSAT (Web Static Analyzer Tool) [Scholtz and Laskowski, 1998]: analysis of usability or accessibility (inspection—guideline review; automated analysis)

- WebSphere Resource Analyzer [IBM, Inc., 2002]: measure web server performance (usability testing—performance measurement; automated analysis)

- WebTango [Ivory and Hearst, 2002a]: structural analysis of web pages and sites and analysis of usability or accessibility (inspection—guideline review; automated analysis)

- WebTrends [NetIQ, 2002]: statistical analysis of log files (usability testing—log file analysis; automated analysis)

- WebVIP (Web Variable Instrumenter Program) [Scholtz and Laskowski, 1998]: log client-side activities (usability testing—performance measurement; automated capture)

- WebViz [Pitkow and Bharat, 1994]: usage-based visualization and animation of log files (usability testing—log file analysis; automated analysis)

- WUM (Web Utilization Miner) [Spiliopoulou and Faulstich, 1998; Spiliopoulou, 2000]: supervised mining of log files (usability testing—log file analysis; automated analysis)

References

Adaptive Technology Research Center. A-Prompt project. Available at
http://aprompt.snow.utoronto.ca/, 2002.

Addy & Associates. Dr. Watson version 4.0, 2000. Available at http://watson.addy.com/.

Christopher Ahlberg and Ben Shneiderman. Visual information seeking: Tight coupling of dy-
namic query filters with starfield displays. In *Proceedings of the Conference on Human
Factors in Computing Systems*, pages 313–317, Boston, MA, April 1994. New York: ACM
Press.

Ghassan Al-Qaimari and Darren McRostie. KALDI: A computer-aided usability engineering
tool for supporting testing and analysis of human-computer interaction. In J. Vanderdonckt and A. Puerta, editors, *Proceedings of the 3rd International Conference on Computer-
Aided Design of User Interfaces*, Louvain-la-Neuve, Belgium, October 1999. Dordrecht, The
Netherlands: Kluwer Academic Publishers.

AlertSite. Web site monitoring by alertsite. Available at http://www.alertsite.com/index.html,
2002.

Patrick Allen, John Bateman, and Judy Delin. Genre and layout in multimodal documents:
Towards an empirical account. In *American Association for Artificial Intelligence Fall Sym-
posium on Using Layout for the Generation, Analysis, or Retrieval of Documents*, Cape Cod,
Autumn 1999. Available at http://www.gem.stir.ac.uk/downloads/allen-bateman-delin.PDF.

AnyBrowser.com. AnyBrowser.com: Your Source for Browser Compatibility Verificaiton, 2002.
Available at http://www.anybrowser.com/ScreenSizeTest.html.

Architectural and Transportation Barriers Compliance Board. Electronic and information technology accessibility standards. Federal Register, 2000. Available at
http://www.access-board.gov/sec508/508standards.htm.

autowebmaker. Automated site creation - Autowebmaker. Available at
http://www.autowebmaker.com/, 2003.

Beth Bacheldor. Push for performance. *Information Week*, September 20:18–20, 1999.

Albert Badre and Sharon Laskowski. The cultural context of web genres: Context vs. style. In
Proceedings of the 7th Conference on Human Factors & the Web, Madison, WI, June 2001.
Available at http://www.optavia.com/hfweb/7thconferenceproceedings.zip/Laskowski.pdf.

Sandrine Balbo. Automatic evaluation of user interface usability: Dream or reality. In Sandrine
Balbo, editor, *Proceedings of the Queensland Computer-Human Interaction Symposium*,
Queensland, Australia, August 1995. Bond University.

Philip J. Barnard and J. D. Teasdale. Interacting cognitive subsystems: A systemic approach to
cognitive-affective interaction and change. *Cognition and Emotion*, 5:1–39, 1991.

Philip J. Barnard. Cognitive resources and the learning of human-computer dialogs. In John M. Carroll, editor, *Interfacing Thought: Cognitive Aspects of Human-Computer Interaction*, pages 112–158. MIT Press, Cambridge, MA, 1987.

Abdo Beirekdar, Jean Vanderdonckt, and Monique Noirhomme-Fraiture. A framework and a language for usability automatic evaluation of web sites by static analysis of HTML source code. In Christophe Kolski and Jean Vanderdonckt, editors, *Proceedings of the 4th International Conference on Computer-Aided Design of User Interfaces*, pages 337–348, Valenciennes, France, May 15-17 2002. Dordrecht, The Netherlands: Kluwer Academic Publishers. Available at http://www.isys.ucl.ac.be/bchi/publications/2002/Beirekdar-CADUI2002.pdf.

Abdo Beirekdar, Jean Vanderdonckt, and Monique Noirhomme-Fraiture. KWARESMI - knowledge-based web automated evaluation with reconfigurable guidelines optimization. In *Pre-Proceedings of the 9th International Workshop on the Design, Specification, and Verification of Interactive Systems*, pages 362–376, Rostock, Germany, June 12-14 2002. Available at http://www.isys.ucl.ac.be/bchi/publications/2002/Beirekdar-DSVIS2002.pdf.

Abdo Beirekdar, Jean Vanderdonckt, and Monique Noirhomme-Fraiture. KWARESMI - knowledge-based web automated evaluation with reconfigurable guidelines optimization. In *Proceedings of the 2nd International Conference on Universal Access in Human-Computer Interaction (UAHCI2003)*, Crete, Greece, June 22-27 2003. Mahwah, NJ: Lawrence Erlbaum Associates.

Bettina Berendt and Myra Spiliopolou. Analysis of navigation behavior in web sites integrating multiple information systems. *VLDB Journal*, 9(1):56–75, 2000.

Michael Bernard and Melissa Mills. So, what size and type of font should I use on my website? *Usability News*, Summer, 2000. Available at http://wsupsy.psy.twsu.edu/surl/usabilitynews/2S/font.htm.

Michael Bernard, Chia Hui Liao, and Melissa Mills. The effects of font type and size on the legibility and reading time of online text by older adults. In *Proceedings of the Conference on Human Factors in Computing Systems*, volume 2, pages 175–176, Seattle, WA, March 2001.

Marilyn Hughes Blackmon, Peter G. Polson, Muneo Kitajima, and Clayton Lewis. Cognitive walkthrough for the web. In *Proceedings of the Conference on Human Factors in Computing Systems*, volume 4 of *CHI Letters*, pages 463–470, Minneapolis, MN, April 2002.

Marilyn Hughes Blackmon, Muneo Kitajima, and Peter G. Polson. Repairing usability problems identified by the cognitive walkthrough for the web. In *Proceedings of the Conference on Human Factors in Computing Systems*, pages 497–504, Fort Lauderdale, FL, April 5–10 2003.

BMC Software. SiteAngel. Available at http://www.bmc.com/siteangel/, 2002.

Jose Borges and Mark Levene. Data mining of user navigation patterns. In *WEBKDD*, pages 92–111, 1999.

Jose A. Borges, Israel Morales, and Nestor J. Rodriguez. Guidelines for designing usable world wide web pages. In *Proceedings of the Conference on Human Factors in Computing Systems*, volume 2, pages 277–278, Vancouver, Canada, April 1996. New York: ACM Press.

Jose A. Borges, Israel Morales, and Nestor J. Rodriguez. Page design guidelines developed through usability testing. In Chris Forsythe, Eric Grose, and Julie Ratner, editors, *Human Factors and Web Development*. Lawrence Erlbaum Associates, Publishers, Mahwah, NJ, 1998.

Neil Bowers. Weblint: quality assurance for the World Wide Web. In *Proceedings of the Fifth International World Wide Web Conference*, Paris, France, May 1996. Amsterdam, The Netherlands: Elsevier Science Publishers. Available at http://www5conf.inria.fr/fich_html/papers/P34/Overview.html.

Dan Boyarski, Christine Neuwirth, Jodi Forlizzi, and Susan Harkness Regli. A study of fonts designed for screen display. In *Proceedings of the Conference on Human Factors in Computing Systems*, volume 1, pages 87–94. New York: ACM Press, 1998.

Giorgio Brajnik. Automatic web usability evaluation: Where is the limit? In *Proceedings of the 6th Conference on Human Factors & the Web*, Austin, TX, June 2000.

Alex G. Büchner and Maurice D. Mulvenna. Discovering internet marketing intelligence through online analytical web usage mining. *SIGMOD Record*, 27(4):54–61, 1998.

A. G. Büchner, M. Baumgarten, S. S. Anand, M. D. Mulvenna, and J. G. Hughes. Navigation pattern discovery from internet data. In *WEBKDD*, San Diego, CA, 1999. Available at http://www.acm.org/sigs/sigkdd/proceedings/webkdd99/papers/paper13-buchner.pdf.

Michael D. Byrne, Bonnie E. John, Neil S. Wehrle, and David C. Crow. The tangled web we wove: A taxonomy of WWW use. In *Proceedings of the Conference on Human Factors in Computing Systems*, volume 1, pages 544–551, Pittsburg, PA, May 1999. New York: ACM Press.

Stuart K. Card, Thomas P. Moran, and Allen Newell. *The Psychology of Human-Computer Interaction*. Hillsdale, NJ: Lawrence Erlbaum Associates, Inc., 1983.

Stuart K. Card, Peter Pirolli, Mija Van Der Wege, Julie B. Morrison, Robert W. Reeder, Pamela K. Schraedley, and Jenea Boshart. Information scent as a driver of web behavior graphs: Results of a protocol analysis method for web usability. In *Proceedings Conference on Human Factors in Computing Systems*, pages 498–505, 2001.

C. Cardoso, S. Keates, and P.J. Clarkson. Designing for inclusivity - assessing the accessibility of everyday products. In *Proceedings of the CWUAAT Conference*, 2002.

Center for Information Technology Accommodation. Section 508: The road to accessibility. Available at http://www.section508.gov/index.cfm, 2002.

Andrew Chak. Usability tools: A useful start. *Web Techniques*, August:18–20, 2000.

S. Chaudhuri and U. Dayal. An overview of data warehousing and olap technology. *SIGMOD Record*, 26(1):65–74, 1997.

Aline Chevalier and Melody Y. Ivory. Can novice designers apply usability criteria and recommendations to make web sites easier to use? In *Proceedings of the 10th International Conference on Human-Computer Interaction*, 2003. In press.

Aline Chevalier and Melody Y. Ivory. Web site designs: Influences of designer's experience and design constraints. *International Journal of Human-Computer Studies*, 58(1):57–87, 2003.

Aline Chevalier. *Le rôle du contexte et du niveau d'expertise des concepteurs de sites web sur la prise en compte de contraintes*. PhD thesis, University of Provence, France, 2002.

Ed H. Chi, Peter Pirolli, and James Pitkow. The scent of a site: A system for analyzing and predicting information scent, usage, and usability of a web site. In *Proceedings of the Conference on Human Factors in Computing Systems*, pages 161–168, The Hague, The Netherlands, April 2000. New York: ACM Press.

Ed H. Chi, Peter Pirolli, Kim Chen, and James Pitkow. Using information scent to model user information needs and actions on the web. In *Proceedings of the Conference on Human Factors in Computing Systems*, volume 1, pages 490–497, Seattle, WA, March 2001. New York: ACM Press.

Ed H. Chi, Adam Rosien, and Jeffrey Heer. Lumberjack: intelligent discovery and analysis of web user traffic composition. In *WEBKDD*, Edmonton, Canada, July 23 2002.

Ed H. Chi, Adam Rosien, Gesara Supattanasiri, Amanda Williams, Christiaan Royer, Celia Chow, Erica Robles, Brinda Dalal, Julie Chen, and Steve Cousins. The bloodhound project: Automating discovery of web usability issues using the infoscent^{TM} simulator. In *Proceedings of the Conference on Human Factors in Computing Systems*, pages 505–512. New York: ACM Press, April 5–10 2003.

Ed H. Chi. Improving web usability through visualization. *IEEE Internet Computing*, 6(2):64–71, March/April 2002.

Kevin Christian, Bill Kules, Ben Shneiderman, and Adel Youssef. A comparison of voice controlled and mouse controlled web browsing. In *Fourth Annual ACM Conference on Assistive
Technologies*, pages 72–79. New York: ACM Press, 2000.

M. Coltheart. The MRC psycholinguistic database. *Quarterly Journal of Experimental Psychology*, 33:497–505, 2001.

Tim Comber. Building usable web pages: An HCI perspective. In Roger Debreceny and Allan
Ellis, editors, *Proceedings of the First Australian World Wide Web Conference*, pages 119–
124, Ballina, Australia, April 1995. Ballina, Australia: Norsearch. Available at
http://www.scu.edu.au/sponsored/ausweb/ausweb95/papers/hypertext/comber/.

Computer Science and Telecommunications Board. *More Than Screen Deep: Toward Every-
Citizen Interfaces to the Nations Information Infrastructure*. National Academy Press, Washington, D.C., 1997.

R. Cooley, J. Srivastava, and B. Mobasher. Web mining: Information and pattern discovery on
the world wide web. In *Proceedings of the 9th IEEE International Conference on Tools with
Artificial Intelligence (ICTAI'97)*, November 1997.

Robert Cooley, Bamshad Mobasher, and Jaideep Srivastava. Data preparation for mining world
wide web browsing patterns. *Knowledge and Information Systems*, 1(1):5–32, 1999.

Michael Cooper, Quentin Limbourg, Céline Mariage, and Jean Vanderdonckt. Integrating universal design into a global approach for managing very large web site. In Alfred Kobsa and
Constantine Stephanidis, editors, *Proceedings of the 5th ERCIM Workshop on User Interfaces
for All*, pages 131–150, Dagstuhl, Germany, November 28 – December 1 1999. Available at
http://ui4all.ics.forth.gr/UI4ALL-99/Cooper.pdf.

Joelle Coutaz. Evaluation techniques: Exploring the intersection of HCI and software engineering. In R. N. Taylor and J. Coutaz, editors, *Software Engineering and Human-Computer Interaction*, Lecture Notes in Computer Science, pages 35–48. Heidelberg, Germany: Springer-
Verlag, 1995.

Kara Pernice Coyne and Jakob Nielsen. Beyond alt text: Making the web easy to use for users
with disabilities. Nielsen Norman Group Report, 2001.

Creative Good. White paper one: Building a great customer experience to develop brand, increase loyalty and grow revenues. Available at http://www.creativegood.com/creativegood-
whitepaper.pdf, 1999.

Crunchy Technologies. Crunchy ebusiness network. Available at
http://www.crunchy.com/tools/index.html, 2002.

John Cugini and Jean Scholtz. VISVIP: 3D visualization of paths through web sites. In *Proceedings of the International Workshop on Web-Based Information Visualization*, pages 259–263,
Florence, Italy, September 1999. Institute of Electrical and Electronics Engineers.

CustomerCentric Solutions. Netgenesis enterprise web analytics. Available at
http://www.customercentricsolutions.com/content/solutions/ent_web_analytics.cfm, 2002.

Flavio de Souza and Nigel Bevan. The use of guidelines in menu interface design: Evaluation of
a draft standard. In G. Cockton, D. Diaper, and B. Shackel, editors, *Proceedings of the Third
IFIP TC13 Conference on Human-Computer Interaction*, pages 435–440, Cambridge, UK,
August 1990. Amsterdam, The Netherlands: Elsevier Science Publishers.

O. M. F. De Troyer and C. J. Leune. WSDM: a user centered design method for Web sites.
Computer Networks and ISDN Systems, 30(1–7):85–94, April 1998.

Deep Debroy. Interface design: Exploring data generated by the webtango tools. *Berkeley EECS
Research Journal,*, Spring:11–13, 2002. Available at
http://www.ocf.berkeley.edu/~berj/BERJ_sp02.pdf.

Mark C. Detweiler and Richard C. Omanson. Ameritech web page user interface standards and
design guidelines. Ameritech Corporation, Chicago, IL, 1996. Available at
http://www.ameritech.com/corporate/testtown/library/standard/web_guidelines/index.html.

Alan Dix, Janet Finlay, Gregory Abowd, and Russell Beale. *Human-Computer Interaction*. Upper Saddle River, NJ: Prentice Hall, second edition, 1998.

DO-IT. Working together: Computers and people with learning disabilities. Available at http://www.washington.edu/doit/Brochures/Technology/atpwld.html, 2002.

DO-IT. Working together: Computers and people with mobility impairments. Available at http://www.washington.edu/doit/Brochures/Technology/wtmob.html, 2002.

DO-IT. Working together: Computers and people with sensory impairments. Available at http://www.washington.edu/doit/Brochures/Technology/wtsense.html, 2002.

DO-IT. Working together: People with disabilities and computer technology. Available at http://www.washington.edu/doit/Brochures/Technology/wtcomp.html, 2002.

Martin Dodge. Mapping how people use a website. *Mappa Mundi Magazine*, June 2001. Available at http://mappa.mundi.net/maps/maps_022/.

DreamInk. Demographics and statistics for web designers – DreamInk web design tutorial. Available at http://dreamink.com/design5.shtml, 2000.

M. Carl Drott. Using web server logs to improve site design. In *Proceedings of the 16th International Conference on Systems Documentation*, pages 43–50, Quebec, Canada, September 1998. New York: ACM Press. Available http://drott.cis.drexel.edu/SIGDOC98/Logpaper2.html.

Curtis E. Dyreson. Using an incomplete data cube as a summary data sieve. *Data Engineering Bulletin*, 20(1):19–26, 1997.

Easiwebmaker. Easiwebmaker - automated site creation and management tools. Available at http://www.easiwebmaker.ie/, 2003.

Valerie J. Easton and John H. McColl. Statistics glossary v1.1. Available at http://www.stats.gla.ac.uk/steps/glossary/index.html, 1997.

Ame Elliott. Flamenco image browser: Using metadata to improve image search during architectural design. In *Proceedings of the Conference on Human Factors in Computing Systems*, volume 2, pages 69–70, Seattle, WA, March 2001.

R. Darin Ellis and Sri H. Kurniawan. Increasing the usability of online information for older users: A case study in participatory design. *International Journal of Human-Computer Interaction*, 12(2):263–276, 2000.

Jennifer English, Marti Hearst, Rashmi Sinha, Kirsten Swearingon, and Ping Yee. Examining the usability of web site search. Submitted for publication, 2001.

Enviz, Inc. Enviz Insight. Available at http://www.enviz.com/solutions/insight.html, October 2001.

K. Anders Ericsson and Herbert A. Simon. *Protocol Analysis: Verbal Reports as Data*. Cambridge, MA: MIT Press, revised edition, 1993.

Michael Etgen and Judy Cantor. What does getting WET (Web Event-logging Tool) mean for web usability. In *Proceedings of the 5th Conference on Human Factors & the Web*, Gaithersburg, Maryland, June 1999. Available at http://www.nist.gov/itl/div894/vvrg/hfweb/proceedings/etgen-cantor/index.html.

Oren Etzioni. The world-wide web: Quagmire or gold mine? *Communications of the ACM*, 39(11):65–68, 1996.

Exodus. Monitoring & management services. Available at http://www.exodus.net/solutions/management/performance_monitoring.html, 2002.

Pete Faraday and Alistair Sutcliffe. Providing advice for multimedia designers. In *Proceedings of the Conference on Human Factors in Computing Systems*, volume 1, pages 124–131, Los Angeles, CA, April 1998. New York: ACM Press.

Peter Faraday. Visually critiquing web pages. In *Proceedings of the 6th Conference on Human Factors & the Web*, Austin, TX, June 2000.

Pete Faraday. Attending to web pages. In *Proceedings of the Conference on Human Factors in Computing Systems*, Extended Abstracts, pages 159–160. New York: ACM Press, 2001.

Christelle Farenc and Philippe Palanque. A generic framework based on ergonomics rules for computer aided design of user interface. In J. Vanderdonckt and A. Puerta, editors, *Proceedings of the 3rd International Conference on Computer-Aided Design of User Interfaces*, Louvain-la-Neuve, Belgium, October 1999. Dordrecht, The Netherlands: Kluwer Academic Publishers.

Christelle Farenc, Véronique Liberati, and Marie-France Barthet. Automatic ergonomic evaluation: What are the limits. In *Proceedings of the 3rd International Conference on Computer-Aided Design of User Interfaces*, Louvain-la-Neuve, Belgium, October 1999. Dordrecht, The Netherlands: Kluwer Academic Publishers.

David K. Farkas. Representing website design. In *Proceedings of the WinWriters Online Help Conference*, Seattle, WA, February 15–19 2003. Available at http://www.uwtc.washington.edu/people/faculty/farkas/FarkasRepresentingDesign-WW03.ppt.

Vincent Flanders and Michael Willis. *Web Pages That Suck: Learn Good Design by Looking at Bad Design*. San Francisco, CA: SYBEX, 1998.

Jennifer Fleming. *Web Navigation: Designing the User Experience*. O'Reilly & Associates, Sebastopol, CA, 1998.

B.J. Fogg, Jonathan Marshall, Alex Osipovich, Chris Varma, Othman Laraki, Nicholas Fang, Jyoti Paul, Akshay Rangnekar, John Shon, Preeti Swani, and Marissa Treinen. Elements that affect web credibility: Early results from a self-report study. In *Proceedings of the Conference on Human Factors in Computing Systems*, number Extended Abstracts, pages 287–288, The Hague, The Netherlands, April 2000. New York: ACM Press. Available at http://www.webcredibility.org/WebCredEarlyResults.ppt.

B. J. Fogg, Jonathan Marshall, Othman Laraki, Alex Osipovich, Chris Varma, Nicholas Fang, Jyoti Paul, Akshay Rangnekar, John Shon, Preeti Swani, and Marissa Treinen. What makes web sites credible?: a report on a large quantitative study. In *Proceedings of the ACM CHI'01 Conference on Human Factors in Computing Systems*, volume 1, pages 61–68, Seattle, WA, March 2001.

Shannon Ford and Dan Boyarski. Design@Carnegie Mellon: A web story. In Gerrit van der Veer, Austin Henderson, and Susan Coles, editors, *Proceedings of the Conference on Designing Interactive Systems: Processes, Practices, Methods, and Techniques (DIS-97)*, pages 121–124, New York, August 18–20 1997. ACM Press.

Freshwater Software. SiteSeer. Available at http://www.freshwater.com/SiteSeer.htm, 2002.

Benjamin J. Fry. Organic information design. Master's thesis, 2000.

Jeanette Fuccella. Using user centered design methods to create and design usable web sites. In *ACM 15th International Conference on Systems Documentation*, pages 69–77, 1997.

Rodney Fuller and Johannes J. de Graaff. Measuring user motivation from server log files. In *Proceedings of the 2nd Conference on Human Factors & the Web*, Redmond, WA, October 1996. Available at http://www.microsoft.com/usability/webconf/fuller/fuller.htm.

George W. Furnas. Effective view navigation. In *Proceedings of Conference on Human Factors in Computing Systems*, volume 1, pages 367–374, Atlanta, GA, March 1997. New York: ACM Press.

W. Gaul and L. Schmidt-Thieme. Mining web navigation path fragments. In *Proceedings of the Workshop on Web Mining for E-Commerce – Challenges and Opportunities*, August 2000.

GNU Software Foundation. Wget. Available at http://www.gnu.org/software/wget/wget.html, 1999.

G. Griffiths, B. D. Hebbron, M. A. Lockyer, and B. J. Oates. A simple method & tool for web engineering. In *Proceedings of the 14th International Conference on Software Engineering and Knowledge Engineering*, pages 755–761. New York: ACM Press, July 2002.

Mark Guzdial, Paulos Santos, Albert Badre, Scott Hudson, and Mark Gray. Analyzing and visualizing log files: A computational science of usability. GVU Center TR GIT-GVU-94-8, Georgia Institute of Technology, 1994. Available at http://www.cc.gatech.edu/gvu/reports/1994/abstracts/94-08.html.

GVU Center. 8th WWW survey. Available at http://www.gvu.gatech.edu/user_surveys/survey-1997-10/, 1997.

GVU Center. 10th WWW survey. Available at http://www.cc.gatech.edu/gvu/user_surveys/survey-1998-10/, 1998.

Marti A. Hearst. Next generation web search: Setting our sites. *IEEE Data Engineering Bulletin*, 23(3), 2000.

Jeffrey Heer and Ed H. Chi. Mining the structure of user activity using cluster stability. In *Proceedings of the Workshop on Web Analytics, SIAM Conference on Data Mining*, Arlington, VA, April 2002.

Jeffrey Heer and Ed H. Chi. Separating the swarm: categorization methods for user sessions on the web. In *Proceedings of the Conference on Human Factors in Computing Systems*, pages 243–250. New York: ACM Press, 2002.

Brian Helfrich and James A. Landay. QUIP: quantitative user interface profiling. Unpublished manuscript, 1999. Available at http://www.nano-sim.org/quip.

Hagan Heller and David Rivers. Design lessons from the best of the world wide web. In *Proceedings of ACM CHI 96 Conference on Human Factors in Computing Systems*, volume 2 of *Tutorial 12*, pages 350–351, 1996.

Hagan Heller and David Rivers. So you wanna design for the web. *interactions*, 3(2):19–23, 1996.

HiSoftware. AccRepair. Available at http://www.hisoftware.com/access/repair.html, 2002.

HiSoftware. AccVerify. Available at http://www.hisoftware.com/access/vIndex.html, 2002.

Harry Hochheiser and Ben Shneiderman. Using interactive visualizations of WWW log data to characterize access patterns and inform site design. *Journal of the American Society for Information Science and Technology*, 52(4):331–343, 2001.

James Hom. The usability methods toolbox. Available at http://www.best.com/ jthom/usability/usable.htm, 1998.

Jason I. Hong, Jeffrey Heer, Sarah Waterson, and James A. Landay. Webquilt: A proxy-based approach to remote web usability testing. *ACM Transactions on Information Systems*, 19:263–285, July 2001.

Anita W. Huang and Neel Sundaresan. A semantic transcoding system to adapt web services for users with disabilities. In *Fourth Annual ACM Conference on Assistive Technologies*, pages 156–163. New York: ACM Press, 2000.

IBM, Inc. About the websphere resource analyzer. Available at http://www-4.ibm.com/software/webservers/appserv/doc/v40/ae/infocenter/was/06060012.html, 2002.

Imageware, Inc. Doctor HTML v6. Available at http://www2.imagiware.com/RxHTML/, 2001.

International Organisation for Standardisation. *ISO9241 Ergonomic Requirements for Office Work with Visual Display Terminals (VDTs), Part 11: Guidance on Usability*. International Standard. Geneva, Switzerland, 1998.

International Organisation for Standardisation. *ISO16071 Ergonomics of Human-System Interaction - Guidance on Software Accessibility*. Technical Specification. Geneva, Switzerland, 2002.

Melody Y. Ivory and Aline Chevalier. A study of automated web site evaluation tools. Technical Report 02-10-01, University of Wasington, Department of Computer Science and Engineering, 2002. Available at ftp://ftp.cs.washington.edu/tr/2002/10/UW-CSE-02-10-01.pdf.

Melody Y. Ivory and Marti A. Hearst. State of the art in automating usability evaluation of user interfaces. *ACM Computing Surveys*, 33(4):470–516, December 2001.

Melody Y. Ivory and Marti A. Hearst. Improving web site design. *IEEE Internet Computing*, 6(2):56–63, March/April 2002.

Melody Y. Ivory and Marti A. Hearst. Statistical profiles of highly-rated web site interfaces. In *Proceedings of the Conference on Human Factors in Computing Systems*, volume 4 of *CHI Letters*, pages 367–374, Minneapolis, MN, April 2002.

Melody Y. Ivory, Rashmi R. Sinha, and Marti A. Hearst. Preliminary findings on quantitative measures for distinguishing highly rated information-centric web pages. In *Proceedings of the 6th Conference on Human Factors & the Web*, Austin, TX, June 2000. Available at http://www.tri.sbc.com/hfweb/ivory/paper.html.

Melody Y. Ivory, Rashmi R. Sinha, and Marti A. Hearst. Empirically validated web page design metrics. In *Proceedings of the Conference on Human Factors in Computing Systems*, volume 1, pages 53–60, Seattle, WA, March 2001.

Melody Y. Ivory, Jennifer Mankoff, and Audrey Le. Using automated tools to improve web site usage by users with diverse abilities. *IT&Society*, 1(3), Winter 2003. Available at http://www.stanford.edu/group/siqss/itandsociety/v01i03/v01i03a11.pdf.

Melody Y. Ivory. *An Empirical Foundation for Automated Web Interface Evaluation*. PhD thesis, University of California, Berkeley, Computer Science Division, 2001.

Melody Y. Ivory. Automated web site evaluation. Available at http://webtango.ischool.washington.edu/talks/awse.pdf, 2003.

Melody Y. Ivory. Characteristics of web site designs: Reality vs. recommendations. In *Proceedings of the 10th International Conference on Human-Computer Interaction*, 2003. In press.

Melody Y. Ivory. Using design knowledge to teach web designers. Available at http://webtango.ischool.washington.edu/talks/designknowtalk.pdf, 2003.

Melody Y. Ivory. Web site usability engineering. In Munindar P. Singh, editor, *Practical Handbook of Internet Computing*. Boca Raton, FL: CRC Press, 2003. In press.

Raj Jain. *The Art of Computer Systems Performance Analysis*. New York: Wiley-Interscience, 1991.

Bonnie E. John and David E. Kieras. The GOMS family of user interface analysis techniques: Comparison and contrast. *ACM Transactions on Computer-Human Interaction*, 3(4):320–351, 1996.

Jeff Johnson. *GUI Bloopers Don'ts and Do's for Software Developers and Web Designers*. San Francisco, CA: Morgan Kaufmann Publishers, 2000.

E Kaasinen, A Matti, J Kolari, S. Melakoski, and T. Laakko. Two approaches to bringing internet services to WAP devices. *Proceedings of the 9th International World Wide Web Conference*, 2000. Available at http://www9.org/w9cdrom/228/228.html.

Jean Kaiser. Browser-safe colors. *Web Design*, June 15, 1998. Available at http://webdesign.about.com/compute/webdesign/library/weekly/aa061598.htm.

David J. Kasik and Harry G. George. Toward automatic generation of novice user test scripts. In *Proceedings of the Conference on Human Factors in Computing Systems*, volume 1, pages 244–251, Vancouver, Canada, April 1996. New York: ACM Press.

Keynote Systems, Inc. Keynote red alert, 2002. Available at http://www.redalert.com/.

Keynote Systems, Inc. Keynote loadpro, 2003. Available at http://www.keynote.com/solutions/solutions_pt_loadpro_tpl.html.

N. Kim and B. J. Fogg. World wide web credibility: What effects do advertisements and typos have on the perceived credibility of web page information? Unpublished thesis, Stanford University, 1999.

Jinwoo Kim and Byunggon Yoo. Toward the optimal link structure of the cyber shopping mall. *International Journal of Human-Computer Studies*, 52:531–551, 2000.

M. Kitajima, M.H. Blackmon, and P. G. Polson. A comprehension-based model of web navigation and its application to web usability analysis. In S. McDonald, Y. Waern, and G. Cockton, editors, *People and Computers XIV - Usability or Else! (Proceedings of HCI 2000)*, pages 357–373, 2000.

Vinodkumar P. Kizhakke. MIR: A tool for visual presentation of web access behavior. Master's thesis, 2000.

Matthew Klee and Will Schroeder. Report 2: How business goals affect site design. In *Designing Information-Rich Web Sites*. Bradford, MA: User Interface Engineering, 2000.

Teuvo Kohonen. *Self-Organizing Maps*. Springer Series in Information Sciences. Berlin: Springer, 1997.

Raymond Kosala and Hendrik Blockeel. Web mining research: a survey. *ACM SIGKDD Explorations Newsletter*, 2(1):1–15, 2000.

Thomas K. Landauer and Susan T. Dumais. A solution to Plato's problem: The latent semantic analysis theory of the acquisition, induction, and representation of knowledge. *Psychological Review*, 104:211–240, 1997.

Lori Landesman and Will Schroeder. Report 5: Organizing links. In *Designing Information-Rich Web Sites*. Bradford, MA: User Interface Engineering, 2000.

Kevin Larson and Mary Czerwinski. Web page design: Implications of memory, structure and scent for information retrieval. In *Proceedings of the Conference on Human Factors in Computing Systems*, volume 1, pages 25–32, Los Angeles, CA, April 1998. New York: ACM Press.

Averill M Law and David W Kelton. *Simulation Modeling and Analysis*. Industrial Engineering and Management Science. McGraw-Hill International Edition, 1991.

Andreas Lecerof and Fabio Paternò. Automatic support for usability evaluation. *IEEE Transactions on Software Engineering*, 24(10):863–888, October 1998.

Rick Levine. Guide to web style. Sun Microsytems, 1996. Available at http://www.sun.com/styleguide/.

Clayton Lewis, Peter G. Polson, Cathleen Wharton, and John Rieman. Testing a walkthrough methodology for theory-based design of walk-up-and-use interfaces. In *Proceedings of the Conference on Human Factors in Computing Systems*, pages 235–242, Seattle, WA, April 1990. New York: ACM Press.

James Lin and James A. Landay. Damask: A tool for early-stage design and prototyping of multi-device user interfaces. In *Proceedings of The 8th International Conference on Distributed Multimedia Systems*, pages 573–580, San Francisco, CA, 2002.

Jonas Lowgren and Tommy Nordqvist. Knowledge-based evaluation as design support for graphical user interfaces. In *Proceedings of the Conference on Human Factors in Computing Systems*, pages 181–188, Monterey, CA, May 1992. New York: ACM Press.

Lycos, Inc. Tripod. Available at http://www.tripod.lycos.com/, 2003.

Patrick J. Lynch and Sarah Horton. *Web Style Guide: Basic Design Principles for Creating Web Sites*. Princeton, NJ: Yale University Press, 1999. Available at http://info.med.yale.edu/caim/manual/.

Gene Lynch, Susan Palmiter, and Chris Tilt. The Max model: A standard web site user model. In *Proceedings of the 5th Conference on Human Factors & the Web*, Gaithersburg, Maryland, June 1999.

Jock Mackinlay. Automating the design of graphical presentations of relational information. *ACM Transactions on Graphics*, 5(2):110–141, 1986.

Macromedia. Macromedia exchange - 508 accessibility suite extension detail page. Available at http://www.macromedia.com/cfusion/exchange/index.cfm#loc=en_us&view=sn121& viewName=Dreamweaver%20ExtensionextID=671605&catID=30&lc_id=21293, 2001.

Rohit Mahajan and Ben Shneiderman. Visual and textual consistency checking tools for graphical user interfaces. *IEEE Transactions on Software Engineering*, 23(11):722–735, November 1997.

Jennifer Mankoff, Anind Dey, Udit Batra, and Melody Moore. Web accessibility for low bandwidth input. In *Proceedings of ASSETS 2002*, pages 17–24. New York: ACM Press, July 2002.

William C. Mann and Sandra A. Thompson. Rhetorical structure theory: A theory of text organization. Technical Report RS-87-190, USC/Information Sciences Institute, 1987.

Shirley Martin. Cluster analysis for web site organization: Using cluster analysis to help meet users' expectations in site structure. *internetworking*, 2(3), December 1999. Available at http://www.internettg.org/newsletter/dec99/cluster_analysis.html.

F. Masseglia, P. Poncelet, and M. Teisseire. Using data mining techniques on web access logs to dynamically improve hypertext structure. *ACM SigWeb Letters*, 8(3):1–19, 1999.

J. May and P. J. Barnard. Supportive evaluation of interface design. In C. Stary, editor, *Proceedings of the First Interdisciplinary Workshop on Cognitive Modeling and User Interface Design*, Vienna, Austria, December 1994.

S. E. Mead, V. A. Spaulding, R. A. Sit, B. Meyer, and Walker. Effects of age and training on world wide web navigation strategies. In *Proceedings of the Human Factors and Ergonomics Society 41st Annual Meeting*, pages 152–156. Santa Monica, CA: Human Factors Ergonomics Society, 1998 1997.

Craig S. Miller and Roger W. Remington. A computational model of web navigation: Exploring interactions between hierarchical depth and link ambiguity. In *Proceedings of the 6th Conference on Human Factors & the Web*, Austin, TX, June 2000. Available at http://www.tri.sbc.com/hfweb/miller/article.html.

Craig S. Miller and Roger W. Remington. Effects of structure and lable ambiguity on information navigation. In *Proceedings of the Conference on Human Factors in Computing Systems*, Extended Abstracts, pages 630–631, Minneapolis, MN, April 2002.

R. Molich, N. Bevan, S. Butler, I. Curson, E. Kindlund, J. Kirakowski, and D. Miller. Comparative evaluation of usability tests. In *Proceedings of the UPA Conference*, pages 189–200, Washington, DC, June 1998. Usability Professionals' Association, Chicago, IL.

R. Molich, A. D. Thomsen, B. Karyukina, L. Schmidt, M. Ede, W. van Oel, and M. Arcuri. Comparative evaluation of usability tests. In *Proceedings of the Conference on Human Factors in Computing Systems*, pages 83–86, Pittsburg, PA, May 1999. New York: ACM Press.

Gerald M. Murch. Colour graphics — blessing or ballyhoo? *Computer Graphics Forum*, 4(2):127–135, June 1985.

National Cancer Institute. Research-based web design & usability guidelines. Available at http://usability.gov/guidelines/, 2001.

National Institute of Standards and Technology. Overview websat. Available at http://zing.ncsl.nist.gov/WebTools/WebSAT/overview.html, 2001.

NetIQ. Webtrends reporting center. Available at http://www.netiq.com/products/wrc/default.asp, 2002.

NetRaker. The NetRaker suite. Available at http://www.netraker.com/info/applications/index.asp, 2000.

Mark W. Newman and James A. Landay. Sitemaps, storyboards, and specifications: A sketch of web site design practice. In *Proceedings of Designing Interactive Systems: DIS 2000*, pages 263–274, New York, August 2000.

Jakob Nielsen. *Usability Engineering.* Boston, MA: Academic Press, 1993.

Jakob Nielsen. Response times: The three important limits. Available at http://www.useit.com/papers/responsetime.html, 1994.

Jakob Nielsen. Web usability: Why and how. *Users First!*, September 14, 1998. Available at http://www.zdnet.com/devhead/stories/articles/0,4413,2137433,00.html.

Jakob Nielsen. User interface directions for the Web. *Communications of the ACM*, 42(1):65–72, January 1999.

Jakob Nielsen. *Designing Web Usability: The Practice of Simplicity.* Indianapolis, IN: New Riders Publishing, 2000.

Jakob Nielsen. Beyond accessibility: Treating users with disabilities as people. Available at http://www.useit.com/alertbox/20011111.html, 2001.

NIST Visualization and Usability Group. CIFter project. Available at http://zing.ncsl.nist.gov/cifter/, 2001.

Noldus Information Technology. Systems for ergonomics research and usability testing. Available at http://www.noldus.com/solutions/usability/usab_intro.html, 2003.

Donald A. Norman. *The Design of Everyday Things.* Doubleday, New York, 1990.

Open Software Foundation. *OSF/Motif Style Guide.* Number Revision 1.1 (for OSF/Motif release 1.1). Englewood Cliffs, NJ: Prentice Hall, 1991.

Michael G. Paciello and Mike Paciello. *Web Accessibility for People With Disabilities.* CMP Books, Gilroy, CA, 2000.

Paessler GmbH. Webserver stress tool 6. Available at http://www.paessler.com/WebStress/webstress.htm, 2003.

Laila Paganelli and Fabio Paternò. Intelligent analysis of user interactions with web applications. In *Proceedings of the 7th International Conference on Intelligent User Interfaces*, pages 111–118. New York: ACM Press, 2002.

Fabio Paternò and Giulio Ballardin. Model-aided remote usability evaluation. In A. Sasse and C. Johnson, editors, *Proceedings of the IFIP TC13 Seventh International Conference on Human-Computer Interaction*, pages 434–442, Edinburgh, Scotland, August 1999. Amsterdam, The Netherlands: IOS Press.

F. Paternò, C. Mancini, and S. Meniconi. ConcurTaskTrees: Diagrammatic notation for specifying task models. In *Proceedings of the IFIP TC13 Sixth International Conference on Human-Computer Interaction*, pages 362–369, Sydney, Australia, July 1997. Sydney, Australia: Chapman and Hall.

Pennsylvania's Initiative on Assistive Technology. Wave 2.0. Available at http://www.wave.webaim.org:8081/wave/index.jsp, 2001.

Thomas A. Phelps. *Multivalent Documents: Anytime, Anywhere, Any Type, Every Way User-Improvable Digital Documents and Systems.* PhD thesis, University of California, Berkeley, Computer Science Division, 1998.

Thomas A. Phelps. The multivalent browser. Available at http://http.cs.berkeley.edu/~phelps/Multivalent/, 2001.

Peter Pirolli and Stuart Card. Information foraging in information access environments. In Irvin R. Katz, Robert Mack, Linn Marks, Mary Beth Rosson, and Jakob Nielsen, editors, *Proceedings of the Conference on Human Factors in Computing Systems*, pages 51–58, New York, May 1995. ACM Press.

Peter Pirolli. A web site user model should at least model something about users. *internetworking*, 3(1), March 2000. Available at http://www.internettg.org/newsletter/mar00/critique_max.html.

James E. Pitkow and Krishna A. Bharat. Webviz: A tool for world wide web access log visualization. In *Proceedings of the First International World Wide Web Conference*, Geneva, Switzerland, May 1994.

Julie Ratner, Eric M. Grose, and Chris Forsythe. Characterization and assessment of HTML style guides. In *Proceedings of the Conference on Human Factors in Computing Systems*, volume 2, pages 115–116, Vancouver, Canada, April 1996. New York: ACM Press.

Klaus Reichenberger, Klaas Jan Rondhuis, and Jörg Kleinz adn John Bateman. Effective presentation of information through page layout: A linguistically-based approach. In *Electronic Proceedings of the ACM Workshop on Effective Abstractions in Multimedia*, San Francisco, CA, November 1995. Available at http://www.cs.uic.edu/ ifc/mmwsproc/reichen/page-layout.html.

RetroAccess. Retroaccess – AccessEnable. Available at http://www.retroaccess.com/access_enable.cgi, 2002.

Xavier Roche. Httrack website copier – offline browser. Available at http://www.httrack.com/, 2001.

Louis Rosenfeld and Peter Morville. *Information Architecture for the World Wide Web*. O'Reilly & Associates, Sebastopol, CA, 1998.

Mary Beth Rosson, Susanne Maass, and Wendy A. Kellogg. Designing for designers: an analysis of design practice in the real world. In *Proceedings of the SIGCHI/GI conference on Human factors in computing systems and graphics interface*, pages 137–142. New York: ACM Press, 1987.

Mary Beth Rosson, Wendy Kellogg, and Susanne Maass. The designer as user: building requirements for design tools from design practice. *Communications of the ACM*, 31(11):1288–1298, 1988.

Sane Solutions, LLC. NetTracker log file analysis and usage tracking software. Available at http://www.sane.com/products/NetTracker/, 2002.

Darrell Sano. *Designing Large-Scale Web Sites: A Visual Design Methodology*. Wiley Computer Publishing, John Wiley & Sons, Inc., New York, 1996.

C. H. Sauer and K. M. Chandy. *Computer Systems Performance Modeling*. Englewood Cliffs, NJ: Prentice Hall, 1981.

Paul Sawyer and Will Schroeder. Report 4: Links that give off scent. In *Designing Information-Rich Web Sites*. Bradford, MA: User Interface Engineering, 2000.

Paul Sawyer, Richard Danca, and Will Schroeder. Report 6: Myths of page layout. In *Designing Information-Rich Web Sites*. Bradford, MA: User Interface Engineering, 2000.

Tara Scanlon and Will Schroeder. Report 1: What people do with web sites. In *Designing Information-Rich Web Sites*. Bradford, MA: User Interface Engineering, 2000.

Tara Scanlon and Will Schroeder. Report 7: Designing graphics with a purpose. In *Designing Information-Rich Web Sites*. Bradford, MA: User Interface Engineering, 2000.

Dominique Scapin, Corinne Leulier, Jean Vanderdonckt, Céline Mariage, Christian Bastien, Christelle Farenc, Philippe Palanque, and Rémi Bastide. A framework for organizing web usability guidelines. In *Proceedings of the 6th Conference on Human Factors & the Web*, Austin, TX, June 2000. Available at http://www.tri.sbc.com/hfweb/scapin/Scapin.html.

Jean Scholtz and Sharon Laskowski. Developing usability tools and techniques for designing and testing web sites. In *Proceedings of the 4th Conference on Human Factors & the Web*, Basking Ridge, NJ, June 1998. Available at http://www.research.att.com/conf/hfweb/proceedings/scholtz/index.html.

Karen A. Schriver. *Dynamics in Document Design*. Wiley Computer Publishing, John Wiley & Sons, Inc., New York, 1997.

Matthew Schwartz. Web site makeover. *Computerworld*, January 31, 2000. Available at http://www.computerworld.com/home/print.nsf/all/000126e3e2.

Andrew Sears. AIDE: A step toward metric-based interface development tools. In *Proceedings of the 8th ACM Symposium on User Interface Software and Technology*, pages 101–110, Pittsburg, PA, November 1995. New York: ACM Press.

Nathan Shedroff. Recipe for a successful web site. Available at http://www.nathan.com/thoughts/recipe, 1999.

Nathan Shedroff. *Experience Design 1*. Indianapolis, IN: New Riders Publishing, 2001.

Ben Shneiderman, Jonathan Lazar, and Melody Y. Ivory. Introduction. *IT&Society*, 1(3), Winter 2003. Available at http://www.stanford.edu/group/siqss/itandsociety/v01i03/abstract.html.

Ben Shneiderman. Designing information-abundant web sites: Issues and recommendations. *International Journal of Human-Computer Studies*, 47(1):5–29, 1997.

Ben Shneiderman. *Designing the user interface: strategies for effective human-computer interaction*. Reading, MA: Addison-Wesley, third edition, 1998.

Ben Shneiderman. *Leonardo's Laptop: Human Needs and the New Computing Technologies*. Cambridge, MA: The MIT Press, 2002.

Gurminder Singh and Mark Green. Designing the interface designer's interface. In *Proceedings of the 1st annual ACM SIGGRAPH symposium on User Interface Software*, pages 109–116. New York: ACM Press, 1988.

Rashmi Sinha, Marti Hearst, and Melody Ivory. Content or graphics? an empirical analysis of criteria for award-winning websites. In *Proceedings of the 7th Conference on Human Factors & the Web*, Madison, WI, June 2001. Available at http://www.optavia.com/hfweb/7thconferenceproceedings.zip/Sinha.pdf.

Rashmi Sinha. Survey software review. Available at http://sims.berkeley.edu/~sinha/teaching/Infosys271_2000/surveyproject/surveysoftware.html, 2000.

Sidney L. Smith and Jane N. Mosier. Guidelines for designing user interface software. Technical Report ESD-TR-86-278, The MITRE Corporation, Bedford, MA 01730, 1986.

Sidney L. Smith. Standards versus guidelines for designing user interface software. *Behaviour and Information Technology*, 5(1):47–61, 1986.

Myra Spiliopolou and Carsten Pohle. Data mining for measuring and improving the success of web sites. *Data Mining and Knowledge Discovery*, 5(1/2):85–114, 2001.

Myra Spiliopoulou and Lukas C. Faulstich. WUM: a Web Utilization Miner. In *Workshop on the Web and Data Bases (WebDB98)*, pages 109–115, 1998.

Myra Spiliopoulou, Carsten Pohle, and Lukas Faulstich. Improving the effectiveness of a web site with web usage mining. In *WEBKDD*, San Diego, CA, 1999. Available at http://www.acm.org/sigs/sigkdd/proceedings/webkdd99/papers/paper18-myra.ps.

Myra Spiliopoulou. Web usage mining for web site evaluation. *Communications of the ACM*, 43(8):127–134, 2000.

Jared M. Spool, Tara Scanlon, Will Schroeder, Carolyn Snyder, and Terri DeAngelo. *Web Site Usability: A Designer's Guide*. Morgan Kaufmann Publishers, Inc., San Francisco, CA, 1999.

Jared M. Spool, Matthew Klee, and Will Schroeder. Report 3: Designing for scent. In *Designing Information-Rich Web Sites*. Bradford, MA: User Interface Engineering, 2000.

Jaideep Srivastava, Robert Cooley, Mukund Deshpande, and Pang-Ning Tan. Web usage mining: Discovery and applications of usage patterns from web data. *SIGKDD Explorations*, 1(2):12–23, 2000.

SSB Technologies. Infocus. Available at http://www.ssbtechnologies.com/products/InFocus.php, 2002.

Lincoln D. Stein. The rating game. Available at http://stein.cshl.org/~lstein/rater/, 1997.

Terry Sullivan. Reading reader reaction: A proposal for inferential analysis of web server log files. In *Proceedings of the 3rd Conference on Human Factors & the Web*, Boulder, CO, June 1997. Available at http://www.research.att.com/conf/hfweb/conferences/denver3.zip.

Jim Thatcher. Section 508 web standards & WCAG priority 1 checkpoints: A side-by-side comparison. Available at http://jimthatcher.com/sidebyside.htm, 2002.

The International Academy of Arts and Sciences. The Webby Awards 2000 judging criteria. Available at http://www.webbyawards.com/judging/criteria.html, 2000.

Yin Leng Theng and Gil Marsden. Authoring tools: Towards continuous usability testing of web documents. In *Proceedings of the 1st International Workshop on Hypermedia Development*, Pittsburg, PA, June 1998. Available at http://www.eng.uts.edu.au/~dbl/HypDev/ht98w/YinLeng/HT98_YinLeng.html.

Harold Thimbleby. Gentler: A tool for systematic web authoring. *International Journal of Human-Computer Studies*, 47(1):139–168, 1997.

Thomas Tiedtke, Christian Märtin, and Norbert Gerth. AWUSA – a tool for automated website usability analysis. In *PreProceedings of the 9th International Workshop on the Design, Specification, and Verification of Interactive Systems*, Rostock, Germany, June 12-14 2002. Available at http://www.uni-paderborn.de/cs/ag-szwillus/lehre/ss02/seminar/semband/MarcoWeissenborn/WebUsabilityTools/AWUS1605.pdf.

UsableNet. LIFT online. Available at http://www.usablenet.com, 2000.

UsableNet. LIFT - Nielsen Norman Group Edition. Available at http://www.usablenet.com/products_services/lfd_nng/lfd_nng.html, 2002.

UsableNet. UsableNet - products & services. Available at http://www.usablenet.com/products_services/products_services.html, 2002.

UWEC. UWEC psychology online, 2003. Available at http://zeb.uwec.edu/POL/participantHomePage.do.

Douglas K. van Duyne, James A. Landay, and Jason I. Hong. *The Design of Sites: Patterns, Principles, and Processes for Crafting a Customer-Centered Web Experience*. Boston: Addison-Wesley, 2002.

Vividence Corporation. Customer experience management: The Vividence approach and methodology. Available at http://www.vividence.com/resources/public/what+we+do/methodology/method.pdf, March 2002.

Pawan R. Vora. Design/methods & tools: Designing for the web: A survey. *interactions*, 5(3):13–30, 1998.

Michael Vorburger. About ALTifier web accessibility enhancement tool. Available at http://www.vorburger.ch/projects/alt/, 1999.

WatchFire. Bobby worldwide. Available at http://bobby.watchfire.com/bobby/html/en/index.jsp, 2002.

Web Criteria. Max, and the objective measurement of web sites, 1999.

WebPartner. Stress testing. Available at http://www.webpartner.com/st_main.html, 2002.

Andy Whitefield, Frank Wilson, and John Dowell. A framework for human factors evaluation. *Behaviour and Information Technology*, 10(1):65–79, 1991.

Tim Wilson. The cost of downtime. *InternetWeek.com*, July 30, 1999. Available at http://www.internetwk.com/sitereliability/sitelead.htm.

World Wide Web Consortium. Web content accessibility guidelines 1.0. Geneva, Switzerland, 1999. Available at http://www.w3.org/TR/WAI-WEBCONTENT/.

World Wide Web Consortium. Evaluating web sites for accessibility. Available at http://www.w3.org/WAI/eval/, 2001.

World Wide Web Consortium. How people with disabilities use the web. W3C Working Draft, 2001. Available at http://www.w3.org/WAI/EO/Drafts/PWD-Use-Web/.

World Wide Web Consortium. W3C HTML validation service. Available at http://validator.w3.org/, 2001.

World Wide Web Consortium. Evaluation, repair, and transformation tools for web content accessibility. Available at http://www.w3.org/WAI/ER/existingtools.html, 2002.

World Wide Web Consortium. W3C CSS validation service. Available at http://jigsaw.w3.org/css-validator/, 2002.

K.-L. Wu, P. S. Yu, and A. Ballman. Speedtracer: a web usage mining and analysis tool. *IBM Systems Journal*, 37(1):89–105, 1997.

Yahoo! Inc. Yahoo! GeoCities. Available at http://geocities.yahoo.com/home/, 2003.

Ka-Ping Yee, Kirsten Swearingen, Kevin Li, and Marti Hearst. Faceted metadata for image search and browsing. In *Proceedings of the Conference on Human Factors in Computing Systems*, pages 401–408. New York: ACM Press, April 5–10 2003.

Osmar R. Zaïane, Man Xin, and Jiawei Han. Discovering web access patterns and trends by applying OLAP and data mining technology on web logs. In *Advances in Digital Libraries*, pages 19–29, 1998.

Panayiotis Zaphiris and Lianaeli Mtei. Depth vs. breadth in the arrangement of Web links. Available at http://www.otal.umd.edu/SHORE/bs04, 1997.

Zhijun Zhang. Usability evaluation methods. Available at http://www.pages.drexel.edu/~zwz22/UsabilityHome.html, 1999.

Zona Research, Inc. The economic impacts of unacceptable web site download speeds, 1999.

Steve Zurier. A question of balance. *InternetWeek.com*, February 15, 1999. Available at http://www.internetwk.com/trends/trends021599.htm.

About the Author

Dr. Melody Y. Ivory is an Assistant Professor in the Information School as well as an Adjunct Assistant Professor in the Department of Computer Science and Engineering at the University of Washington. Dr. Ivory received a BS in computer science and mathematics from Purdue University and received MS and PhD degrees in computer science from the University of California at Berkeley. Her primary research and teaching interests are in human computer interaction, specifically enabling users to easily interact with information. She has conducted extensive research on automated web site evaluation and has developed methodologies and tools to facilitate automated web site evaluation.

Photo courtesy of Dowell Eugenio, Information School, University of Washington.

Index

195

HUMAN-COMPUTER INTERACTION SERIES

KLUWER ACADEMIC PUBLISHERS – DORDRECHT / BOSTON / LONDON